DEEPER SECRETS OF HUMAN EVOLUTION
IN LIGHT OF THE GOSPELS

DEEPER SECRETS OF HUMAN EVOLUTION
IN LIGHT OF THE GOSPELS

Twelve lectures held in Berlin, Stuttgart,
Zurich and Munich between 11 October and 26 December 1909

TRANSLATED BY CHRISTIANA BRYAN

INTRODUCTION BY TOM RAVETZ

RUDOLF STEINER

RUDOLF STEINER PRESS

CW 117

Rudolf Steiner Press
Hillside House, The Square
Forest Row, RH18 5ES

www.rudolfsteinerpress.com

Published by Rudolf Steiner Press 2021

Originally published in German under the title *Die tieferen Geheimnisse des Menschhietswerdens im Lichte der Evangelien* (volume 117 in the *Rudolf Steiner Gesamtausgabe* or Collected Works) by Rudolf Steiner Verlag, Dornach. Based on shorthand notes that were not reviewed or revised by the speaker. This authorized translation is based on the third German edition (2017)

Published by permission of the Rudolf Steiner Nachlassverwaltung, Dornach

A catalogue record for this book is available from the British Library

ISBN 978 1 85584 592 3

Cover by Morgan Creative
Typeset by Symbiosys Technologies, Vishakapatnam, India
Printed and bound by 4Edge Ltd., Essex

Contents

Lecture 1
Berlin, 11 October 1909 (Notes)
Buddha and the two Jesus children

The prehistory of Christ. The three spiritual streams meeting in the Christ event: the first connected with Buddha, a second with Zarathustra and a third represented by the ancient Hebrew culture. Buddha and the teaching of love and compassion. The descent of the Nirmanakaya-Buddha into the Jesus child of Nazareth. The incarnation of Zarathustra in the Jesus child of Bethlehem. The twelve-year-old Jesus in the Temple. The subsequent convergence of the two families. The confluence of Zarathustrianism and Buddhism and their union in Jesus of Nazareth.

Lecture 2
Berlin, 18 October 1909 (Notes)
The Gospels. Buddha and the two Jesus children

The Nazarene Jesus child. The Nirmanakaya of Buddha. Influence of Buddhism in Christianity. The Bethlehem Jesus child. Ancestry of both Jesus children. Confluence of the Zarathustrian and Buddhist streams in the twelve-year-old Jesus of Nazareth. The integration of the ancient Hebrew stream. It was Buddha's mission to bring the teaching of compassion and love, but Christ is the power of love itself. The factor upon which all evolution rests.

Deeper Secrets of Human Evolution in Light of The Gospels

Lecture 3
Berlin, 2 November 1909
Four differing perspectives in depicting Christ in the four Gospels

The being of Christ Jesus: light and love. World concepts in the Gospel of John, mood of sacrificial devotion in Luke's Gospel. The spiritual force of the earthly Sun lives in the Gospel of Mark; the system of all concealed natural and spiritual forces of the world. The Gospel of Matthew depicts the Christ as a harmonious image of the human being and the mysteries of human history.

LECTURE 4
BERLIN, 9 NOVEMBER 1909
The Mission of the Ancient Hebrew people

The faculty of thoughtful judgement; recognizing the Godhead in its external manifestation, without clairvoyance, as developed by the ancient Hebrews. Abraham's particular constitution has to be inherited through heredity for this purpose. The connection of a mathematical world conception with inner imagination takes place through Moses in Egypt. His laws are consolidated in Arabia. Contact with the lore of Eastern Magi takes place in Babylonian Captivity. Recapitulation of ancient Hebrew destiny in the appearance of the Bethlehem Jesus. The kingdom of humanity or the Kingdom of Heaven.

LECTURE 5
BERLIN, 23 NOVEMBER 1909
Preparing for an understanding of the Christ event
The Mission of the Ancient Hebrew people

The confluence of spiritual streams of antiquity in Jesus of Nazareth. The withdrawal of ancient clairvoyance and of the significance of blood relationships in the face of emergent influences: use of the I; the Kingdom of Heaven. Preparations for this by the Nazirites. The Baptism of St John. Children of the Snake and the image of the Lamb. John the Baptist as the fulfilment of a new age in which the spiritual world illumines the human soul through phenomena of the outer world.

LECTURE 6
STUTTGART, 13 NOVEMBER 1909
On the right relationship with anthroposophy

Completion of a seven-year cycle in the German Theosophical Society. The necessity to communicate the findings of spiritual research before developing higher faculties of vision; testing these findings with thinking. Visionary clairvoyance and the capacity for thorough thinking. Why earlier incarnations are not remembered. Why the Gods caused humankind to arise. How a thinking and a non-thinking visionary clairvoyant sees phenomena of the spiritual

world. Thinking gives substance enabling a grasp of spiritual content. Simple brain convolution in clear thinkers. The dangers of visionary clairvoyance. Training the power of judgement; future recalling of present incarnation.
Pages 56-77

LECTURE 7
STUTTGART, 14 NOVEMBER 1909
The Gospels

Four varying depictions of the Christ event in the four Gospels: St John portrays Christ from the perspective of thinking, St Luke from a feeling aspect, St Mark from the perspective of willing and St Matthew, in harmonizing all three qualities, depicts the human Christ Jesus. The confluence of Buddhism, Zarathustrianism and the spiritual stream of the ancient Hebrews in Christianity. Buddha's doctrine of compassion and love. The legend of Buddha. The future Maitreya Buddha. The mission of Abraham and the ancient Hebrew people. The sacrifice of Isaac. What underlies Jacob's cultural mission in Egypt. Zarathustra's reincarnation as Zaratos in ancient Chaldea. The two Jesus children. The Solomon and Nathan lines in the house of David. Simeon, reincarnated Asita.
Pages 78-102

LECTURE 8
ZURICH, 19 NOVEMBER 1909
The Matthew Gospel and the enigma of Christ

The four Gospels and the four categories of pre-Christian initiation. Abraham's mission and that of the ancient Hebrew people. Sacrificing Isaac. Joseph in Egypt. The Ten Commandments of Moses. The paths of the Magi and the Soloman Jesus as a repetition at a higher level of the path taken by the Jewish people. The Bodhisattvas and the future understanding of Christ.
Pages 103-121

THE HUMAN I, GOD WITHIN AND THE GOD OF OUTER REVELATION

LECTURE 9
MUNICH, 4 DECEMBER 1909
Group Souls and Individuality

The qualities of group souls and those of an I. The spiritualization of language. Identifying core human qualities through anthroposophical thinking. The elaboration of the human I.
Pages 122-138

Publisher's Note

THE present lectures cover the theme of the Pre-History of the Great Christ Event, forming a continuation of themes treated of in Rudolf Steiner's previous lecture cycle, *The Gospel of St Luke* (Basel, 15–26 September, 1909).

The words *Theosophy* and *theosophical* used by Rudolf Steiner in the sense of his anthroposophically-orientated spiritual science have been replaced in the following subject-specific passages with the words *anthroposophy, anthroposophical, spiritual science/scientific* and *spiritual knowledge.*

Introduction

Ｉｎ the Middle Ages, theology was seen as the Queen of the Sciences. The Bible was the unquestioned source of the highest knowledge. Missionaries were able to convince sceptical listeners merely by telling them the stories of the miracles in the New Testament. Human beings could perceive God's word of power, or God's Spell (as preserved in our word 'gospel') in the sermons of the monks. When the Enlightenment began to subject scripture to the same critical scrutiny as every other text, this showed not only that human beings had shaken off the last shackles of priestly authority, but also that the last vestiges of the capacity to apprehend spiritual realities directly had died out. When scholars could only draw on thinking that was oriented to the sense-perceptible world, they could find in the gospels nothing but sense-perceptible realities.

Biblical theology has moved on since the nineteenth century, which was dominated by the search for the elusive 'Q' or Quelle, the source from which Matthew, Mark and Luke are supposed to have copied, adding their own thoughts as they wrote their gospels. One approach that grew up in the 1970s, the Bible as Literature, fulfils one of Steiner's suggestions about how we can approach scripture, namely that we look at the secrets of its composition. Other commentaries explore the Bible stories in their archetypal, mythical reality, which can lead to similarly fruitful discoveries. With all this, the question of truth is left undecided. However enriching the results of these approaches may be, we could apply the same methods to Shakespeare or Tolstoy with equal profit, without having to believe that Hamlet was a historical figure, or that Pierre Bezukhov took a pistol through the streets of Moscow in order to assassinate Napoleon.

Discovering the truth of the gospels *for us* does not dissolve the tension between dogmatic acceptance and the critical approach. For this, we need to find a different way of knowing, one that could participate in the world from which the evangelists drew their inspiration. Long before Rudolf Steiner started to speak about the results of his spiritual researches, as he does in the lectures in this volume, he wrote extensively about the need to find ways of knowing that would allow the things that we are investigating to reveal their essence. This is the method that Owen Barfield described as the quest for 'a systematic investigation of phenomena by way of participation'. (*Saving the Appearances, A Study in Idolatry*, 1988, p. 137). Steiner's writings and lectures are an invitation to develop such participative knowing.

Bearing this historical challenge in mind, we can better understand a recurring motif of Steiner's lectures on the gospels and other sacred texts of humanity. This is what he calls the 'independence' of the research whose results he brings. He contrasts this with conventional biblical scholarship, which analyses the texts, seeking to understand them in their context and drawing on many other disciplines including history, archaeology and philology, to piece together what the authors of the gospels might have meant. In the lectures in this volume, he describes the source from which he can draw as the Akashic Record; in the language of the gospels, this is the living library to which St John refers at the very end of his gospel, which contains all the deeds of Christ that no written book could encompass.

Whilst Steiner's capacity to develop his cognitive faculties to the point where he could consult this continually evolving library was exceptional, what he is describing here applies more generally. Understanding is always a two-way process: we bring something towards the text or the person that we wish to understand. The fact that the lectures in this volume are presented to us in English reminds of the fact that some mediation is necessary between the words that Steiner spoke and our receiving them. Even if we are able to read the German original, we need to be aware that we were reading notes taken with varying degrees of competence and care; furthermore, if we had a perfect recording of Steiner's words, we would still be hearing words and concepts that have developed their meaning over a century, along with references to events and personalities who were well-known to Steiner's audience, but not to us.

Reading and understanding any text is a creative act. To take this seriously means that we cannot in good conscience say: 'We know because Rudolf Steiner said...' (any more than we can say 'We know because St Matthew said...'). In the sixth lecture, speaking with a certain exasperation, Steiner asks his listeners to overcome any feeling of subservience, which might lead to our treating his research results with the dogmatic acceptance that humanity has worked so hard to overcome. Instead, he addresses us as fellow-researchers. Using what Steiner often calls healthy common sense and taking our own research questions as our starting point, we will be able to meet his insights with our understanding.

The central theme of the lectures collected here is the gospels, particularly the Gospel of St Matthew. They were held for members of the German Section of the Theosophical Society in 1909, at the middle-point of Steiner's exposition of the gospels: the great cycles on St John and St Luke have been held; the cycles on Matthew and Mark are still to come. In the third lecture, Steiner criticizes the tendency, evidently prevalent among his audience, to receive the cycles he had already given as passive consumers. Sadly, the tendency that Steiner bemoans in his followers has not been overcome in the century since.

The question of the two Jesus-children, which Steiner speaks about particularly in the first two lectures of this volume, is a case in point. Steiner took the infancy narratives of St Matthew and St Luke far more seriously than modern biblical scholarship, which tends to discount their value as historical descriptions, seeing them rather as typical of the legends that surround the birth of a hero or religious leader. However, there is a danger that we receive Steiner's insights in a somewhat sensational way, as if his intention were to shock traditional Christians. In fact, the insight into the two narratives comes as part of a far wider picture. Opening great vistas onto the cultural and spiritual development of humanity, Steiner allows us to sense what was necessary for the incarnation of Christ, the representative and future human being. Both St Paul and Iraneus, one of the so-called 'Church Fathers', speak of the incarnation of Christ as a recapitulation of everything that human beings had developed in pre-Christian ages. Steiner fills out this beautiful thought with more detail. He saw that in Christ, the kingly aspect of human culture, which allows us to master the earth, had to be united with the priestly aspect, through which we develop devotion to the divine. These had to combine in turn with the heritage of Abraham, progenitor of brain-bound thinking.

Beholding this broad sweep of history and feeling the necessity of such a recapitulation, we might find ourselves asking: How could such very different human qualities be united in one human being? Turning then to Steiner's lectures, we find his explanations, including the light he sheds on the very different stories told in the gospels of Matthew and Luke. If we then read the gospel passages for ourselves, we may find that the texts speak to us differently than they did before. Instead of having to accept the Incarnation as a miraculous irruption from the heavenly world which we could never hope to comprehend, we can see a process of development that we can follow inwardly. Then we could say that we have found our own independent standpoint from which to read the gospels, which yield up far deeper worlds of meaning than we might have found had we read them without deepening our own questions. Having done all this, we may find it easier to build a bridge to other sincerely seeking Christians, who would be put off by sensational talk of two Jesus-children, but who may share our longing to comprehend how the Incarnation could come about.

In the third lecture, Steiner points to another way in which we can deepen our participatory knowing, which arises from the fact that he develops his themes over the course of many lecture cycles. The lecture cycles on the gospels were intended to lead his listeners into relationship with spiritual beings of the highest order. Through St John, we encounter the world of the Cherubim, bearers of divine wisdom; through St Luke, we encounter the Seraphim as the manifestations of the fiery love that is at the heart of all being. Steiner's hope was clearly that his audience would live into these worlds actively. However, he was forced to change the intended sequence of lecture cycles because he noticed that his audience took the revelations contained in each one as the final word. He sensed that to bring the Gospel of St Mark, which would lead us into the world of the Thrones, would only bring more confusion. For this reason, in lectures 4 and 5, he turns to the Gospel of St Matthew, which embodies the zodiacal sign of Waterman, the one who combines and harmonizes the other three beings. The lecture cycle on the Gospel of St Matthew was held the following year, in 1910. That on St Mark was only held in 1912.

Following the course that Steiner set out as active readers a century later, we can heal through our own process of cognition an ancient wound in the history of the Church. In the fourth century, the Church was grappling with the question: Who was the divine being who incarnated as Jesus Christ? Was he God's agent in creation, a creature like us, yet far greater than us in his power? This was the view of Arius. Or do we encounter in Jesus Christ the Son of God himself, one of the three persons of the Holy Trinity, which lies beyond creation and time, as the source and direction of the world? This was the view of Athanasius, which became Christian dogma. Steiner did not bring a single, simple dogmatic statement as an answer, to compete with the creeds of the churches. Rather, the insights he brings in successive lecture cycles on the gospels and other topics allow us to grasp with living understanding the spiritual beings at work in Jesus Christ. If we stopped here, it would suggest an Arian Christology: Christ originates in the world of the spiritual hierarchies, not in the realm that gives them their being. When Steiner speaks about the one who unites those beings at work in the gospels of Mark, Luke and John, rather as the human ego integrates the mental, emotional and volitional life into one coherent centre, we are invited to meditate on how the Son of God, the second person of the Trinity, is at work in the totality of the hierarchies.

In the sixth lecture, Steiner criticizes the tendency, evidently prevalent amongst his audience, to think that hearing and reading his insights relieved them of any need to remain contemporaries and to master the scientific and practical learning of their day. Now that more than 100 years separate us from the moment when he gave his lectures, his words are all the more pressing. In the case of those readers who are reading this lecture cycle out of an interest in the gospels, I recommend reading the gospels themselves (not always a given) and obtaining at least one up-to-date commentary, perhaps on the Gospel of St Matthew. Readers who wish to go deeper may find that literature in the field of New Testament Background Studies enriches their appreciation of the gospels and also provides interesting resonances with some of the insights that Steiner brings in these lectures. Even this would only be scratching the surface. It is worth mentioning here the astonishing fact that in the middle of the twentieth century, just as it seemed as if the gospels had lost all their freshness and vitality for modern humanity, the discoveries of the Dead Sea Scrolls and the Nag Hammadi library came as a gift to broaden the horizons of those seeking to understand the biblical texts. It would be a sad omission, of just the kind that Steiner bemoans, if we thought that we knew the world of the gospels and contemporary scholarship without taking account of these finds. An excellent guide on this path is Andrew Welburn, whose painstaking research demonstrates how some of the Nag Hammadi texts bear out statements that Steiner made, over thirty years before they were recovered.

In the last two lectures in this collection, Steiner shows us where the path of participative knowing might lead. Speaking about the Christmas tree, he meditates on Christ's words: 'See, I am with you until the end of days.' He then outlines a task:

> We are called – especially through anthroposophical spiritual development – not to propagate a dead, rigid Christianity but to develop for the future an ever-new Christianity, a Christianity that brings forth ever new wisdom and knowledge. [my translation]

Reading such words can stir our soul. However, if we had merely read the lectures in this volume passively, the task of developing such a living understanding of Christianity might seem beyond us. If we have taken the first steps on the path of participative cognition that Rudolf

Steiner lays out before us, we could feel that we are indeed developing such an understanding. This can allow us to hear the closing words of the final lecture in this volume as a challenge to which we can rise:

> Feel ... that it is up to your souls to resolve to become worthy instruments for the development of humanity into the future, in the sense we have outlined! Feel the whole weight and gravity of this anthroposophical resolve: we are not to be anthroposophists for our own sake; rather, if we take into account what has just been said, we are to be anthroposophists out of a sense of duty towards humanity; duty towards humanity's task and towards humanity's mission. [my translation]

Tom Ravetz
August 2021

Lecture 1

BERLIN, 11 OCTOBER 1909 (NOTES)

BUDDHA AND THE TWO JESUS CHILDREN

For the first time, in the last lecture course in Basel[1] we were able to speak about a subject hitherto not broached within the German Section,[2] albeit the Christ event itself has often been spoken of, especially in connection with the Gospel of St John. By linking this event with the Gospel of St Luke, as we did in Basel, we were able to explore what we can call Christ's prehistoric life. Here we are dealing with extremely complex relationships. As we heard, a high Sun Being incorporated itself into the body of Jesus of Nazareth and lived there for three years between the Baptism in Jordan and the Mystery of Golgotha. This lofty Christ Being has often been spoken about. However, an elaboration of what came alive in our souls as the personality of Jesus of Nazareth, who absorbed this high Being into himself, can only be attempted when it is linked to the Gospel encompassing the history of Jesus's childhood. His development from childhood until the Baptism in Jordan formed the main theme of the Basel lectures. Even in this biographical prehistory we have before us a most intricate web of relationships. The greatest of these, one has to reflect, is far from easy to grasp or portray. The structure of the world cannot be drawn in a few sketchy strokes nor grasped in a few convenient concepts.

The personality who received the Christ Being into himself in his thirtieth year is a complex entelechy. Only on the basis of the Akashic Record can an accurate view be gained as to why the life of Jesus is so diversely presented in the various Gospels.

Today something of the life of Jesus of Nazareth will be outlined in order to provide an overview of what was explored in more detail in the Basel lectures. The Gospel of St Matthew is intended to form part of the lectures for members this winter, potentially also that of St Mark.

Against this background the Christ event takes on a completely new dimension for us. We hear a small indication of this as an addendum to St John's Gospel as a pointer to what can initially only be treated in outline.

The Akashic Chronicle, accessible to clairvoyance, reveals in living picture-script what has taken place over time. The nature and course of spiritual communication is generally such that facts from the Akashic Chronicle can be spoken about without linking them to a specific record. Only later will it be shown that all this can be found again in certain records, such as the Gospels, which in turn can only be rightly understood through recourse to the Akashic Record.[3]

Spiritual streams which had previously gone their separate ways throughout world history flowed together in Palestine. With reference to the Gospel of St Luke one can speak of three spiritual streams that met in the Christ events. One of these is connected with Buddha, another with Zarathustra and a third embedded in ancient Hebrew culture. These three currents flowed together into a palpable event, which is to say into the Christ event itself. These spiritual streams are usually spoken of in far too abstract a way. They manifest, in fact, in exceptional beings who have to be constituted in such a way that they can support the confluence of such streams. For this reason we need to accurately research such beings in relation to their inner constitution.

The Buddhist stream reached its apotheosis in Gautama Buddha. He had been previously incarnated, but his incarnation in the sixth century BCE was of particular significance for his being. It was then that he first became what we may call a Buddha. Before this he was a Bodhisattva, a great teacher of humankind, a personality who, over time, acquired new capacities. We ourselves once lived in ancient Egypt, equipped with quite different faculties from those we possess today: some of these old capacities atrophied, new abilities were added.

Anyone not taking a development such as this into account can gain no objective view of the world. Nowadays, for instance, human beings can of themselves grasp certain logical and moral laws, can use their own judgement to recognize this or that. However, this was not the case in ancient times. In those days, for instance, humans could locate nothing of a moral-ethical nature within themselves and would not have understood such a concept, however well explained in modern parlance. A completely different faculty would need to have been addressed. This is why there are certain axioms of human verity today, such as teachings concerning compassion, teachings of love, which could not have been detected three thousand years ago. Today an inner voice tells us about the laws of compassion and love. In those days, human beings would have sought in vain for any such inner voice. Instead human beings had, to put it crassly, to have ideas of compassion and love *suggested into them*, inculcated into them by evocation.

The being whose task it was over thousands of years to cause compassion and love to flow into humanity from higher spiritual regions was that very Bodhisattva who then incarnated in India as Buddha. As a human being in the physical world he would not have found compassion or love present within himself. However, Bodhisattvas would, through their initiation, have risen into spiritual realms where they could be imbued with teachings of compassion and love and could then bring these downwards to earth. The moment does eventually arrive when humanity, from then onwards, has matured sufficiently to find for itself what was once caused to flow into them. Such was the case with compassion and love.

As this Bodhisattva rose to become Buddha, sitting under the Bodhi tree in the sixth century BCE, great and important processes were taking place not only within him but throughout the world. At that time the laws of compassion and love arose within this Buddha-become-human, that is to say a circumscribed exposition of these laws arose in him by means of the Eightfold Path. In that the Buddha could become aware of these teachings within himself, humanity was endowed with the possibility of likewise experiencing them in future ages. Since then some human beings have indeed been able, following the example of the great Buddha, to experience this themselves and to live a life that—with equal vitality—crystallizes such teachings from out of the Eightfold Path.

Only when a significant number of human beings have become mature enough to experience what Buddha underwent long ago will these capacities become a fully integrated feature of humankind. This is how, mission by mission, spiritual substance is transferred downwards to our world from lofty spiritual spheres. In around three thousand years from now sufficient numbers of human beings will have matured enough to tread the Eightfold Path and only then will compassion and love have become truly incorporated and inherent in humanity. At that point new events and missions will descend from spiritual realms into the physical world.

In antiquity Buddha enabled teachings of compassion and love to stream into humanity and now these are alive and working in human beings, Buddha having given them their initial impetus. Once a Bodhisattva has mastered his task, after some three thousand years' activity he becomes a Buddha who has fulfilled a given mission for humanity.

What then became of this Buddha, whose mission it was to bring compassion and love to humanity, once he had left his physical body? The name Buddha always signifies a last, final incarnation. He only needed his Gautama incarnation in order to fulfil his mission. Since that time it has not been possible for that Bodhisattva individuality, having attained Buddhahood, to descend into a physical body again. He can only descend as far as an etheric body and is therefore only visible to clairvoyance today. When such a form without physicality is taken on by an individuality it is called a Nirmanakaya; it is the means by which that being is able to carry forward the mission with which it was entrusted as a Bodhisattva. In this way the great Christ event was prepared for by this reigning Buddha, now in Nirmanakaya form.

As parents, Mary and Joseph of Nazareth gave birth to a child whose name was Jesus. This child was of such a unique disposition that the Nirmanakaya-Buddha could muse: this child is physically constituted in such a way that it contains the potential to take humanity a quantum step forwards in its development if he, Buddha, would bestow upon it his own bequest. He therefore sank down, in Nirmanakaya form, into that Jesus child. This Nirmanakaya form should not be imagined as an enclosed shape such as the physical bodies we inhabit but rather that what would otherwise be mere forces have here become exceptional entities. This grouping of entities is held together in higher worlds by the ego, the I, of the underlying individuality concerned, in a similar way to that in which our faculties of thinking, feeling and willing are bound together in us. It is this host of entities combined within the Nirmanakaya-Buddha that the clairvoyant sees.

Analogies for this exist in nature, too: for instance, in the Gall Wasp,[4] the fore and rear bodies are connected only by the thinnest of shafts. If one imagines this shaft as invisible, one appears to have two separate yet connected entities. Similar connectivity exists within a beehive or a colony of ants.

Relationships of this kind were well known to the writer of St Luke's Gospel. He too was aware that the Nirmanakaya-Buddha was descending into the Jesus child. He expressed this by saying: When the child was born in Bethlehem a host of angels descended from the spiritual worlds who announced to the shepherds what had taken place. Those shepherds had, for certain reasons, become clairvoyant at that moment.

At first the child Jesus developed slowly, showing no outward sign of exceptional qualities that would have indicated a mighty spirit. However, a deep inwardness and soulfulness soon emerged, an animated life of feeling becoming apparent. A clairvoyant would have seen the Nirmanakaya-Buddha floating above the child. We are told in Indian legend that an old sage went to Buddha and recognized that in him a Bodhisattva was being called to full Buddhahood. The old man burst into tears because he would no longer live to experience the Buddha himself. Asita, as the old sage was called, was reborn and was again an old man at the time when Jesus was young. He was in fact the Simeon of St Luke's Gospel who saw before him Jesus on the occasion of his presentation in the Temple as that same Bodhisattva now become true Buddha, and could therefore say: *Lord, now lettest thou thy servant depart in peace for mine eyes have seen thy salvation.* Thus, five hundred years later, the sage saw what he could not have seen until then.

If one traces the origin of Jesus in the Gospel of St Luke and compares it with the Jesus described in St Matthew's Gospel, distinct differences are noticeable that have been completely overlooked by science. The right conclusion as to why their ancestry differs can, of course, be found in the Akashic Chronicle: they are, and must be, different.

At around the same time as Jesus was born there lived another set of parents, also called Mary and Joseph, who also gave birth to a son in Palestine called Jesus; there were two Jesus children, two sets of parents, both with the same names. One of these Jesus children is from Bethlehem—he lived with his parents in Bethlehem. The other child and his family lived in Nazareth. The first Jesus stems from the line of David via Solomon. The Nazarene Jesus, on the other hand, comes from the lineage of Nathan, also of the house of David. Where St Luke speaks primarily of the first Jesus, St Matthew speaks of the other Jesus child. The child from Bethlehem showed quite different characteristics in his early years from the Nazarene child. This first child was well developed in all outwardly discernible capacities and could, for example, speak from birth onwards, even though his words were largely incomprehensible to those around him. The other child, by contrast, showed a greater tendency to inwardness.

The Bethlehem child now bore, incarnated within him, the great Zarathustra of old. As is known, this Zarathustra had bequeathed his astral body to Hermes and his ether body to Moses. His ego had been reincarnated in Chaldea six hundred years before Christ as Nazarathos or Zaratos and now, finally, as Jesus. This Jesus child had to be taken to Egypt in order to relive for a while impressions of surroundings known to him, while inwardly revivifying them. We should absolutely not believe that this Jesus, of whom St Luke speaks, is the same individual as the Jesus spoken of by St Matthew. On the orders of Herod, all children under two years old were to be killed. John the Baptist would have been affected by this decree had not enough time elapsed between his birth and that of Jesus.

In his twelfth year the ego being of the Bethlehem Jesus child, that is the Zarathustra-I, moved across into the other Jesus boy, that is, from age twelve onwards the previous I of the Nazarene Jesus no longer inhabited him whereas the I of Zarathustra now did. The Bethlehem boy died as soon as this I had withdrawn from him. St Luke describes this transfer of the Zarathustra ego into the child from Nazareth in his account of the twelve-year-old Jesus in the Temple. It was inexplicable to his parents that their boy should speak with such wise authority. He was their only child. The other set of parents, however, had other children: four boys and two girls. Both families were later to become neighbours in Nazareth and would eventually meld into a single family. The father of the Bethlehem family was already an old man when Jesus was born and he died shortly afterwards. This mother moved with her children to Nazareth, to the other family.

It was in this way that the Buddha in his Nirmanakaya form worked together with the I of Zarathustra within Jesus of Nazareth; Buddha and Zarathustra working in concert within this child.

St Matthew speaks initially about the Bethlehem Jesus in his Gospel. Here the wise Magi from the Orient appear at his birth, led by a star to the place where Zarathustra was reincarnating.

Lecture 2

BERLIN, 18 OCTOBER 1909 (NOTES)

THE GOSPELS, BUDDHA AND THE TWO JESUS CHILDREN

Last time I was describing the contents of the lecture cycle given in Basel, where we were focusing on St Luke's Gospel. There we alluded to a question someone might ask: now that so much has been said about St John's Gospel and the picture of Jesus Christ it contains, can one possibly, in respect of the other Gospels, say anything quite as enlightening, something that would make an impression as deeply moving as did St John's Gospel?

Were this to be the case, a description of the other three Gospels would not be descriptions in the sense of spiritual research. Because what we seek in spiritual-scientific research should not be taken as some kind of documentary report; it should not just arrive like any other sort of transferred material but should instead be seen as a subject that can be researched with tools of the spirit.

The spiritual researcher sets himself the task of investigating how the events of Palestine present themselves, without recourse to any reports. Without reference to—or consideration of—any literature, the research begins. Afterwards, the researcher tries to demonstrate how the same truth shines towards us as it does from existing records.

In connection with St Luke's and St John's Gospels, we have chosen to retrieve from the vast vista of the Akashic Chronicle what can be rediscovered in those very Gospels of St Luke and St John. Inasmuch as one avails oneself of the results of the spiritual researcher's activity, as described, it is as if one encounters the Gospels anew. I indicated that one has the opportunity to discuss quite different aspects of St Luke's Gospel from those treated of in the Gospel of St John. This latter begins with the personality of Jesus of Nazareth from the time when he was thirty years old. Here that high Sun Being, the Christ Being, approaches us and we are concerned with the last three years of the life of Christ Jesus.

St Luke, on the other hand, gives us an insight into that momentous process which enabled the mighty Being of the Christ to flow into the personality of Jesus of Nazareth, an insight that shows the confluence of Zarathustrianism and Buddhism, and we saw how these two powerful spiritual streams met and united precisely within Jesus of Nazareth. We encountered him last time as a human personality, born as a child endowed with an exceptionally inward disposition, albeit one that could not have led his peers to an understanding of the outer physical world. Shining forth above this personality who appeared before us in the form of the Nathan Jesus child, the actual Jesus of Nazareth, we see what we called the Nirmanakaya of the Buddha as the aura of this child. Nirmanakaya is the form taken on by Buddha after his ultimate incarnation, in which he attained Buddhahood. We emphasized that our Western teachings fully confirm the contents of Eastern teachings, namely that the individuality who manifested in the sixth century BCE was indeed a Bodhisattva.

Such a Bodhisattva attains Buddhahood in a particular embodiment, and in this state their individuality has reached a stage of development that it no longer needs to be incarnated in a physical, earthly body. It is a momentous achievement when an individual no longer reincarnates. That this can be so depends not only on the level of development achieved but on the nature of that individuality. After that incarnation this Bodhisattva-Buddha had no further corporeal embodiments to fulfil and so he did not incarnate, but was from then onwards manifest in the lowest contiguous level of being, namely in the ether or life body. Buddha no longer descended to material corporeality but only to the level of an ether body.

An ether body of the kind in which such an individuality continues their onward development looks—if it is seen at all—nothing like a physical body, which forms an undifferentiated, self-contained unity. An ether body of the sort described, into which the Buddha descended, does not form any such enclosed spatial unity but is a multiplicity of separate entities. Let us bring to mind how the constituent elements of the human being split apart when that individual makes gradual progress, a process described in *Knowledge of the Higher Worlds*. What coheres as a unity within a normal human being as the forces we call thinking, feeling and willing then exist separately, as it were, self-sufficiently. The person gains sovereignty over what they have now become: a three-fold entity or what we could call a *multiplicity*, as is elaborated in my book *Occult Science, an Outline*.

In the case of the Buddha and his subsequent incarnations we have before us an ether body consisting of non-cohering beings. In normal human beings it is only the principle of the physical body that holds the ether body together.

When such a Bodhisattva-Buddha reappears in an ether body there is manifest—if indeed it becomes visible—a whole array or host of beings. Just such a host is described by the writer of St Luke's Gospel when he speaks of the angels appearing to the shepherds in the fields. It was this very ether body, also called Buddha's Nirmanakaya, which hovered over the Nazarene Jesus child. And this—the totality of all that Buddha ever was—becomes the inspirer of what now streams forth and infuses itself into Christianity. We see here how Buddhism flowed into Christianity. We need to think about this quite concretely and not as an abstraction. Whoever wants to understand how this took place in reality must be able to point to the concrete event when the Buddha, already elevated to the next stage of advancement, integrates himself into Christianity, and this is the event described in St Luke's Gospel as the appearance of the host of angels, which is the Nirmanakaya of the Buddha.

We then heard how a second Jesus child existed, whom we called the Bethlehem Jesus, and how he was none other than the reincarnated Zarathustra, an extraordinarily precocious child in whom Zarathustra was re-embodied. This is described in the Gospel of St Matthew and it portrays the individuality especially well understood by Matthew: the being who brought into Christianity the Zarathustrian stream. This is why it is also described to us how this child's hereditary origin is via the royal Solomon line of the house of David, whereas the Jesus of St Luke's Gospel originates in the priestly Nathan line, also of the house of David.

If we want to understand Christianity in its profound significance, we need to be clear that the most important spiritual streams in the world had to converge within it. We see that the royal line of David divides into a Solomon and a Nathan line. In the Solomon line, kingly qualities are perpetuated, in the Nathan line priestly qualities. Regal qualities come to the fore primarily in the first two periods of human life, qualities that radiate from an informed mastery of such world connections as bring the human being into harmony with the world. This can only take place when the forces of the physical and ether bodies are properly developed. As Zarathustra had developed primarily these forces to a state of inner completion, he had, until the age of twelve, to make use of forces emanating from physical and ether sources. He was especially endowed with these attributes as a result of traits inherited through the Solomon line. For his intended task, however, he needed those great powers that support the I, those of the astral body, powers that could only be granted him through lines of inheritance many generations in the making. Had Zarathustra remained in a body possessing such exceptionally developed physical and etheric elements until he was aged thirty, he would have been unable to deepen his essential being to the extent that he did. At the age of twelve he therefore translocated into the Nazareth Jesus so that, from age twelve onwards, the individuality of Zarathustra could co-dwell within the same child as was inhabited by the Nirmanakaya Buddha. It is in this way that the confluence of these two streams took place in Jesus of Nazareth during his twelfth year.

The third stream to join these was the ancient Hebrew stream. Only through this triple confluence could the individuality arise who was to receive the Christ into himself. We can ask ourselves how this ancient Hebrew spiritual stream flowed into the other streams, how indeed we can conceive of the essential properties of this old Hebrew spiritual stream. Let us first remind ourselves of what we heard about Buddha's development. What transpired in that a Bodhisattva becomes a Buddha?

The individuality incarnated as the Bodhisattva-Buddha had the task of transmitting the teachings of compassion and love from epoch to epoch. If we want to understand this we need to be aware that human beings of ancient times existed in a completely different state of consciousness. We should avoid being as short-sighted as modern science, which believes that the same faculties have always existed in humanity, that they gradually developed from primitive beginnings and that humanity used to subsist on the same level as animals. This is simply not so. What we identify as thinking, feeling and willing have not always existed. The further back we go in human evolution, the more it appears to our present state of consciousness as a dim, dreamy clairvoyance. For this reason, everything that needed to be disseminated by way of teachings or moral principles had to be transmitted by means quite different from those of today. Nowadays one can set forth certain moral principles and people understand them. When a person hears any such principle, they can say: yes, my own reason confirms it. For this to pertain, one's own reason and conscience need to be developed. It can be tangibly proven in external history that conscience began at a specific point. Aeschylus[5] did not yet mention conscience. The distinct soul force of conscience emerged at a precise point in history and was absent before that point.

Before humanity possessed a conscience, before logical thinking existed, any appeal to rational thinking or conscience would have been like speaking to a stone or a plant.

In those days, when souls needed strength and impetus, this had to be infused into them. Anything concerning love, for instance, had to be induced by suggestion through the individuality of the Bodhisattva whom we later call Buddha. The time eventually came when human beings were able to gain their own sense of the meaning of love and compassion and their own insight into the Eightfold Path. These laws, with which humanity had once been endowed from on high, could only be realized as teachings once Buddha was present, and for this in turn to become a reality, the Bodhisattva had to become Buddha.

Every kind of human evolution has to take place at a particular time and in a particular people, from whom a number are singled out for their comprehension of such teachings. Some may find a contradiction between this and what was said earlier when it was stated that it was Christ's mission to spread love. When something such as this is said, it is essential to listen very closely. It lay within Buddha's mission to introduce the teaching of love and compassion, but Christ *is* that power of love. He himself brought love. There is a difference between conveying a teaching and *being* that teaching itself, oneself exemplifying it.

This teaching was brought by Buddha precisely so that the power of love was enabled to stream downwards and reveal itself on earth through a mighty Sun Being. It was equally essential that this power of love should manifest on earth within a people that had undergone a development different from that in which Buddha had lived.

What differentiates what Buddha contributed to world evolution from what the individuality of Moses could bring? We rightly call what the Buddha contributed the great law of Dharma. Buddha introduced his teachings in such a way that people would recognize them as being locatable within their own souls. Moses introduced laws in a completely different way, namely as commandments. For the people to whom Moses gave his laws it would not have been possible to present them as being rooted within individual souls; they had to be divine laws sent from on high. Whereas Buddha said: you will find the teachings I give you in the deepest forces of your soul, Moses said: the coming God confers these laws upon you.

Laws needed to be given on the basis that one people was deemed to be at a younger stage of development than another, that certain forces had not yet matured. All development follows the maxim that nothing proceeds in a straight line.

We usually conceive of development as a later event following a preceding one. But this is not how development works. It comes about on the basis of other preconditions. If we observe a growing plant we see the germ or seed, then the stem growing upwards, we see how leaves and finally the blossom emerge. At this point development ceases to be linear—subsequent evolving from previous—and pollination occurs. A new influx into the process is needed: a grain of pollen from another plant. Spiritually, the most diverse forces and states now stream together.

In Palestine, Zarathustrianism and Buddhism had to unite with another stream, one which could infuse them with comparatively youthful forces. For many long ages the law of Jehovah had held sway within this people. Had they lived at a stage when Buddha could have appealed to their individual souls in 600 BCE, they would not later have had the requisite youthful forces to contribute. They still needed to receive laws from their godhead that did not appeal to their individual souls. This Levantine people needed to be held at an earlier stage of consciousness.

A hypothetical analogy can be made concerning the individual. Imagine that someone wanted to enforce creativity at a certain age. This should clearly not be attempted! For this a child would have to be brought up atypically, because if I try to teach him something at age seven that would normally be taught later, I have deprived him of developing other soul faculties later in life. If I wait until he is ten, when he presents with more matured forces, he retains his youthful freshness and can evince a later creativity that would otherwise have been destroyed.

You see how this pertained in the Near East. The Hebrew people were held back in just such a way. They could not yet absorb Buddha's teachings of compassion and love but were given this in the form of a commandment. They did not receive the call of Buddha to develop—of themselves—the teachings of compassion and love. There was only one place in world progress, where people were then most advanced, that the Bodhisattva-Buddha could convey his teaching. Once quite different strengths had developed elsewhere, this spiritual stream would join the others in another place.

Where do we need to look to find what flows down through the generations of a people? Upon what does this depend? By what means does the individual assume whatever is incumbent upon their people?

Until the age of seven human beings are sheathed in an etheric mantle which they then slough off. However, they remain enveloped in an astral sheath, which is similarly sloughed off at puberty. It is only then that the astral body is born. Between the ages of twelve and fifteen, when the astral body is born, it contains all the forces held in common with folk identity. The astral sheath, which is now cast off, contains all attributes until then harboured inwardly, traits held in common with—and characteristic of belonging to—a particular people. What happens to the sheath that is cast aside? This astral sheath containing folk characteristics unites with those sheaths similarly cast off by ancestors. Here is something resembling a chain.

While the individual still has this sheath until the age of fourteen he is a link in the chain that reaches back to his ancestors. To which degree of ancestry does this extend? To the forty-second degree, to the six-times-seventh degree! This is how humans are connected with their ancestors, and this was well known in ancient times. It is also known today within spiritual science. Because humans are connected in this way with their ancestors the ancient Egyptians ensured that in their Book of the Dead the human soul appeared before forty-two judges.

If a particular quality or trait is to come to the fore that enables an individual to be embedded within a people, all the related ancestors must be aligned in such a way that each member of the chain brings that trait to expression. If Zarathustra was to incarnate, then it had to be into a sheath that bore the fundamental features of his people.

This is why St Matthew describes Zarathustra as being born as the forty-second descendant after Abraham, born into a line that contained all the characteristics of his people. This is how those influences entered the third stream [of which we have been speaking].

LECTURE 3

BERLIN, 2 NOVEMBER 1909

FOUR DIFFERING PERSPECTIVES IN DEPICTING CHRIST IN THE FOUR GOSPELS

OBSERVATIONS made in connection with the Gospels of St John and St Luke[6] and the associated reflections on which we focused can be characterized in no other way than by saying that they originate from the following perception: that the Being whom we name as Christ Jesus—in so far as modern human understanding can conceive of this entelechy at all—is a Being of such magnitude, such all-encompassing might, that no study can proceed from one-dimensional statements as to who Christ was nor what significance his presence entails for each individual human spirit, for every single human soul. Amid our considerations this would have appeared irreverent in face of the world's most vast mystery. Our observations are characterized by an attitude of awe and reverence. Awe and reverence are words that can express the following attitude: you yourself should not laud too highly human comprehension when faced with this ultimate of mysteries. Try never to estimate anything too highly—not even that which spiritual science, however towering, can offer and regardless of the lofty regions to which it can extend—when you encounter this, the greatest mystery of all life. And do not believe that human words are equal to the task of expressing anything more than a tentative, solitary approach to this greatest of mysteries. All the lectures held over the past three years had as their central focus the words that also appear in St John's Gospel: *I am the Light of the World*. The whole aim of the lecture series on St John's Gospel was to understand these words. Those lectures may serve to give a gradual measure of understanding—by making them our own, even if only in the form of an inkling—of what is written in St John's Gospel itself: *'I am the Light of the World'*.

If you see a light shining, have you understood, by gazing into it, what light is? By knowing the colour or other qualities of that light, do you grasp what is shining? Do you know the Sun by looking upwards and receiving white sunlight as a revelation? Could you not imagine that it means comprehending something more than light within what radiates: the radiating itself? Because the being of whom we were speaking could say of himself: 'I am the *Light* of the World', we were required to understand that word, yet by so doing we have understood no more than this Being's articulation of his life: *'I am the Light of the World'*. Everything offered here by way of thoughts in connection with the Gospel of St John was needful in order to show that the Being who encompasses world wisdom is indeed the light of the world. But this Being is far more than could be characterized in our St John's Gospel studies. Anyone who thinks they have understood or encompassed the Christ Jesus on the basis of the lectures given on St John's Gospel or who believes that they have an inkling based on this single expression of his life cannot hope to have understood the immensity of this radiant Being.

There then followed the lectures on St Luke's Gospel and here we learnt of a different aspect. If one could in some manner use the words: *'I am the Light of the World'* as a tool for understanding our reflections on the John Gospel, when looking at the Gospel of St Luke—if deeply enough fathomed—one could paraphrase these words: *'Father, forgive them, for they know not what they do'* or: *'Father, into thy hands I commit my spirit'*. What Christ Jesus is—and here I mean not only the light of the world but who he is as the Being who brings the greatest possible gift of devotion, who can encompass within himself the potential for such sacrificial surrender as unites all things and Beings without loss of identity—but also that Being who contains the utmost imaginable devotion, who is also the fount of compassion and love that streams forth warmly over all future human and earthly life. Everything contained within those words of his gives us a second aspect to the Being we call Christ Jesus.

In this way we characterized the Being capable in his compassion of making real the greatest sacrifice and who, through the power of his radiance, shines upon all human existence. We have described light and love as revealed within the Being of Christ Jesus. Whoever takes our observations on the St John and St Luke Gospels in their widest connotation can to some extent gain an inkling of what in Christ Jesus signifies *light*, what in him is *love* and what is *compassion*. We have sought to comprehend in Christ Jesus two qualities in their universal magnitude. What we had to say about Christ as the spiritual light of the world that pours itself into all things as eternal wisdom, so as to live and weave in them, can give rise to the kind of spiritual vision that shines towards us out of St John's Gospel; and there is no attainable wisdom towards which one could strive that is not contained in some form within the Gospel of St John. All the wisdom of the world is to be found within this Gospel because John, who could observe all the wisdom of the world within Christ Jesus, could see it not only as it came about in remotely ancient times but also as it will be enacted in the farthest future. This is why, in descriptions connected with St John's Gospel, one glides eagle-like high above all human existence and in like manner one floats aloft when unfolding those vast concepts that make possible an understanding of St John's Gospel with its comprehensive insight into processes taking place within human souls. This all-embracing world ideation occupies that Sophia which flows to us when we unite our contemplation with St John's Gospel. What flows from St John's Gospel is then revealed to us, itself circling at eagle-height above everything taking place in daily, hourly and immediate human destiny.

If, descending from these heights, one views the individual human soul from hour to hour, from day to day, from year to year, from century to century, from millennium to millennium, looking particularly at those forces we call human love, then one can see this love as it wells and weaves over millennia in living human hearts and souls. On the one hand one sees how this love can accomplish the greatest, most heroically significant deeds for humanity, on the other how humankind's greatest sacrifices flow from a love for one being or another, for one cause or another. One then sees how this love accomplishes the human heart's highest goals and yet can be something of a double-edged sword. Take a mother; she loves her child deeply and tenderly. The child commits some misdemeanour. The mother loves her child and cannot bring herself to punish it, so deep is her love. The child commits another offence; again her heartfelt maternal love does not allow her to punish it. And so it continues and the child grows up to be a wastrel and troublemaker for the rest of his life. When touching on such deep issues, it is preferable to bring examples from times long gone rather than from the present. In the first half of the nineteenth century, there was one such mother who loved her child dearly. It must be expressly stated that nothing can be valued above love, that love is one of the most supreme human qualities in all circumstances. This mother loved her child to the extent that she could not bring herself to punish it for a minor theft within the family. A second theft followed without consequence and the child later became a notorious poisoner as a result of unwise, misguided maternal love. Love can perform boundless deeds when permeated with wisdom. This is precisely the significance of the love that flowed from Golgotha into the world: that it was united, within one Being, with the light of the world and with wisdom itself. If we contemplate Christ Jesus in light of these two qualities we recognize that love is the loftiest force in the world. We must also acknowledge how, in the deepest sense, love and wisdom belong together.

What have we gleaned in presenting these observations on the Gospels of St John and St Luke? We have learned nothing more than that the unique attribute of Christ Jesus, which one can call the light of the world, the universal warmth of love, flowing in him as in no other Being in the world, is something no human power of understanding can ever penetrate or encompass.

Whereas we were speaking of great and mighty thoughts in relation to St John's Gospel, ideas that soar, eagle-like, far above and beyond human minds, when following St Luke's Gospel one finds a quality that speaks continually and directly to every human heart.

What is so telling in St Luke's Gospel, what fills us with such warmth, is the outer expression of love, an understanding of the love willing to sacrifice itself, to give itself so totally that it wills nothing more than utmost self-surrender.

In seeking a picture for the mood or state of soul with which thoughts on St Luke's Gospel justifiably face us, we can feel something akin to the feeling that comes over us from Mithraic depictions of the sacrificial bull hurrying to the site of his sacrifice. We see it ridden by a human being; above it are depictions of cosmic events while below we are shown the course of earthly events. The human being hews his axe into the body of the bleeding sacrificial bull, who gives up its life so that the human being can overcome what he needs to overcome. Seeing the sacrificial bull beneath the human being, whose onward development relies on its sacrifice, sets the right underlying tone or feeling in relation to our contemplation of St Luke's Gospel. What the sacrificial bull has signified—throughout all time for those among humanity who have understood its inherent meaning—an expression of love, of an ever-intensifying love, will understand something of the depictions of love given during our St Luke studies, where nothing other than this second quality of Christ Jesus was being described. Does anyone fully know another being through just two of their qualities? Because we are confronted in this Being with the greatest of all mysteries, an understanding of two characteristics was essential as a beginning. Nevertheless, nobody should imagine that, on the basis of two such traits, they can themselves adequately conceive of this Being.

We have described two qualities of Christ Jesus and have not stinted in offering what we could to a dawning comprehension of the mighty significance of these two qualities. Yet we harbour too much reverence and awe in face of this Being himself to imagine we have even an inkling of the further qualities residing in him. Now there is a third aspect—one which relates to something not yet spoken of in our movement—which can only be characterized in general outline. One could say: in depicting the Christ in St John's Gospel, he is described as acting not only as an elevated Being, but as a lofty Being who is served by the realm of the wisdom-filled Cherubim.

This is how he is pictured in the setting of St John's Gospel, evoking a sense of Cherubim soaring aloft at eagle height. Characterizing him in the sense of St Luke's Gospel, one would describe him in terms of the warm fire of love that wells forth from the heart of Christ, of what he means for the world through working in the heights where the Seraphim are to be found. This fire of love streams throughout the world from the Seraphim and it is Christ Jesus who imparts this loving fire to us on earth.

Now to the third aspect we wanted to describe: Christ's meaning for the earthly world is not only that he brought the light of wisdom, the warmth of love, not only that he brought cherubic and seraphic elements into earthly existence but that he *was* and he *is*—when one beholds him in all his power—working through the realm of the Thrones for our Earth. It is through this that all strength and power is introduced into the world, so as to accomplish everything to do with wisdom, to do with love. These are the highest of the hierarchies: Cherubim, Seraphim and Thrones. The Seraphim lead us into the depths of the human heart with their love and the Seraphim raise us up to the heights of eagles. Wisdom rays forth from the realm of the Cherubim. Devotional love becomes sacrifice, as symbolized by the sacrificial bull. Strength, pulsating throughout the universe, strength that engenders the power to make real the creative force that throbs throughout the world: this is represented for us by the whole symbolism of the lion. The strength that is drawn towards the earth by Christ Jesus, the strength that rights everything, that brings order to all things, denoting the heights of evolved power, this is what St Mark illustrates for us as a third attribute of Christ Jesus.

When we speak—in the mood of St John's Gospel—of the high Sun Being whom we call Christ as the light of the earthly Sun in a spiritual sense, when we speak—in the mood of St Luke's Gospel—of the warmth of love welling forth from the earthly Sun of Christ, then we must speak—in the mood of St Mark's Gospel—of the power of the earthly Sun itself in its spiritual aspect. All the concealed and manifest forces present on earth, weaving to and fro, all those terrestrial forces and powers appear before us when witnessing events as portrayed through St Mark's Gospel.

Could one but guess, however tentatively, how the ideas, how the earthly thoughts of Christ, came to earth, would one understand them if one could rise up to the heights in the sense of St John's Gospel? Could one but feel the wafting warmth of sacrificial love, could one feel the warmth of St Luke's Gospel streaming through oneself? If one could sense Christ's thinking in St John's Gospel, Christ's feeling in St Luke's Gospel, then one would learn of Christ's willing through St Mark's Gospel. Here one learns to know those individual forces through which Christ makes real for us both love and wisdom.

We will have gained an additional inkling of three qualities by adding to our considerations of the Gospels of St John and St Luke those of St Mark, too. One would then be able to say: We approached you in awe, O Christ, and experienced a sense of your thinking, your feeling and your willing as these three powers of your soul floated above us, exemplifying the loftiest of earthly paradigms.

We have set out our studies thus far as though we were observing someone on a small scale, as a microcosm, noting that they consist of sentient, intellectual and consciousness souls and then exploring the qualities of each of these. Taking the words consciousness soul in relation to Christ, we could say: an intimation of this is given to us in St John's Gospel. The mind or intellectual soul of Christ is presented pictorially through St Luke's Gospel and the sentient soul is described—in all its strength of will—by the Gospel of St Mark. If we can really encompass all this, it will resolve for us both the manifest and hidden forces of nature surrounding us, concentrated as they are in the individuality of Christ, and in turn shed light on all the forces in existence.

In St John's Gospel we extended ourselves into this individuality's thinking; in St Luke's Gospel we immersed ourselves in the feelings of this Being. Because in the latter one does not need to penetrate so deeply into his individuality, our observation was less difficult than comprehending what we encounter in St Mark's Gospel, namely the hidden structure of all natural and spiritual forces of the cosmos. This can all be found in the Akashic Record and will be reflected back to us when we allow the colossal document of St Mark's Gospel to work upon us. We will then gain an intimation of all that is concentrated within the single individuality of Christ, of all that is otherwise dispersed throughout all the beings in the world. We will come to understand in its loftier brilliance what we have already learnt about the fundamental orientation and principles of the various individuals described. As the secrets of world-willing contained in St Mark's Gospel are revealed, we will approach in awe the central fulcrum of the universe, Christ Jesus, and will gradually gain a sense of his thinking, his feeling and his willing.

When we contemplate thinking, feeling and willing acting together in concert, we gain an approximate image of the whole human being. Yet we are also bound to see thinking, feeling and willing as separate entities within the individual. Summarizing, our vision even here would be insufficiently far-ranging to gain an overview of everything. While our task is made comparatively easier by observing these three capacities separately, our picture will pale on seeing all three faculties intermingled within the human soul. We separate them for our own benefit because we lack the strength to observe them in combination; when trying to combine them the image pales.

If one has observed the three Gospels of John, Luke and Mark and acquired an inkling of the thinking, feeling and willing of Christ Jesus then one can see, in essence, the harmony these three qualities can achieve. However, this is the point at which the picture becomes unclear and fades because no human strength is equal to synthesizing what for us has been presented separately. For in being there is unity without separation—at last, and only now, are we able to synthesize this as a unity, a single entity. This is when the picture fades for our vision. Yet what then appears to us is all that Christ Jesus was as an earthly, human being.

Contemplating what Christ Jesus was as a human being, how he acted as a human being in the thirty-three years of his earthly existence, can now be developed with reference to St Matthew's Gospel. The contents of this Gospel furnish us with an image of self-contained harmony. If, in St John's Gospel, we described a divine God-human belonging to the entire cosmos, we depicted a unique, self-sacrificing Being of love, as portrayed by St Luke, and then in St Mark's Gospel we encountered an embodiment of cosmic will, so in the Gospel of St Matthew we have a true image of the Palestinian individual who lived as a human being for thirty-three years and in whom the synthesized essence of all the aspects described by the other three evangelists is distilled. In the Matthew Gospel we meet the figure of Christ Jesus as an utterly human being, as that unique earthly human whom one is unable to understand unless one has been prepared by studying the other three Gospels. Though the individual may pale for us, this paler image nevertheless mirrors what we have so far learnt from our studies. St Matthew's Gospel provides the only image of Christ that can yield an insight into his personality.

This is how matters now stand, which we had, of necessity, to characterize differently in our earlier approach to the first Gospel. Now that we have characterized two further Gospels, we can explore how they relate inwardly to one another, how we can gain an insight into Christ Jesus when, on the basis of our previous studies, we approach the human being who became what he did become through Christ Jesus. The God-Man draws near to us through St John and, as a corollary to St Luke's Gospel, this Being unites within himself—in the form of teachings of compassion and love—the streams from all directions that had evolved out of Zarathustrianism and Buddhism. Everything pre-existing came towards us in relation to Luke's Gospel. When we consider the Matthew Gospel, what comes to the fore in all its exactitude and immediacy are his own folk roots in the ancient Hebrew people: the man Jesus as he lived in accordance with his origins in the Hebrew people. We will recognize why the blood of this ancient people had to be the means by which it could contribute to earthly humanity precisely through the blood of Christ Jesus.

When we consider the Matthew Gospel we encounter Hebrew antiquity, its mission and the significance of this people for the whole world, for the birth of a new epoch: the birth of Christianity issuing from the ancient Hebrew world. As we learn of powerfully comprehensive ideas through St John's Gospel, as we gain a feeling for the warmest, most boundless sacrificial love through St Luke, an inkling of the forces of all beings and all realms through St Mark's Gospel, we now acquire knowledge of—and a feeling for—what lives in humanity and its earthly evolution through Christ Jesus in Palestine. What Christ Jesus was as a human being, what he still is, all the secrets of human history and its becoming: all this is contained in the Gospel of St Matthew. Whereas Mark represents the secrets of all beings and realms of Earth and the cosmos—as connected with the Earth—one finds the mysterious secrets of human history and destiny in St Matthew's Gospel. We learnt of the concept of Sophia from St John, of the mysteries of sacrifice and love from Luke's Gospel, about the forces of the cosmos and the Earth from Mark's Gospel, so we hear of human life, human history, human destiny, by studying St Matthew's Gospel.

We would now be in a position to investigate St Mark's Gospel had we, over the past seven years of our spiritual-scientific movement, been able to spend four years working on guiding principles and three years deepening these as a way of shedding light on various spheres of life. Then we could, as it were, have crowned the entire edifice with a contemplation of Christ Jesus in the context of the Matthew Gospel. However, as human life is not perfect and as this has not been the case—at least not for those within this spiritual-scientific movement—it is therefore not possible, without causing confusion, to move instantly to an exploration of St Mark's Gospel itself. To imagine, on the basis of the John or Luke Gospels, that any real knowledge of Christ Jesus could follow would be a mistake. Similarly, one might believe that one could, unilaterally, make use of everything that might be said in relation to the Mark Gospel. Misunderstandings would then be more numerous than before. For these reasons another way needs to be found. What should now follow, as far as this is possible in the near future, is a study of St Matthew's Gospel. To this end we will not yet plumb the mighty depths of St Mark's Gospel, thereby avoiding the misconception that to describe just one aspect of a person is tantamount to describing the entire being. Misunderstandings will thus be avoided. We will therefore present—as far as is possible—the ancestry of Christ in the ancient Hebrew people or what we can also call the birth of Christianity in Palestine. Over the coming days, our study will focus on the Matthew Gospel, avoiding, as we have, the idea that a single trait can adequately describe an entire being. This will make it easier to follow what is to be said in relation to the St Mark's Gospel.

Lecture 4

BERLIN, 9 NOVEMBER 1909

THE MISSION OF THE ANCIENT HEBREW PEOPLE

In the last lecture we discussed how we would structure our studies of the Gospels and the reasons were given for our intention to set forth some aspects of St Matthew's Gospel. In some respects this is to describe the most human elements of Christ Jesus that we encounter in this Gospel. On the other hand, we are given a comprehensive overview of the historical events that show how Christ Jesus emerges out of humanity itself. As this Gospel reveals to us how the greatest event of earthly evolution has emerged out of history, we can reasonably guess that the deeper secrets of human advance lie precisely in this Gospel.

Today I will again expressly emphasize that what is said on this occasion is sensitive and that it is easy to do serious harm to our spiritual-scientific movement by one-sidedly sharing these mysteries with all and sundry. The greatest, most grateful tact needs to be exercised in relation to this. It is not too much to expect each one of you to find it within your forbearance only to speak of any Christ-picture once you are in possession of all four aspects, as characterized in the four Gospels. From our study of St Luke's Gospel we could see how the two great pre-Christian streams of Zarathustrianism and that which reached its pre-Christian zenith in Buddhism flowed together, pouring themselves out into that great Christian stream of spiritual life on Earth.

The Gospel of St Matthew initially speaks of something quite different: namely, to show how the physicality into which the individuality of Zarathustra incarnated emerged from out of the ancient Hebrew people. It sets itself the task of showing the part played by the ancient Hebrew people in the universal evolution of humanity. One might imagine, when the individuality of Zarathustra had incarnated in the Jesus of Bethlehem, that only the physical essence was born out of the Hebrew folk and that nothing more is being asserted than that Zarathustra is reincarnated into a Hebrew physical body. Were one to give this assertion even a nuanced credence, it would result in a false understanding of the truth.

Observations such as this make it clear that an individuality such as Zoroaster-Zarathustra needs physical embodiment as an instrument. If an individuality descends from the highest heights, from the most divine of spiritual worlds, and is incarnated into unsuitable embodiment, then nothing more than that body's inherent potential as an instrument can be created by the incarnating being. False nuances of feeling, as mentioned earlier, can give rise to manifold misunderstandings. In the Theosophical movement it was long not understood that the human body is the temple of the human soul. We need to take into account what has so often been emphasized here: that the human I dwells within three sheaths, each of which is older than the human I itself. This I is an Earth-entity, the youngest of the three components. The astral body has its origins on the ancient Moon, the ethereal, etheric or life body originates on Old Sun, which is three planetary cycles ago. The physical body is in its own way the most complete component and has four planetary ages behind its evolution. The physical body has been fashioned over aeons of time so that it is now the most perfected instrument available to the human ego, enabling it in its task of eventually raising itself back to spiritual heights. Were the physical body to be as incomplete as the astral body and the I, human development on earth would not be tenable.

If you take this seriously, you will no longer entertain any falsely nuanced association with the concept that Zarathustra was born *out of* the Hebrew people. This people was necessarily constituted as it was, so that it was able to offer the physical basis for a being such as Zarathustra. If we imagine that this being has, since his time as the teacher of a proto-Persian people, been developing ever higher, we must also say that it was essential to provide a bodily instrument of a quality commensurate with this Being's lofty stature. A fitting instrument had to be available to him. Throughout the evolutions of Saturn, Sun, Moon and Earth, the Gods have been at pains to shape and configure the universal human form. From this we may draw the inference that the more intimate and individual the preparations for a human body, the more extra spiritual-divine work is entailed in furnishing a body with the exceptional qualities then needed to serve Zarathustra.

In order for this to come about, the entire history of the ancient Hebrew peoples had to take the course that it took. The Akashic Chronicle shows us that the contents of the Old Testament do in fact coincide with historical records. Everything within the ancient Hebrew folk had, as it were, to be configured in such a way as to find its zenith in the individuality of the Bethlehem Jesus. Exceptional processes had to be invoked. Forces most capable of being developed by humanity—necessarily developed—had to be extracted from the sum total of post-Atlantean culture so that humanity could replace their ancient clairvoyant faculties with them. The ancient Hebrew peoples were destined to offer just such a physicality, structured into the very fabric of the brain so as to enable what we call worldly knowledge to be established without clairvoyant influence. Such was to be the mission of this nation. Abraham, the progenitor of this people, was just such an individual whose physicality was chosen as a fitting instrument for reasoned thinking. Everything previously of great significance and stature had been framed by the after-effects of ancient clairvoyance, but now an individuality with the best-suited brain was called to observe matters with reasoned thinking and without being harried or compelled by clairvoyant imaginations and intuitions. An exceptionally configured brain was essential in supporting an individual destined as was Abram or Abraham.

The following also corresponds with the Akashic Record, namely the direction from which Abraham came: westwards from beyond the Euphrates, towards Canaan. Abraham was summoned, as we are told in the Bible, from Ur in Chaldea. Whilst the after-echoes of a dimming clairvoyance still lingered in Egyptian and Chaldean-Babylonian cultures, an individual from the Chaldean people was selected who was no longer reliant on such visionary capacities but who based his observations on events in the outer world. A culture was to be introduced whose fruits are still embodied in our Western civilization. Synthetic thinking and mathematical logic were introduced by Abraham and right into medieval times he was regarded in a certain sense as the initiator of arithmetic. The entire configuration of his thinking was such that it saw the world in terms of relative measure and number.

A personality constituted in this way was predisposed to a living relationship with such a Godhead as would manifest through the medium of the outer world. Other Gods, with the exception of Yahweh, appeared in the inner recesses of the soul and Imagination, Intuition and related faculties had to be developed in order to gain understanding of them. In ancient India one could gaze out and see the sun rising, see the kingdoms of Earth, the processes in the airy regions, those of the sea and so on. Yet all this was regarded as a great illusion—as Maya, in which the Indian could have seen no trace of the divine once he had attained to this through inner Imagination—had he not afterwards sought to bring this into relationship with the outer world. Just as for Zarathustra, too, we should be aware that he would not have been able to reveal the great Being of the Sun had not Ahura Mazdao also arisen within him. But we see this particularly in the Egyptian Gods, who originate deep within soul experience and are subsequently brought into relation with outer phenomena.

This is the standpoint from which all pre-Hebrew divinities are to be regarded. Yahweh or Jehovah, however, is the one God who observes us externally, who approaches humankind from the outside, revealing himself in wind and weather. Inasmuch as human beings penetrate everything present in the world by way of measure, number and weight, to this extent do they move closer to the God Yahweh. In earlier ages this was the reverse. Brahma was initially recognized within the soul and from thence brought outwards into the world. Yahweh, conversely, is first encountered externally and can only be verified by subsequent inner experience. This is the spiritual counter-image of what we can call the union of Yahweh with Abraham. Here was a man whose personality could grasp and understand Yahweh or Jehovah, a man whose physical constitution was such that the deity pervading, enlivening and weaving throughout world phenomena could comprehend it.

Through the unique attributes of this man, Abraham, we are now concerned with deducing the mission of an entire people. It was essential that Abraham's spiritual entelechy be transferred to others, something dependent on physical means; for every impulse that needs to be brought to outer expression is reliant on a quite specific configuration of the physical body. The ancient religions, built as they were on a basis of dimming clairvoyance, did not need to rely so heavily on whether individual components of a brain were formed in this way or that. Comprehension of Jehovah, however, was strongly bound to the physical configuration of the brain. Only via the route of heredity within a people connected by blood relatedness could such characteristics be transferred.

Something quite special had to take place. Abraham needed descendants who passed on that unique physical constitution which, previously, the Gods themselves had formed and which found its culminating pinnacle in Abraham. The shaping of physical bodies now had to be undertaken over many generations, independently of human ken, so as to continue the formative work, hitherto the charge of the Gods. A brain capable of comprehending Jehovah had to be arrived at through physical heredity and the union of Jehovah with Abraham transmitted onwards into descendants. An extraordinary devotion to Jehovah was entailed in this process, an exceptional devotedness on the part of Abraham as an individuality, because the potential for progressively developing a particular constitution is dependent on the extent to which it is used as intended. If one wants to make a hand skilled for a particular purpose, for instance, this can only be successful to the extent that the hand is cultivated in accordance with its intended design or purpose. In order to foster the physical basis for a Jehovah-compatible brain, devotedness in addition to Jehovah-comprehension had to be present in the highest imaginable degree.

This was in fact the case. We are told in the Bible how it took place. Devotion is at its greatest when one sacrifices what one is oneself to become in future. Abraham is to sacrifice his son Isaac to Yahweh-Jehovah. In doing this he would have sacrificed the entire future of the Hebrew people, everything that he was and everything with which he was tasked with bringing about worldwide. Abraham was the first to comprehend Jehovah. To show his complete surrender to this task he has to devote himself utterly to its demands. In sacrificing his only descendant he renounces all future propagation of his line throughout the world.

His devoted renunciation went as far as sacrificing Isaac; it was his will so to do. Isaac is then returned to him. What does this mean? It means something quite awe-inspiring. Isaac is returned to him by Jehovah himself. In other words, Abraham carries out the mission with which his individuality is tasked to the extent that he is willing to devolve his mission to posterity—not on his own account—but on his son's, as a gift from Yahweh-Jehovah. If you think about it, you will see here a fact of world significance illuminating to a boundless extent the secrets of humanity's historical evolution.

Let us see how events proceed. Through his dedicated surrender to Jehovah, it becomes possible for all that the Gods had hitherto created to really endure over time. Physical humankind was born out of cosmic existence. What we know as physical embodiment on Earth is interwoven as number, measure and weight with laws over which the realm of stars holds sway. Humanity is born from out of the starry worlds and bears within it the laws of the starry heavens. These laws of the stellar heavens had, as it were, to be inscribed into the blood flowing onwards through the generations of ancient Hebrew peoples originating in Abraham. Everything within the old Hebrew peoples had to be regulated in such a way as to allow the onward flow of lawfulness—as expressed in number, measure and weight and as it had formed human physicality—from out of cosmic unity and in the form of laws pertaining in stellar realms.

We see this expressed in a severely distorted passage in the Bible where it is stated[7] that God wished to make the Israelites as numerous as the stars in the heavens. What is in fact meant is that, in the way they reproduced and dispersed across the earth down the ages, God intended the laws and numerical ratios to hold sway that also pertain in the stars on high. The Hebrew people was to be aligned—in the stream of its hereditary transmission—in accordance with the numerical harmony of the stars.

We see how this takes place. Isaac had two sons, Jacob and Esau. We see how, in all that flows via the blood of generations, those belonging to the line of Esau are set aside, discontinued and a more fitting bloodline is brought to the fore and further modified. Jacob had twelve sons—corresponding with the twelve divisions of the Zodiac through which the Sun passes on high—enacting the ordering of each constellation in turn. This has an inner lawfulness, an inner principle. In the lives and processes of heredity visible in the Hebrew peoples, a reflection of the number and measure reigning in the heavens can indeed be discerned. Abraham was prepared to sacrifice his son Isaac, fully re-dedicating himself to his mission from Jehovah. A ram or a lamb was sacrificed in place of Isaac. What does this signify?

Something of extraordinary depth is concealed here. The human physicality destined to reproduce and embody capacities capable of grasping measure and number in the world were, in accordance with mathematical logic, to be preserved and received as a gift from Jehovah. To maintain this capability in unalloyed form, however, it was essential to eliminate all forms of dim, atavistic clairvoyance, to renounce all manner of Imaginations, Intuitions and the influx of all such revelations as persisted in other archaic religions well into Chaldean and Egyptian times. All bequests from the spiritual world had to be rejected. The last such spiritual gift that remained when all others had become obscure is denoted in the mystical symbolism of the ram. The two horns of the ram denote the renunciation of the two-petalled lotus flower, the last of the gifts of clairvoyance to be sacrificed after all such aptitudes had long since been discarded. To achieve the physicality required in Isaac, the final clairvoyant capacity, the gift of the ram, had to be renounced.

The people continued to live out their mission in such a way that precisely such faculties as Abraham possessed were inheritable down the generations. When any clairvoyance resurfaces atavistically, whenever one or another is able to see into the spiritual world, a reaction sets in that rejects the personality concerned; they are cast out and not tolerated within their community. Hostility towards this gift of the ram is expressed in enmity, as exemplified by Joseph. His dreams were prophecies illumined by the spiritual world. He is therefore quite naturally outlawed, banished for having the very gift that is to be eradicated from the mission of the Hebrew people. He is shunned by his brethren for having inherited a resurgent aspect of ancient clairvoyance. This is why Joseph is exiled to Egypt: he has deviated from the mission of his people.

What we are told is very significant! Now we see why the personality representing all that the Hebrew people could only look back upon as something existing before Abraham, how what exists in the personality of Joseph is related to illustrate by exception the characteristics so essential to the fulfilment of the ancient Hebrew peoples' evolutionary mission. The door had been closed to the world that had—through latent clairvoyance—led to the religions of India and Persia. The portal had been sealed. Now people looked—via measure and number—to Jehovah, to the one entity who could rightly order the world. The only known certainty was that everything externally visible, everything manifest in the world, was an emanation of Jehovah-Yahweh, the world creator, and was one and the same as the human I, was synonymous with human ego-hood. Yet no Imaginations, no individual inner experiences of this fact surfaced within these native communities. In those times—I must emphasis this—no individual experience of this fact could occur. It had to be learnt through outer experience. In other words, this had to be learnt amongst a people who could still experience such things.

Joseph thus became the binding link between the ancient Hebrews and the Egyptians, with a people, in other words, from whom knowledge could be gained of experiences no longer accessible to Hebrews. Whatever can be synthesized by means of one's own inner experience—knowledge and experience of the external world with those of inner imagination—could then only be absorbed by aligning oneself with a people still experiencing this to a high degree, a people such as the Egyptians.

Inner capacities such as these had to be harmonized with those of mathematical logic. Only someone still possessing something of this imaginative quality could introduce logic to the Egyptians and Joseph, having this ability, was the most apt link. He could serve the Egyptians in that he had two gifts: the old clairvoyance from the time of Abraham, which could access the realm of Egyptian striving, as well as what they lacked by way of mathematical logic, being unable to implement in physical life what their imagination revealed. Pharaoh was incapable of ordering matters as this new, previously absent, faculty dawned. Imagination was plentiful but, when a certain level of disorder set in, the additional faculty of thinking in terms of number and measure was lacking in the Egyptians, yet present in Joseph. He was in a position to give sage and timely advice at the Egyptian court and was the most fitting connection between Hebrews and Egyptians. In this way he could bring it about that the Yahweh-Jehovah teachings which had hitherto been a synthesis of external reality—like a mathematical world concept—now gained the colour and imaginative content abundant in Egypt.

It was Moses who made the harmonious correlation between ancient Egyptian experience and knowledge of world-conditions and contexts. Once made, the Hebrews could be led back to process in their own ways what they had experienced—or rather had undergone—in Egypt. It is a matter of the following: that a gift remained unalloyed by other peoples and that an idiosyncratic blood-configuration remained unadulterated. On the other hand, whatever ancient peoples had achieved had to be salvaged. What has been handed down from ancient times is the wisdom alive in the Egyptians that has been inculcated, incarnated and literally embodied by Moses into the old Hebrew peoples with their predisposition to mathematical-logical faculties. Then again, the Hebrew people had to be torn away in readiness for inheriting what could only be transferred through Abraham's people.

And so they lived on. In ever refining essential preconditions and aligning their blood ever more closely with these preconditions, the time came when it became possible, in accordance with the lines of heredity down the generations, to realize the physical vessel for the Jesus child and make it suitable for the personality of Zoroaster–Zarathustra to inhabit it. To this end the people had to be made powerfully robust.

If, in the sense of the Matthew Gospel, we trace the times of the Kings and Judges and the various destinies of the ancient Hebrew peoples we will see how the conditions and relationships revealed by this people often stray and yet were essential in bringing about what had necessarily to be brought about. It was especially important that this people underwent the misfortune expressed as the Babylonian imprisonment. We will see how their unique folk characteristics developed and how, after encountering the ancient traditions present in Babylon from an opposing perspective, they were then ready to be reunited with all that they had left behind. That is one thing. The other is that, just when the Hebrew people were led into a confluence with the Babylonians, a great and mighty teacher from the East was teaching there and that some of the most outstanding among the Hebrews had the opportunity to live in the light of this great teacher. This is the time when Zarathustra was teaching as Nazarathos or Zaratos in the very region to which the Jews had been led. Some of the greatest prophets came under his influence and he was able to achieve much: as much, in fact, as was required at the point when the people's blood configuration had already been to a certain degree effective yet now needed specific external influences.

One cannot go far wrong if one compares this entire evolution with the gradual and incremental development of an individual. A child is born and grows up to its seventh year in the physical care of its parents. Influences on a physical level predominate here, followed by those enabling the etheric body to be born in a timely way. This stage focuses primarily on shaping memory to the end that everything developing in the ether body can be properly strengthened. A third period can be characterized as the astral body beginning to connect with the external world and absorbing what we can term the necessary powers of judgement or the ability to discriminate.

The ancient Hebrew people experienced this journey in a unique way. They underwent the first period during the time between Abraham and the first kings, and this can be compared with the first seven years of an individual childhood. Everything is done to consolidate the unique characteristics of blood. Everything we are told about Abraham's travels, of the elaboration of the twelve tribes, how the laws of Moses were incorporated, about the tribulations in the desert, can be compared with all that streams into the individual from their physical surroundings. The second phase that follows cements their inner life and is characterized by the dominion of the kings until their captivity in Babylon. After this the influences of Chaldea and those of the oriental Magi become active upon the Hebrew people. The spiritual leader who lived between 600 and 550 BCE, and who was already allowing this Eastern content to flow into the Hebrew peoples, was none other than the individual we know as Zarathustra. Even then he was working towards the preparation of a suitable physical vessel through increasing potential and creating ever more suitable conditions for a fitting physical body to evolve through the generations from Abraham onwards. All this ultimately enabled Zarathustra to reincarnate within this stream.

St Matthew portrays this progression in an especially wonderful and truthful way, introducing a threefold element. There are three times fourteen generational elements: fourteen from Abraham to David, fourteen from David to the Babylonian Captivity and again fourteen from Babylon until Christ Jesus. Here are three times fourteen—forty-two—generations that reveal how the physical embodiment of Jesus contained the essence of the combined destinies of the ancient Hebrew peoples from Abraham downwards. Now a human being arises who brings to expression all those qualities garnered down the generations through lines of heredity, who expresses spiritually the workings of his soul by synthesizing them all within his single human personality. Hebraic evolution in its entirety since Abraham was to be gathered up into this one individuality and find its zenith in the Jesus described in St Matthew's Gospel. How could this come about? This is only possible by recapitulating all preceding evolution at a soul level.

Zarathustra sets out from the region of Ur in Chaldea, whence Abraham originates, emanating spiritually from the Mysteries. This is where the golden star first appears and proceeds on its course with the local Magi following it. The same takes place on a spiritual plane as took place physically through Abraham. The path Abraham took is taken spiritually by the star followed by the Magi. This is in fact the incarnating Zarathustra himself, treading the path Abraham took and descending to his birthplace. This is the moment when the individuality of Zarathustra incarnates in the Jesus child of Bethlehem and which is known to the Magi. They follow the star that is their great teacher, Zarathustra, who is incarnating.

We are now faced with the fact that this trail actually continued, that contained within the personality of that Jesus child the entire evolution of the Hebrew people is encompassed. We see firstly that on a spiritual level the sacrifice of Isaac is re-enacted. In spirit this is repeated through the sacrificial gifts of the three Magi from the East: gold, frankincense and myrrh are their offerings. We also see that again something appears that reminds us of the earlier events of the ancient Hebrew people. Connected with the birth of this Jesus child is an image of the destinies of the ancient Hebrews. A certain Joseph, with his heritage of dreaming, is the connecting link between the Hebrew and Egyptian peoples. Here again is a Joseph given to dreaming and his dreams tell him not only that Jesus is to be born but also that he must flee to Egypt with the child.

Now Zarathustra's path leads onward and into the body of the Jesus child. Just as he had followed the path travelled in the physical world by Abraham—from Ur in Chaldea to Canaan—now he continues on his way to Egypt. Likewise, the Jesus child is brought back from Egypt, just as the Hebrews had been led back. Thus we see in the appearance of Jesus of Bethlehem—only later called Jesus of Nazareth—a recapitulation of the folk destiny of the ancient Hebrew people right up to their homecoming out of Egypt into the promised land of Palestine. The external history of the Hebrew people that had played out over many long centuries is now reprised in the destiny of that human individuality representing Zarathustra in the body of the Bethlehem Jesus. Taken as a whole, this is the secret of humanity's entire history, as related in the Matthew Gospel. One does not understand human history at all if one does not take account of the fact that in the individual destinies of great leading individuals—each of whom have their unique mission—human evolution over centuries is repeated, that they incorporate in one incarnation the essence of all that has been developing in humankind over many long centuries. Christ Jesus had naturally to encompass far more than this but his physical embodiment had to be prepared for, and this could only take place in the extraordinary ways described.

How do matters now stand regarding the short time in which a recapitulation of the entire Hebrew people is to take place within the personality of Jesus? What characterizes this time in history? Let us gather together the various evolutionary facts I have sought to align for your imaginations. Combining these we see: humanity proceeded from out of a primeval state in which what bound people together in love were the ties of blood. Those drawn together by blood loved one another and marriage took place within closely related family groupings. There was no bond of love other than this in ancient times and because of this, love was bound to blood relations. These closely-related marriages formed the basis for life in ancient times. But then these close ties were increasingly loosened in the most varied of regions of the Earth and we can trace how it was seen as exceptional when men and women of different hereditary or tribal lines intermarried, when marriage was widened after such initial closeness. All the myths, sagas and legends, such as, for instance, the Song of Gudrun, characterize this as unusual, impressive and worthy of remark. In this realm of human development two streams are active. One, a divine-spiritual principle whose active aim it had always been to lead humanity as a single entity, unified through blood-relatedness. Opposing this was another, a luciferic principle, which aimed to make individuals self-reliant, each as great and powerful as possible. Both principles have to be active within human nature and both are essential to human evolution.

Now both these powers were working in the course of humanity's progress: divine-spiritual powers and those retarded luciferic powers remaining behind on the Moon who wished to prevent humankind from losing the identity that would make them completely independent. These two forces have always been active within human evolution. These powers have caused the human I or ego, which is a product of Earth, to be forever wrenched to and fro. On the one hand, humanity was inspired to general human love, on the other towards inner self-reliance. At a certain point something of a crisis was reached in relation to the divergent activity of these two forces. This human crisis, this decision, took place when, as a result of the deeds of the Roman Empire, a large swathe of earthly humanity was thrown together. This was indeed a decisive moment in human evolution, a moment when the hitherto unresolved issue of close—or wider—intermarriage was to be determined. Human beings stood in danger of losing their I-identities through remaining within the single-tribe marriage context or instead losing all connection with humanity at large and becoming isolated, self-reliant and egotistic individuals. This was a pivotal moment.

What needed to happen at this moment? Something quite particular. The human I first had to become sufficiently mature to develop what we can call independence and freedom and—of itself and in freedom—to unfold a soul-spiritual love that could exist independently of blood ties. The human ego was at a watershed. It had to become completely unfettered and self-aware. This was the situation faced in the ancient world by most people on Earth with the exception of those in the Orient: the necessity to bring about a new birth of their I, a new birth through which each I—born of itself—could attain to the love it had itself engendered. Such an I was to develop love on the basis of freedom and freedom out of love. Fundamentally, only when a person becomes a true human being do they attain to this. A true human being is indeed one who has achieved this birth of their I. This is because those who love solely on the basis of blood ties are compelled to love and merely express on a higher level what also exists, at a lower level, in the animal kingdom. Only at the point we have just described did real potential for human development present itself; this was the stage at which the influence enabling humans to attain true humanity spread across the world, making of people veritable humans.

Remember, if you will, what I have told you countless times: that the individual, by virtue of his very being, consists of three members: a physical body in common with minerals, an etheric or ethereal body in common with plants and an astral body, hitherto also the seat of a love experienced in common with animals. Through fully developing their I or ego, human beings have become the crown of earthly creation. The rest of creation have names externally bestowed on them and are in this sense objects. The I has a name that it can only bestow upon itself. Divinity speaks in the I. Terrestrial conditions no longer pertain in the ego. Only the spirit realm speaks in the human ego. Spirit speaks from out of the heavens once such an ego or I has fully realized itself. One could say that previously three kingdoms existed: mineral, plant and animal and that another realm can be added, which had albeit raised itself above that of the animal but had not yet attained completion, which had not yet received into itself a celestial element. This is the realm which contains all that does not exist in earthly realms, contains all that can be gathered up within an I and was once called, in the tradition of biblical parlance, the Kingdom or Kingdoms of Heaven and frequently rendered as the 'Kingdom of God'.

This heavenly realm is none other than a paraphrase of the term 'the realm of humanity'. When referring to mineral, plant or animal kingdoms, we could—in the sense of the Bible—add as a fourth domain: the 'Kingdom of Heaven'. The human realm is in reality—in the sense of the Bible—a heavenly realm. Those who once gazed via the Mysteries into the entire course of human evolution could have said the following: Look back into olden times, to the time when humanity was becoming human, and you will see that the Kingdom of Heaven did not yet exist on earth. Now the time has come when the Kingdom of Heaven is to appear on Earth. This is what the forerunner of Christ Jesus proclaimed and what Christ Jesus himself declared: 'The Kingdom of Heaven is nigh'. In this they were characterizing their times in the very deepest sense. And it was precisely then that the birth of Christ Jesus had to take place. He was to bring to Earth those very forces by means of which the human I would be able to gain the qualities described. The entire evolution of humankind can thus be divided into two parts: a pre-Christian age in which the Kingdom of Heaven did not yet exist on Earth and an age in which the Kingdom of Heaven was then to be found on Earth: in the human kingdom in its highest sense.

The ancient Hebrew people were chosen to provide the physical corporeality, the physical sheaths which had been in preparation as an entity to receive the bearer of the Kingdom of Heaven.

These are the secrets that reveal themselves when one focuses on historical questions in the context of St Matthew's Gospel. We can add to the two streams contributing to Christianity and characterized earlier—Zarathustrianism and Buddhism—a third stream: the Hebrew stream, the contribution of the ancient Hebrew peoples. We can now say: there used to be leaders such as Buddha and Zarathustra, who wanted to bring the offering of their religious streams. For this a temple needed to be raised and it could only be built by the ancient Hebrew people. These were the people who built the bodily temple of Jesus and this was the temple into which those two tributary streams could flow. Zarathustra was the first to sacrifice himself by incarnating into this prepared body. The Buddha then made the sacrifice of allowing his own Nirmanakaya to flow into the other Jesus. In this way these two streams found their confluence.

In giving you some additional thoughts today, which are by way of being somewhat conclusive in nature, I have only been able to provide fleeting sketches of these deep mysteries. Just to convey such conclusive lines of thought, I have been obliged to characterize them rather schematically. Later we will continue to explore the mission of the ancient Hebrew people and the unique emergence of the Christ Jesus from this people. We will encounter the inimitable as it emerges from history, from the temporal course of evolution, and encounter a Being of eternal consequence, a Being having significance of eternal duration. The advent will gradually reveal itself—emerging from a transitory, ephemeral world—of that which will endure forever.

Lecture 5

BERLIN, 23 NOVEMBER 1909

PREPARING FOR AN UNDERSTANDING OF THE CHRIST EVENT

THE MISSION OF THE ANCIENT HEBREW PEOPLE

By way of contributing to our studies of the St Matthew Gospel, we touched on the mission of the ancient Hebrew people and the emergence of Christ Jesus from this people. Our observations in this connection were intended gradually to create some clarity as to how the various spiritual streams flowed together to collectively vouchsafe the great spiritual stream of Christianity for the onward progress of the Earth. The part that fell to the ancient Hebrew people in the evolution of all humanity could only be shown in brief outline last time. One cannot understand the Gospel of Matthew without going at least some way into the other elements of this people. So that we understand each other quite clearly, we need to bring to the forefront of our souls of what this mission consists. We saw how this differed from the mission of other pre-Christian peoples, which were still associated with what we can call the results of humanity's clairvoyance, which could be found among all peoples of antiquity. This is something one can also call ancient wisdom.

Similarly, and characterizing it sketchily, we can say that in ancient Atlantis all human beings could see into the spiritual world. Though only the initiated had the most advanced experience of this, most people were to at least some extent familiar with it because, in certain intermediate states, the Atlantean human being had clairvoyant experience of some spiritual realms. This faculty was to be replaced with what we now know as the predominant state, namely, activated reasoning, a grasp of the outer world with our physical senses, in short, life in the outer world. This was developing slowly and gradually throughout pre-Christian ages such that we can say: the ancient Indian people still possessed considerable remains of ancient clairvoyance. What the holy Rishis taught was inherited from even more ancient wisdom. Even in the second post-Atlantean cultural epoch in Persia, what the pupils and followers of Zarathustra knew was based on wisdom handed down from Atlantis. Ancient Chaldean astronomy is imbued with this primal wisdom, as is the wisdom of the Egyptians. The sort of science based upon post-Atlantean scientific faculties would have been totally incomprehensible to the ancient Egyptian or Chaldean mind. Science, which expresses itself in concepts and ideation of a physical nature, did not yet exist. The sort of reflection of which we are capable did not exist.

It is in no way gratuitous to make clear to oneself the difference between a genuine seer of our times and, for instance, one of Chaldea or ancient Egypt. For someone who attains true seership on the basis of conditions pertaining today, it is as follows: they receive what we can call the revelations of the spiritual world, the intuitions, experiences and knowledge from out of spiritual realms, and they must imbue these revelations—on the basis of all they have gained from earthly thinking—with the logical, sensible mode of thought acquired in everyday life. The experiences of a modern seer cannot be grasped in their totality unless they are received into a soul thoroughly schooled in logical and sensible thinking. Modern revelations and intuitive knowledge remain unintelligible, demanding the approach of a soul rigorously trained in logical thinking. Whoever has such revelations without first mustering the requisite will to train their earthly faculties with rational stringency will only achieve the sort of visionary clairvoyance that remains incomprehensible and hence susceptible to error. Today, only souls possessing genuine, intensive willpower to school themselves in rational mode are able to receive in fitting manner the revelations and knowledge accessible through seership today. This is why, in a spiritual movement such as ours, the greatest possible importance must be attached precisely to *not* developing clairvoyance one-sidedly—and thereby allowing one-sided impressions to be received—but that toward such revelation each soul must generate an element. A great deal of logical schooling work has to be undertaken in the furtherance of intentional clairvoyance. The two cannot be separated in our time.

This was quite different for the Egyptian or Chaldean seer. They received their inspiration, albeit via different means, in tandem with their inherent logical laws. They therefore needed no particular logic of their own. Once they had undergone spiritual training, these inspirations would contain ready-formed laws. Today's physical organism is no longer capable of that, having evolved beyond this stage in the course of humanity's onward trajectory.

Bearing this difference in mind, we can then understand what is meant when we say that remnants of ancient clairvoyance were widespread among pre-Christian peoples, with the single exception of the ancient Hebrews, chosen as they were to create a human organism suited to comprehending the outer, physical world in terms of measure, number and so on, and by these means gradually to ascend to the spiritual knowledge contained within the image of Yahweh or Jehovah. This was the crux: that in Abraham a human being was chosen whose brain was a fitting precursor for an entire people who could then inherit this feature from him. No longer would the inspirations be received as if rising up inwardly but rather as a gift originating externally. They received all that stemmed from Abraham not from within but as a revelation from without. Here something very important is indicated in differentiating this people's developmental situation from those of all the other peoples of antiquity; the difference is radical.

You may well think that the old faculties—those previously inherited capacities—might not be lost all at once, but that remnants of it might linger in this people. This is the case with Joseph, who retained something of older faculties in common with other nations, enabling him to be the link between Hebrews and Egyptians, who remained immersed in the spiritual stream of pre-Christian humanity. New faculties could only develop gradually.

Why was a people prepared in such a way? Why were they chosen, endowed with specialized capacities and detached from the rest of pre-Christian evolution? This had to happen in order to prepare humanity for that great impending moment when Christ Jesus was to descend to earth. This was a time when all ancient clairvoyance and blood-relatedness forfeited its significance in face of something completely new that appeared among humanity: full use of the I or ego. Through this radical intermixing of bloodlines much was lost of what had previously been so significant, but in its place full use of the human I was heralded. In this way the true Kingdom of Humanity—or the Kingdom of Heaven—could be added to all other kingdoms.

In general, human beings are not readily inclined to embrace what is new and to recognize it as such. They do not accept events taking place on a spiritual plane without further ado. There was always talk of some prophet or other appearing in future and this was as prevalent in pre-Christian as in more recent times. In the twelfth and thirteenth centuries there was a veritable addiction to prophesy. People emerged here and there prophesying the imminent reappearance of Christ, foretelling where this would take place. At other times isolated incidences of this would crop up. There was discussion of this or that person being the incarnation of a new Christ. Obviously, we need waste no words on these prophesies because, even if they gained some contemporary traction, they lack substance. Such prophesies always contained their own downfall in that they would speak of what was to come but failed to prepare humanity to *recognize* what was being foretold. They did not sufficiently preconfigure human feelings such that they would have understood the imminent event.

For people hearing those prophesies it must have been similar to the grammar school teacher, mentioned by Hebbel[8] in his diaries, who punished a pupil because he could not understand Plato. Hebbel then adds humorously that this pupil was the reincarnated Plato. This is exactly what happens to people who continuously predict a reincarnation of Christ. They would be quite unprepared for the substance of any such event, even if it were to transpire, and would hold Christ to be something other than Christ himself.

This is now to be prevented in advance. One needs to know the following to understand St Matthew's Gospel; so that there are at least some people who understand the Christ event, which is—to characterize it from one perspective—that it was Christ who brought to humanity the possibility henceforth not only to receive physical impressions externally but also to receive spirit from the external world. Individual human beings were to be prepared, and this is what, in fact, took place in Hebrew antiquity: that a few individuals were prepared in a certain way for acquiring an understanding of the Christ event. These people—they were few among the ancient Hebrews—need to be looked at more closely if one wants to understand how preparations for the coming of Christ were cultivated, how those characteristics inherited down the ages from Abraham were rendered adept at comprehending prophetically how the human I was to be introduced by the Redeemer. Those conditioned to see and understand clairvoyantly what had been prepared in the ancient Hebrews and what Christ in reality signified were known as Nazirites. They could perceive in vision all that had been developing among their ancient Hebrew forefathers to enable Christ's birth among them and hence how Christ could be understood. These Nazirites were, in terms of their way of life and their inner configuration—as dictated by their clairvoyant development—bound by strict regulation which, because they belonged in a completely different time, differed substantially from the rules whereby one attains to spiritual knowledge today; yet they nevertheless possessed some similarity with them. Some aspects of Nazirite life were important then but are of secondary importance today, and other aspects would be essential nowadays that were tangential then. For this reason nobody should believe that what previously led to visionary knowledge of Christ would today in like manner lead to any such far-reaching and essential understanding.

A prime requirement of a Nazirite was total abstinence from alcohol and eating anything prepared with vinegar was frowned upon. For those even more strictly adhering to the rules, it was further essential to avoid everything originating in the vine because it was held that in vines the plant-forming principle had overreached a certain point: the point past which more than Sun forces are at work. Sun forces affect the vines but other forces also ripen within it: what develops when the ripening continues into autumn under a Sun waning in strength. Drinks of grape origin were only for those who did not want to follow the path to higher clairvoyance, for those who venerated the God Dionysos while absorbing into themselves forces and capacities that rose up from out of the Earth.

A Nazirite bound by these laws during their training was further prohibited from contact with anything subject to death and in possession of an astral body, in short, with everything of an animal nature. They had to be strictly vegetarian and this was the reason why many confined themselves to eating only carob—or locust bean-derived bread, also known as St John's bread—a food widely used by those aiming to follow Nazirite instruction. They also ate the honey of wild bees—as opposed to domesticated bees—and other nectar-collecting insects. John the Baptist later chose precisely this path, living off locust bean bread and wild honey. In the Gospels it is said that he ate locusts and wild honey, but this is a mistranslation because he would hardly have been able to catch locusts in the desert wilderness—something to which I have previously drawn your attention.

Another fundamental for Nazirites was not to cut their hair for the duration of their training towards clairvoyance, something intimately connected with the evolution of humanity and something it is vital to keep in sight when considering humankind's development. Whatever belongs to the essential nature of the human being can only be understood when one seeks it in spiritual realms. However extraordinary it may sound, we retain in our hair a remnant of certain inward-raying forces, through which in olden days the forces of the Sun shone into human beings. Hair was something full of life that allowed forces of the Sun to ray into humans. You see this expressed, for example, in sculptures of lions—from times when humans were still conscious of such deeper aspects—where the sculptor has not merely created a modern lion with an almost poodle-like mane but a lion of ancient tradition whose mane bushes forth as if replete with—and condensed from—the Sun's rays. People could then reflect that it was entirely possible, in ancient times, that leaving hair uncut could attract forces into oneself, especially if the hair was strong and freshly healthy. However, by the time of the Nazirites, this reality was seen as barely more than symbolic.

Allowing what stood behind the forces of the Sun to stream into oneself represented something of real progress in human evolution. This progress from atavistic clairvoyant vision—streaming upwards within—to a way of thinking and conceptualizing about the outer world was associated with the fact that humans gradually became less hair-covered beings. One has to imagine Atlantean and immediately post-Atlantean humans as having luxuriant hair growth, a sign that they were still strongly irradiated with spiritual light. A choice is described in the Bible between the smooth Jacob and the hirsute Esau. In the latter we see a man descended from Abraham, retaining the last remnants of an earlier stage of development as expressed in his luxuriant hair. The type of man possessing faculties supporting greater interaction with the physical world is represented in the figure of Jacob. He had the gift of cleverness, combined with all the shadier characteristics this entailed, and he consigns Esau to relegation. In this way an offshoot from the main path of evolution is eliminated in Esau. Esau's line continues as the Edomites, in whom ancient human traits persist.

All these things are beautifully expressed in the Bible. Now a consciousness was to arise in humanity that was once again aware of a spiritual life, and this was to emerge among the Nazirites in that they wore their hair long during their schooling. In antiquity the connection of hair with spirit light was even expressed through the words for light and for hair being—with small variation—practically identical. The Hebrew language as a whole tends to draw attention to the deepest secrets of humanity and as such should be regarded as a powerful linguistic revelation of wisdom. This is background to the fact that the Nazirites let their hair grow long. Today, however, this need not be seen as a decisive feature.

During their training the Nazirites were guided towards a specific clairvoyant experience, namely to have an imaginative inkling of the gradual and imminent approach to humanity of Christ. The last of the great Nazirites around the time of Christ is called John the Baptist. He had not only experienced this anticipatory culmination in himself but had enabled all those whom he wished to make truly human to experience it likewise. The culminating experience mentioned is none other than the Johannine baptism. We need to learn to understand it in its evolutionary setting and significance, however. What indeed is this baptism? To what does it lead? Initially, it consists of a person being immersed under water, during the process of which their ether body is loosened from their physical body in the region of the head, whereas normally the two bodies are firmly enmeshed together. You have certainly heard that when people drown they see a tableau of their entire lives as a consequence of their ether body becoming detached from their physical body. In just this way did the person baptized by John experience their life's tableau with all its idiosyncracies, which would otherwise have remained forgotten. He would also have seen the condition of humanity in terms of that particular age, how the physical body develops out of the ether body, the latter acting as its sculptor. This etheric element of the human being, which forms their physical body, could only be observed when in the loosened state described. This is what took place during a Johannine baptism.

Had a person experienced this baptism three thousand years before the era of our reckoning, they would have become conscious of the fact that all the best spiritual qualities with which humankind is endowed must indeed be an ancient inheritance, because in those antique times all bounty received from the spiritual world was experienced as the divine bequest it was. This image was imprinted on the ether body and in turn became a formative force on the physical body. Particularly in those developed in advance of the rest of humanity, baptism would have revealed that all their knowledge rested upon ancient revelation. It was known as beholding etheric soul nature in an image of a snake or Serpent. Those who experienced this were known as Children of the Serpent, having witnessed how luciferic beings descended into human beings; what formed the physical body was a creature of the Serpent.

Now, however, not in a Johannine baptism three thousand years before John the Baptist but in his own times, something quite different transpired: among those baptized there were already some who demonstrated by their nature that human evolution was progressing apace, that the human I, fructified as it is by the outer world, possesses enormous power. Another image emerged, one quite different from that of the Johannine baptisms of yore: the person now saw the creative forces of the ether body no longer in the form of a Serpent but as an image of a Lamb. Such ether bodies were no longer imbued from within with what originated in luciferic forces but were instead completely surrendered to a spiritual world shining into human souls through manifestations of the outer world. This vision of the Lamb was the central experience of the Johannine baptism for those who understood the real meaning of that baptism. These were the same who could reflect: such human beings are quite different; they have become new beings. Those few who experienced Johannine baptism in this way could say: a great and mighty event is occurring, human beings are utterly changed and the human I has gained sovereignty here on Earth! Those whom St John had baptized were prepared in this way to comprehend the signs of the times, to understand that a momentous event was taking place.

This had always been the task of the Nazirites. Through baptism they achieved a state of knowing how imminently the coming of Christ was approaching. They knew this through the qualitative nature of their ether body while it was in a loosened state during baptism. John the Baptist was to show that the time had come when the human I could begin to indwell human nature and this made him John, the fulfilment of antiquity. He gathered a community around himself to whom he could show how the Christ principle would descend now that humanity was turning to align with their I. John the Baptist educated these Nazirites in the highest sense so that prophecy became fulfilment, creating a community around him who could comprehend the approaching Christ event. Only in this way can the words of John the Baptist[9] be rightly understood. These words are to be taken in their infinitely profound sense. It really no longer behoves someone who wishes to occupy themselves with these things nowadays still to see John the Baptist as a raging fanatic who merely rebukes the Pharisees, who calls them a brood of vipers and reproves them: 'Do not presume that in Abraham you have a father; God can bring forth children for Abraham from out of these stones.' From John the Baptist this would have been carping had he not also been glad when the Pharisees and Sadducees came to him to be baptized. Would he have scolded them on arrival? Why would he have done that?

Understanding matters from the inside out, it soon becomes apparent that mere chiding is not behind these harsh words but a lofty sense and deep significance that can only be grasped if one approaches the ancient Hebrews from a particular perspective. From what has been said you will already have gained a sense that in Abraham a man has been chosen who possesses the precise traits necessary and among whose descendants Jesus could, at the allotted moment, be born. For this to happen, what were tendencies in Abraham needed to evolve. We need to be quite clear that for them to unfold, something else always had to be excluded. We saw how Joseph was rejected. But this occurred even earlier with such, for example, as Esau, progenitor-patriarch of the Edomites, because he retained remnants of an ancient inheritance. Only such traits were to persist as inclined towards the designated direction. This is wonderfully expressed in that Abraham had two sons: Isaac, son of Sarah on one side, and then Ishmael. The ancient Hebrew people stem from Isaac. But Abraham had other characteristics as well. Had these persisted through the generations, a rightful inheritance would not have come about. This other heredity had to be radically cast aside, deflected in another direction, namely in that of Ishmael, son of the Egyptian maid Hagar. Two lines of heredity therefore descend from Abraham: one via Isaac and the other via the banished Ishmael who, bearing the blood of an Egyptian woman, had to take on characteristics unsuited to the mission of the Hebrew people.

Now something extraordinary happened. The Hebrew people were to generate what was rightful through heredity and claim their ancient inheritance of wisdom from without. They had to go to Egypt to absorb qualities available there. Moses was able to transmit this to his people because he was an Egyptian initiate. He could not have done this had this wisdom remained in Egyptian form. It would be wrong to imagine that ancient Egyptian wisdom could simply be dropped into all that flowed down from Abraham. This would not have been compatible with Hebrew culture and would have resulted in cultural deformity. Moses brought quite distinctive qualities to his Egyptian initiation and could therefore not extract from it wisdom easily transferable to the Israelites. He only later gave them guidance, indeed only once outside Egypt, on the basis of revelations he received in Sinai.

What, then, is this revelation in Sinai? What did Moses receive there and what could he impart to his people? He bestowed on them something that could indeed be grafted onto the stem of his people because it was uniquely related to them. Once, Ishmael's descendants had migrated to the very region through which Moses and his people were wandering. The characteristics garnered via Hagar were passed on to the Ishmaelites. Though distantly related to Abraham, they had retained far older traits, and these were now found by Moses among these Ishmaelites, who had initiates of a kind in their midst. Through the revelations of this tribal branch he could make the Sinai revelations comprehensible to the Israelites. This is why an ancient Hebrew legend tells of an offshoot of Abraham's line, by the name of Ishmael, being banished into Arabah, namely into the desert. What flourished within this Ishmaelian offshoot was also preserved in the legacy of Moses. The ancient Hebrew people therefore re-accepted, in the form of teachings—the legacy of Moses's revelations in Sinai—what had been excluded from their bloodline. They accepted this back from an external source.

Here again we see the wonderful mission of the ancient Hebrew people, in that everything was to be given them such that it was later received back in the form of a gift. It was as an external gift that Abraham received in Isaac the entire Hebrew people. Similarly, Moses and his people received back—through the descendants of Ishmael—that which they had earlier banished. In exile Ishmael was only to evolve his own unique constitution and in return to accept from his God what had been expelled. In this way Jacob was later reconciled with Esau, through which act the Hebrews could receive back qualities once discarded in Esau.

One needs to read the Bible very carefully if one is really to do justice to the enormous import of the words it contains. Instances such as these course as a characteristic trait throughout Hebrew history. The descendants of Hagar provide features connected with the Commandments of Moses, whereas the bloodline representing Moses's salient features flows from Sarah. Agar or Hagar translates in Hebrew to Sinai, meaning a stone mountain, a mountain of stones, great stones, megaliths. One could also say that great stones or stone Tablets are an outer emblem or corollary of Hagar, in which form Moses received his Commandments, the revelation of his laws. The Commandments for the Jewish people originate therefore not in the finest qualities of Abraham but from Hagar, from Sinai. In this way the danger was averted that those who merely adhered to the Commandments—the Pharisees and the Sadducees—would remain static in their development. These are the ones who, when baptized by John the Baptist, want to see a Serpent instead of a Lamb. What would otherwise be carping by John the Baptist is transformed into a beautiful parable when he calls to the Pharisees and Sadducees: You, who are followers of the Serpent, beware that you see rightly during your baptism! In other words, seeing the Serpent instead of the Lamb. Further, he warns them not to become arrogant on the grounds that Abraham is their father because these are only words in their case; they have sworn on what originated in the stones, the Tablets of Sinai, but this has ceased to be of prime significance. 'Now an I is approaching from out of the cosmos, to come into the world as a new-born I, and this I is what I proclaim to you: I show you how what is to develop out of Jewry, what has truly been handed down through the generations, no longer bears witness in the form of single Tablets of stone from Sinai but upon all that surrounds us. Children of God may appear through this so that the spiritual behind the sense-perceptible will become visible. From these stones, God's word will raise children for Abraham. You do not understand the words: Abraham is our father!'

Only now, after what has been said here, do these words acquire their full meaning for us. Something of this nature does not only need to be read in the Akashic Chronicle but can be found in the Bible.

Compare what St Paul says in his Epistle to the Galatians. What has just been said above is also confirmed by Paul the Apostle. He also states that Hagar or Agar is the same word as Sinai and that a Testament was given in Sinai, beyond which people—on the basis of all that is entailed in descending from Abraham through the ages—are to grow towards comprehending what has entered the world through Christ.

Attention is simultaneously drawn to words that one will have to understand in future. It is such a pity, in an age when intelligence is seemingly so advanced, that so little reflection is devoted to the words of atonement: 'Repent ye'. They could be translated as: Actively transform your senses within yourselves. In the most varied places it is said that John baptized with water in the name of repentance, of atonement, in other words for the changing or transforming of the senses. When those baptized emerged from the water they were to change the sense in which they looked: not back to past traditions but ahead to all that the liberated I—bestowed through Christ Jesus—contained. Their minds were to be led from the old Gods of yore in the direction of new spiritual beings, new Gods. This is the sense in which the aim of Johannine baptism was to re-orientate and transform human senses. John baptized with water in order to call forth in a few individuals the power to understand that the Kingdom of Heaven was nearing, to enable them to recognize who Christ Jesus was.

With this, something has been added to what we have learnt about the mission of the ancient Hebrew people. All this will also gradually lead to a better understanding of Christ. It is quite wonderful how this mission is constituted. We saw how what was predisposed in Abraham could evolve through generations. For this, some elements had to be excluded and those suited to their task further evolved through lines of heredity and capacity. Such capacities could only be acquired externally, and what the people of Abraham could develop—and were chosen so to do—was concentrated in one Being, in Jesus.

The Jewish people needed something onto which they could hold by way of a teaching or tenet. This always approached them from the outside and originated in an aspect of themselves that had earlier been ejected by themselves. Qualities transferred to Ishmael could no longer remain in their blood but could only rightfully remain in their insight or knowledge, and so was received back in the form of the Mosaic laws of Sinai. These laws had fulfilled their purpose once the time had come when the teachings given via the stones, the Tablets, were no longer needed but were to be replaced by the contents of the entire, approaching world of humanity. In this way the time was being prepared for in which, by way of stone Tablets, those people, the sons of God could arise, and beyond all stones, yes, beyond the entire Earth, the spiritual world would be opened.

All these pictures are just fragments contributing to an understanding of the mission of the ancient Hebrew people. Only when this mission is fully understood can one comprehend the towering figure of Christ Jesus as he is portrayed in the Gospel of St Matthew.

LECTURE 6

STUTTGART, 13 NOVEMBER 1909

ON THE RIGHT RELATIONSHIP WITH ANTHROPOSOPHY

WHAT has often been said in the lectures that form the last seven lecture cycles is no mere figure of speech: they correspond with a law of existence. In having completed a seven-year cycle of lectures in the spiritual-scientific life of our movement, I venture to suggest that there should be a few moments of self-reflection in our striving, in our work. This work is only possible if a spiritual movement proceeds in such a way as to align its lawful inner principles with universal principles. Such universal aptness advances in cycles that can be reckoned in units of seven. We count seven planetary states, seven conditions within each of these planetary worlds and so on. Similarly, in a movement such as ours, the number seven plays a part. In a certain sense, our quest over this time returns to its beginnings, in that much has been worked through in the meantime and incorporated into our work content. This striving returns at a higher level, above where it began, but this can only be successful if the deeper aspects of the subject—the legitimacy of its inner principles—has not been neglected.

If you look back at how we have worked over the past seven years, you will notice something: this work has progressed with a certain regularity. What is being said is not exact to the day but, taken as a whole, this is the case. We can be said to have laid the foundations for our work in the first four years, during which we occupied ourselves with acquiring some knowledge of the human being, gaining a certain outline of the ways in which access to the spiritual world can be attained; some time was also devoted to speaking of great cosmic connections or what we may call testing the results of the Akashic Chronicle[10] as it relates to world- or cosmic mysteries.

Those members among us who joined this work later on needed—and will always need—to create the firm foundation for our endeavours that is essential for their eventual achievement. For it is by no means sufficient—for our movement to advance in the right way—simply to assimilate what has been occupying us over the past three years. If you hold something of a rearward review, you will see that the truths and knowledge dealt with in the last three years have been built and enlarged upon, and this applies even to the factual knowledge with which you have—perhaps rather strikingly or shockingly—been faced. If you seek to make a connection with the material we tended in our first four years—as it were the four-fold foundation of the entire edifice—you will see that even what was striking or shocking, what constituted great and comprehensive truths, was nevertheless closely connected with all that took place in those first four years. You will be assured of this connectivity if you review it for yourself. Our younger members would do well to feel the urgent need for a firm foundation to be deeply engraved on their hearts. Increasingly, care has been taken to furnish latecomers with the means of catching up with what has taken place in preceding years. Without such revision, it is actually impossible to keep up with progress. We need to take our spiritual-scientific movement in the deepest sense seriously. In this connection we may be permitted to touch on a theme—especially at this important time—a theme that addresses the ethos, indeed the entire spiritual mode of imagining: How can anthroposophists rightly relate to spiritual science?

What is being said here will become clearer if we frame the question differently: Why is anthroposophy taught in the way that it is? Why is knowledge of higher worlds presented, knowledge that is the result of spiritual research and clairvoyant consciousness? Could this be done differently by starting, for instance, by giving guidance to individual people as to how they should proceed in their own inner life? Guidance as to how they could awaken higher faculties so that they could—through such suggestions—themselves have the opportunity gradually to ascend to spiritual worlds before hearing—as is now the case—about what are known facts in the spiritual world? This was largely the method once cultivated before the advent of our spiritual-scientific movement, in its modern sense of the word. For a long time it was said: there is no great advantage in someone stepping forward onto the world stage to share the results of spiritual research. So one would behave in as modest and reticent a manner as possible in relation to spiritual tidings. One would in fact limit oneself to setting a few rules as to how to develop the dormant forces in people's souls and would then, basically, give no more information than the individual could eventually discover for themselves. The question might now arise: Why is this path alone no longer in use? Why, instead, are the results of spiritual research being shared as anthroposophy?

This has not arisen out of any arbitrary personal penchant, but for good reason. We will understand all the better what we need to understand if we again ask ourselves: What does spiritual science actually convey? It communicates the facts and realities of higher realms, from super-sensory worlds; it shares the results of what clairvoyant consciousness can research in those higher realms.

Now it is the case that someone to whom communications of this sort are vouchsafed and who is not him- or herself clairvoyant, is initially unlikely to be persuaded by facts that can only be verified through direct vision. Such a person takes these communications in but cannot test them through clairvoyant scrutiny. Certainly, that is the case. Yet it would be quite wrong to believe that the non-clairvoyant person receiving such material cannot test this material at all, cannot interrogate it. To believe this would be equally wrong. It is similarly untrue to assert that one can simply absorb the results of spiritual research on the basis of loyalty or faith. Any such communications would be most incomplete, something vital would be lacking, if they were to rely solely upon belief and claim.

What is conveyed here is legitimately researched in an inherently rightful way and—this has often been reiterated—is verifiable with clairvoyant consciousness. If it is queried, however—and, as far as

I am concerned, even if only by a single researcher—once it has been uncovered and communicated, anyone can understand it by engaging their unbiased thinking and their common sense, both of which are available to them here on the physical plane. We could well add: even if not all of those sitting here can necessarily check everything to the most rigorous standards, they can at least give themselves the chance of doing this, given time and capacity—which are merely capacities of this physical plane.

Taking even the most complex issues, as touched upon over recent lectures, such as the incarnation of Zarathustra, challenging concepts associated with the fact that Zarathustra's astral body was transferred to Hermes, that Zarathustra's ether body transmigrated to Moses, nobody could claim that the person who has obtained these realities from spiritual research would expect anyone to accept such facts on the basis of blind faith. No, that certainly is not the case! Were someone to say: That's all well and good, but why would I trust a clairvoyant who claims all this about Zarathustra and his incarnations? I am going to check everything, using all means available to physical humanity here on the physical plane, everything that history tells us, everything contained in stone tablets, everything contained in religious records, all of this I intend to check with the greatest rigour... Someone of this ilk will say: Let us assume that what this seer says is correct; but does it accord with facts that can be externally verified? Then they would re-check everything externally verifiable and would notice that, the more they delved into detailed research, the more would they find facts communicated by the seer to be proven.

Were the word fear to have any relevance at all in this respect, one might say that spiritual-scientific research might potentially fear inexact testing, but it certainly has nothing to fear from those using all that physical research can yield. These latter will see that the more incisive their research, the more the facts concur with those communicated through seership. However, for less complex subjects, such as reincarnation and karma or life between death and rebirth, which lie closer to human ken, the only faculty anyone needs is unbiased, impartial observation of what life itself offers. The more one observes life, the more will one find that what the seer communicates accords with reality; in other words, there are ample opportunities to confirm that what has been won from super-sensory realms is confirmed by physical existence. This is not something just to be lightly accepted but something we should regard as indispensable necessity. We should test against life itself such facts as can only be verified by a few spiritual researchers. We really must stop perpetuating the idea that everything should be taken on trust and belief! No, accept as little as possible on trust and belief but check and check again without bias, totally without bias! This—above all else—needs to be emphasized.

The issue now is that when—or if—such checks are undertaken they should be strenuous. They require thinking, they require of each to make every effort to find proof in the physical world for the findings of spiritual research. And here we come to a subject that we do well to discuss and which resonates with our first question, namely: Is it advisable or even necessary for human beings of today—alongside their essential training in pursuit of spiritual experience, which is justified—is it necessary or even beneficial to engage energetically with our normal means of acquiring knowledge, with the ordinary modes of thinking prevalent in the physical world? In other words: Does the spiritual pupil do well to overcome the comfortable indolence they bring with them in such abundance from the unspiritual world? Do they do well to overcome their slothful habits by seriously expanding their thought-world and—using the very faculties that make humans recognizably human, even in this physical world—mastering their thoughts and putting them to real use? Does this pupil do well, above all, to engage in large bouts of study, particularly in cognitive modalities? It is actually quite difficult to teach present consciousness clearly and precisely what is implied by this activity.

Someone wanting to make progress in an anthroposophical field came to me recently who also wished to school himself to think spiritual thoughts with ever more clarity; he wanted me to recommend some reading matter. By way of thought-schooling material I recommended he study Spinoza's *Ethics*[11] to make him more capable of sharpening the contours of thoughts received in this transferred form. After only a few weeks he wrote to me saying that he could not understand why he needed to study this book as it was a comparatively hefty tome, its narrative primarily aiming to prove the existence of God. He said he had never doubted God's existence and could not see the value of following protracted thought processes to prove it. You see, this is a typical example of the indolence with which so many approach spiritual science. They are quickly satisfied as soon as they have secured some faith. They shun the uncomfortable struggle involved in acquiring—piece by piece—imaginative content and themselves enlarging on it. Nothing more than blind faith is ever the outcome of an attitude such as this. You will see that everything ceases to be blind faith as soon as your thinking begins to be schooled and is not just greedily trying to develop forces leading to an elementary level of clairvoyance.

Certainly nothing said here speaks against striving to evolve forces hidden in the soul. This is good and valuable striving. On the other hand, what needs emphasizing is that, in parallel with physical thought forces given us here in the material world, it is essential to train—however uncomfortably—those tools of knowledge that make us fit for creating our own sharply delineated imaginations and concepts of what we hear transmitted from higher worlds. One might easily believe that even the smallest degree of clairvoyance is preferable to however much sensible grasping of facts from the spiritual world. Someone might say: I have no idea why I am in this society where spiritual things are constantly being related. I would prefer to have however tiny a clairvoyant vision instead.

I know a very educated theosophist whose heartfelt desire it is to stride beyond mere learnedness into actual vision and who expressed it like this: If only I could just once catch sight of the vanishing tail of an elemental being! Certainly, that is quite an understandable wish. Yet that theosophist would never agree to renounce all the spiritual truths he had received in exchange for this glimpse, though even this could happen: that someone would give up everything spiritual they had learnt in exchange for just one seer's glimpse. Holding such a view is extremely misguided and in every respect wrong; because we live in times characterized as being an age of conscious thinking. As has often been pointed out, ancient Indian civilization developed a very different sort of consciousness, one reminiscent of dimly dawning clairvoyance. Only gradually have our modern faculties evolved and we are the first in the sphere of Earth evolution to join in the actual development of the consciousness soul with our faculties of human thinking. This is why it is so vital that spiritual science is drawn down from supra-sense worlds and that it appeals to sensible human thinking.

We need to clarify the following differentiation: a simple visionary needs no special recourse to thinking. Their thinking can be very primitive even though they may be able to see relatively far into the astral realm or even to some extent into the Devachanic plane. They may be quite advanced and see much. The other possible case is that someone knows a very great deal about spiritual truths yet sees nothing, is unable to see at all, is not in a position to see even the vanishing tail of an elemental being. This can also happen. Now let us ask ourselves: How do these two sets of soul capacities relate to each other?

Firstly, we have to highlight two things not to be confused: having something and being conscious of what one has. It is incredibly important to keep this in view. You will understand that question better if we add: You see, in primal times you were all clairvoyant, in common with humanity as a whole, because these were times when people looked far, far back in time, back to the very beginnings of time. And now you might ask: Why do we not remember our previous incarnations if, at the start of time, we could already look backwards?

This should have proved at least one fact to you: for example, the fact that you could previously recall earlier incarnations has not helped your present ability to remember your incarnations. You could raise the question: Will it help our future incarnation if—in terms of memory—we now become visionary clairvoyants? You could focus on one fact: that the old clairvoyance has not helped you to look back in recollection today because it is something you all once possessed. Why are so many people today unable to recall their previous incarnation? This is an extremely important question. A majority of people do not remember their previous incarnations because they had not, at that time, developed capabilities precisely of their self, of their I, of their ego. Because it is not a case of having developed clairvoyant faculties but whether or not what would have been visible then had been developed at all.

However clairvoyant human beings used to be, if they had not concerned themselves with specifically developing faculties of the self—of the I—in other words the ability to think, the ability to differentiate or discriminate, which are the hallmarks of the human I on Earth, that I was nevertheless absent in previous incarnations. Selfhood was absent. What, then, could one retrospectively recall? One would have had to see to it that a self-contained I was present in one's last incarnations. Everything depends on this! Only those people are able to recall their past lives who—during those past lives—worked at their means of thinking, logic and their ability to discern. Such individuals can remember. Someone may have developed however lofty a level of seership, yet if they did not work at their powers of logical thinking and discrimination, they will not remember their earlier life. At that time they failed to set the target at which their memory was later to aim. So you see that, if one understands anthroposophy rightly, one should reflect that the capacity for painstaking thinking cannot be mastered soon enough.

Now you could maintain: If I became clairvoyant, those powers of logical thinking will have been mastered of themselves. That is not the case. Why have the Gods caused human beings to come into being at all? For the reason that they could only evolve capacities within human beings that they could not have advanced in any other way: the power to think, to imagine something in thought in such a way that these thoughts are combined with differentiation. Such abilities can only be shaped on our Earth. They did not previously exist and could only arise in that humanity came about at all.

By way of comparison, we could say: Let us assume you have a seed such as a grain of wheat. However long you contemplate it, it will not germinate into a wheat plant. To do so it needs to be planted in soil and left to grow, allowing growth forces to activate it. What divine beings possessed before the creation of human beings can be compared with that grain of wheat: were it to exist in the form of a thought, it would first need tending by terrestrial human beings on the physical plane. There is no other way for thoughts sent from higher worlds to be tended than for them to flourish through human incarnations. Thus what humans think on this physical plane is unique and must complement such potentialities as approach from spiritual realms. Human beings are in fact essential for this, otherwise the Gods would not have caused them to arise. The Gods made possible the genesis of humanity so that what they had previously possessed could also appear to them in the shape of thoughts formed through human activity.

That this was even possible—that what descended from higher worlds could take the form of thoughts—would never have been possible had not human beings clothed these spiritual gifts with the contours of their own thinking. People who do not want to exercise their thinking on Earth deprive the Gods of something they have been relying upon and they thereby fail in their intrinsically human task, their human assignment. They will only fulfil this mission in their incarnation when they undertake to work rigorously with their thinking.

When one considers this, everything else follows from it. Such revelations and genuine facts about the spiritual world as can take root in the human soul do so in the most varied ways. It is certainly possible—and there are many cases nowadays—for some people to have visionary experiences without being clear thinkers. In fact, the majority of those who have clairvoyant visions tend to be diffuse non-thinkers rather than clear, bright thinkers. However, there is an enormous difference in their experience of the spiritual world between indistinct and clear thinkers. It is a difference which I can express as follows: what is revealed from spiritual worlds impresses itself best into those forms of spiritual imagination towards which we can bring our clearest thoughts. Such thinking provides the best possible vessel.

If we are not thinkers then revelation has to seek alternative forms such as those of a picture, an emblem or symbol. This is the most frequent means of reception among non-thinkers. You will hear how visions are related in terms of symbols and portents by these visionary clairvoyants who are not simultaneously rigorous thinkers.

This is all very nice, but we must become conscious that such subjective experience differs completely depending on whether the vision is received by a clear thinker or by a non-thinker. Non-thinking people will have visions in the form of emblematic symbols—this or that figure appears from the spiritual world. Let's say you see an angelic figure and some symbol expressing this or that, such as a monstrance or a chalice, and you see this as a finished picture in supra-sensible fields. You can be sure that this is not reality but an image.

Even subjective visions of the spiritual world are experienced slightly differently by thinkers and non-thinkers. They do not instantly appear, ready formed, as if shot from a pistol but emerge variously. Take a non-thinking clairvoyant visionary and another who is able to think clearly and who might both have the same vision. In one case the non-thinking visionary sees this or that appearance from the spiritual world while the thinking clairvoyant sees it a little later. The moment they see it, it has already been grasped by his or her thinking. At this point he or she can differentiate and know whether it is truth or untruth. They see it slightly later. The revelation from the spiritual world approaches, however, slightly later and in a *pre-thought-steeped* form that allows the beholder to differentiate between reality and delusion; in other words, she or he possesses something that predates what they see. This is received at the same time as the non-thinking clairvoyant, but is perceived fractionally later. When it is seen, the vision is already infused with thought and judicious appraisal, which enables the beholder to discriminate clearly between apparitions reflecting their subjective wishes and objective veracity. This is the difference between subjective experiences. The non-thinking visionary sees immediately, the thinker slightly later. The vision remains the same as first seen for the non-thinker, however the thinker will be capable of sequencing and contextualizing it within what she or he knows of the ordinary physical world. The two can be properly brought into relation with each other. After all, the physical world is itself a manifestation of the spiritual world.

From this you can see that—if you approach the spiritual world equipped with the instrument of your thought-creating, reflective ability—you will be vouchsafed certainty in your judgement of that world. To this we can add: one might argue about the value of communications from the spiritual world if one has not seen or heard them oneself. To these two opposing situations mentioned let us add a non-clairvoyant third possibility: someone who hears the results of spiritual research that has been gained by way of clear thinking combined with clairvoyant seership. That person absorbs these facts from the spiritual world and understands them to be sensible. The seer capable of thinking has them too, as does every thinking person who has grasped them, however unconscious they may be of having done so. They by no means need to be clairvoyant themselves and yet they can absorb the full value of the content of what is communicated to them.

There is a difference between having something and being aware of what one has. It is not difficult to appreciate the difference between a non-seeing spiritual student and a clairvoyant. Imagine now that you were to be in line for an inheritance but did not yet know about it. It would be of the same equitable value to you today whether you knew about it or not. You might only hear of its existence later and yet its value would remain the same. It is just like this for the person experiencing facts about the spiritual world through anthroposophy. If sensibly seized upon, these facts now remain in their possession and they can await such time as they will themselves become sufficiently conscious of them, bearing in mind, nevertheless, that hearing them is by no means the same as oneself being in possession of first-hand facts. This becomes especially apparent after death. What is of more *use* to human beings—if I may use the trivial word 'use' by way of clarification: having visions in a state of thoughtlessness or receiving—without seeing them in vision— purely spiritual communications?

One might easily think that seeing visions would be a better preparation for death than merely hearing facts derived from the spiritual world. And yet: after death it is of little use to human beings what they have seen by way of visions. But with facts, on the other hand, one is immediately able to set to work to make them one's own if one has grasped them in a sensibly thoughtful way. What is valuable after death is precisely what one has understood, regardless of whether it has been seen in visionary form or not. Taking even the most profoundly initiated: they can see the entire spiritual world but the significance of this is no whit increased if they are not capable of expressing their findings in terms of clear human concepts. After death the only things that will help them are the concepts they have formed here on Earth. These are the seeds for life after death. Of course, if one is a clairvoyant and simultaneously a clear thinker, one can usefully share the fruits conferred by vision. However, after death two non-thinking people, of whom one is clairvoyant and the other only hears what his peer is seeing, find themselves in the identical situation because what we take into our life after death is precisely what we have struggled to master through our own incisive thinking. This ascends as a seed rather than as something we extract from the worlds into which we now go. We receive what we do from spiritual worlds not as a free gift simply to facilitate a more comfortable existence once we leave our earthly abode but so that we convert it into earthly currency. To the extent that we have affected this conversion into earthly currency are we helped after death. That is the essential point here.

Such are connections after death. On the physical plane the relative position of a clairvoyant to a thinking clairvoyant is similar. It is certainly wonderfully instructive to gaze into spiritual realms. But we must nevertheless discern whether such a person is merely looking at these realms in vision regardless of the fact that—without penetrating through the visions with their thinking—they have no defence against delusion. There is no other defence against illusion than clearly thinking through what has been seen. Even apart from this, let us assume that a visionary sees this or that, how she or he sees it—this can be deduced from their descriptions—it will still be imbued with elements of the physical plane. Has anyone ever described to you an angel that bears no features reminiscent of the physical world? It has wings, but then birds also have wings. It has a human upper body in common with every person on Earth. Admittedly, some of the things related may not be constituted quite as on Earth, though elements may still be present, and images can invariably—and justifiably—be related to the physical. But you will note that pictures such as these retain a terrestrial imprint. The shapes and images resembling their physical counterparts, as seen in many a vision, do not belong to the spiritual world but are merely symbolizations or parables of the spiritual world couched in terms of the physical world. I have set this out clearly in the book *Occult Science, an Outline*.[12] There I argue that modern clairvoyance must restrict its graphic, image-forming ability to its pre-development stage, but that it cannot remain static here but must press onwards to a point where even the last vestige of earthly images is discarded. There is, however, a certain danger to the seer once he or she has shed these last remnants. Seeing, for example, an angel after having dispensed with all earthly parallels, there is a danger of seeing nothing at all. When leaving behind all earthly images transposed into the spiritual there is a real danger that nothing more can be seen. What then prevents one from losing all sight on entering the spiritual world proper is the seed that can arise from active thinking. Thought lends its substance to grasping what exists in spiritual worlds. We gain the ability to really live in the spiritual world by equally really grasping—in our sense world—what is no longer shot through with sensory elements. That is: solely and uniquely, our thinking. We cannot take anything with us into the spiritual world other than our thinking. For example, think of a circle, but without the chalk that drew it, solely the thought of the circle. You can ascend to spiritual worlds in this way. But you may not bring anything of the image with you.

I can now explain more fully the subjective process outlined earlier. Let us assume that, again, a monstrance cross is seen in vision. Let me characterize the two clairvoyants—one visionary, one also a thinker—by assuming one of them sees the vision here (a) while the other, the thinker, only sees it here (b):

The thinker only becomes aware of the visionary image from here (b) onwards. Yet he or she apprehends it simultaneously with thinking and can permeate it with thought. At the very moment when the thinking seer permeates the image with thought it becomes unclear for the visionary seer—here at (b)—where it becomes dark and hazy and only reappears after a while. At the very point where image and thought can unite, it becomes dark for the visionary, who is never in a position to bind thought with image. For this reason he or she never has the experience: *You were there with your I.* So this remains an experience inaccessible to the merely visionary seer.

All this goes into the matter in a somewhat more detailed way. It is extremely important to bear all this in mind and to realize how vital it is to train one's thinking to overcome its inherent indolence that causes one to avoid the effort of attaining cognitive knowledge. It is a thousand times better to have encompassed spiritual Imaginations in thinking and then—sooner or later, each according to their karma—to raise oneself by one's own efforts to spiritual realms than to see immediately but to fail to process this vision through thinking; all of which has often been reiterated in the movement known as anthroposophy. It really is a thousand times more preferable to gain knowledge of spiritual science without seeing anything than to see all sorts of things without the opportunity to penetrate them with incisive thought, because this is how they are compromised by uncertainty and instability.

You can express this with even more precision by saying: at present there are clear thinkers with sensible insight into the spiritual-scientific worldview. Why is it that these are the very ones who find it so hard to become clairvoyant? It is comparatively easy for non-thinkers to have a measure of visionary clairvoyance, which easily inclines them to arrogance when faced with thinking, whereas it is relatively hard for thinkers to become clairvoyant. This is the very cliff edge at which a certain veiled disdain sets in. There is hardly anything that feeds arrogance as readily as clairvoyance un-illumined by thinking, and it is so dangerous for the reason that such a clairvoyant generally has no idea that they are arrogant, instead deeming themselves humble. They lack the means to determine how colossally conceited it is to hold others' thinking efforts in such low esteem, while placing the greatest importance on a certain inspired quality. This is the seat of monstrous, masked arrogance.

The question now is: Why is it that—as experience teaches—it is so exceptionally difficult for some thinkers to also become seers?

This is connected with an important fact. What we call the human power of differentiation, of judgement, that very capacity for logical thinking cultivated by thinkers, causes a definite modification of the entire structure of the brain. The physical instrument of one's brain is altered by astute thinking. Physical research is largely ignorant of this but it is nevertheless the case. A brain used by a clear thinker looks different from that of a non-thinker. Being clairvoyant alters this fact little. A non-thinker's brain has complex crenulations or folds whereas that of a developed thinker is relatively less complex and has fewer folds. Thinking is expressed in such simplification of brain gyri or folds but science is unaware of this.

Clear thinking can survey in broad overview rather than involve itself in analysis, hence the greater simplification in the brain of a stringent thinker. Where physical research has accustomed itself to testing thinking under physical conditions, it is soon apparent that physical research confirms what spiritual science states. In examining the brain of Mendelyéyev[13], to whom science attributes the establishment of the periodic system of elements, the truth of what spiritual science says is attested: the gyri or ridges of his brain are simplified. He possessed thinking that was—within certain limits—comprehensive and the physical evidence of this is entirely congruent with what I said. This is not a particularly valuable fact and is just mentioned in passing. So, as I say, changes to the instrument of thinking are evident. These changes call on us to focus on the activity of thinking itself. Nobody is born with all the faculties they may later possess, though they perhaps retain related tendencies. These have to be nurtured and developed so that changes to the brain do indeed take place throughout life. The tool of clear thinking has undergone a metamorphosis throughout a life of thinking and is then changed from its earlier condition.

The fact is that our ether body, which has to be loosened from our physical brain to enable clairvoyant vision, is bound to this physical brain through our activity as thinkers. The work of thinking binds our ether body firmly to our physical brain. If someone—through their karma—does not yet have the strength to loosen their ether body in a timely way, then it may be that they are unable to have much by way of clairvoyant experience during this incarnation. Let us assume that it may have been their karma to be a very clear thinker in their last incarnation. This time, their thinking will not engage their ether body so strongly with their physical brain and they will be able to loosen their ether body relatively easily, precisely because this thought-filled element is the best possible seed for their ascent into spiritual regions and for spiritual research. They must, of course, first have disengaged their ether body from their brain. However, if their brain has become so enmeshed with their ether body due to the incisive chiselling or chasing-in effects of thinking to the point that it is exhausted, karma may make them wait a long time before that ether body can once more be loosened. If they then ascend to the spirit again, they will have done so via logical thinking. It has not been lost; nobody can take away from them this advantage won by their own efforts. This is immensely important because clairvoyance can be lost at any time. I will draw your attention again to the fact that in ancient times you were all clairvoyant. Why do you no longer possess this faculty? Because in those ancient times you were not bound to earthly existence but were unattached and translocated into spiritual worlds. You had not drawn this world down to the level of your capabilities, your clairvoyance having rested upon translocation.

This is what we need to keep in mind. These are the kind of subtleties we should inscribe into our souls. We must be clear that today genuine occult science has the task of conveying the results of clairvoyant, spiritual research that is suffused with thought for the purpose of always clothing these spiritual results in such a way that non-clairvoyant people can readily grasp them through their own thinking. For this they first need to be attached to thinking, hence the difficulty in contrast with old books that treat of revelations from the spiritual world. If you read these ancient books you will—if you approach them in the manner of the modern spiritual scientist— notice something missing. You may find many an excellent revelation in these ancient tomes but the modern person will not be able to make much sense of all this unless he or she is clairvoyant and can properly contextualize such material. However, what spiritual science offers can be processed by each person willing to expend some effort on the task because they can infuse it with elements wrested through physical, earthly thinking; because we grasp concepts that pertain both here and in the spiritual world. Modern natural science speaks of evolution and spiritual science speaks of evolution, too. Once you have understood the concept of evolution, you can understand what spiritual science has to convey. You can have a concept of karma because you can create a thought-fashioned picture for yourself. Granted, you can simply say to yourself, as many a theosophist does: every spiritual cause has a spiritual effect and this constitutes karma. But then you will have no genuine concept of karma. You can also observe the concept of cause and effect by watching billiard balls but this is a false comparison with karma. Try taking an iron ball and throwing it into a barrel of cold water. If the ball is cold the water remains just as it was. If, on the other hand, you heat the iron ball and then throw it into the barrel, the water will become warmer. As a result of an event, such as that of the iron ball, the water is warmed. This is comparable with karma inasmuch as a subsequent situation is affected by an earlier event.

For reasons such as this we must be absolutely clear that anyone who processes the facts of the spiritual world with their own thinking can also communicate those facts in such a way that anyone who has acquired their thinking here on the physical plane can utilize that thinking on subjects conveyed from the spiritual world. They will be able to understand them. We should all take this to heart. We should all understand that it is not just a matter of receiving communications from the spiritual world but that everything depends on whether we receive them in a manner compatible with our present earthly circumstances. Each individual needs to take care that they receive such communications from spiritual realms in no other way. Admittedly, the slothful wish simply to believe what you hear is always present. But this is extremely awful and dire. If someone just wants to believe something it is almost like wanting to be told that light exists when in fact what they need is a light bulb to illuminate a room. They need a light bulb and belief will help them not one jot. It is therefore important to seize hold of the means—the means of reflecting, conscientiously and thoroughly—so that these means represent our initial method of gathering what spiritual science communicates from higher realms. Research of this realm can only be carried out once the requisite faculties have been developed, but grasping what has thus been researched is viable for every person willing to receive it in the right way.

If one thinks in this way, the dangers that are otherwise associated with the anthroposophical movement can be more or less avoided. These dangers, however, assert themselves instantly when people start seeing clairvoyantly without ensuring that they simultaneously enrich knowledge by means of their own thinking. Many have this greed, simply to snatch something from the spiritual world without painstakingly proceeding with the thinking that must be mastered here in the physical world. No God can conceive of the world in thought form unless they are incarnated on our physical Earth; they can do this in other forms but to comprehend our world through thinking can only be achieved here when incarnated. Bearing this in mind, every individual needs to be absolutely clear that dangers are attached to clairvoyance not rightly used.

Whoever develops clairvoyance without using it rightly remains at an astral level, fails to bring the experience down to the physical level, cuts themselves off from the prospect of convincing others and creates a dangerous abyss between their vision and physical reality.

Let us assume that someone has significant visions on the astral plane; these could be quite real, as far as anyone is concerned, and could also occur in non-thinking visionaries. Yet what now happens is that between them and the physical plane an abyss opens up. Imagine that this cloth is the physical plane. The visionary seer is standing on the edge of it. He or she sees their visions. The authentic spiritual world lies beyond the physical world, which is Maya or illusory semblance. This physical plane cannot be removed by the visionary seer. It disappears only for the individual able to remove it by means of their thinking. This is the only way to penetrate beyond the physical plane: by understanding it with your thinking vision. Otherwise the physical plane is present, but you do not see the spiritual world, the genuine spiritual world. This is when the abyss opens up and the physical plane remains present as illusory Maya. This inability to penetrate through physical levels lies in the fact that the brain is unable to switch itself off. If you have learnt to think properly you have no immediate need for your brain. Whilst thinking requires the workings of the brain, thinking activity does not require direct use of the brain. It is nonsense to claim that the brain thinks. I once went for a walk with a young man—some thirty-five years ago—who was studying and who was well on the way to becoming a complete materialist. He said: When I think, my cranial atoms swoop around and every thought has a definite shape; he opined that it was quite ludicrous to assume the existence of something like a soul, which might be doing the thinking, as it was the brain itself doing this. I said to him: Tell me, then, why are you so dishonest as to say '*I* think'—if that is the case? You would need to say: 'my brain is thinking'. You would also need to claim that your brain is eating, your brain is seeing the Sun—that would be more truthful. People like that would soon see what nonsense they carry around with them.

It is not the brain that does the thinking. As I said, this can be explained by all sorts of trivial examples—if one is not a thoroughgoing modern materialist. Thought-filled activity is not directly dependent upon the brain as its tool. Where thinking has become pure, one's brain does not participate. It is only involved in the activity of symbolizing, of symbol-creating.

Imagine a chalk circle: this takes place in your brain. However, if you imagine a pure, symbol-free circle, the circle itself is the active ingredient and is only then conceptualized by the brain. When people have clairvoyant visions, they remain in their ether bodies and do not even reach their physical brains. One can spend one's entire life in visionary states without one's brain evolving. One's ether body will be elaborated but not one's brain. Nor can one bestride the abyss in this way because Maya has not been thoroughly transformed. This can only be achieved by penetrating it with thinking.

Those who despise proceeding through thinking will only evolve faculties that are unable to grasp their object, that do not advance with any real grip, as it were, on the spiritual world proper. As a consequence of this a disparity arises between what is developing in their ether body and their essential nature as a human being. There is complete misalignment here: those visionary faculties are incompatible with the brain. The brain is coarse because the person concerned has not taken the trouble to ennoble their brain through thinking. A hindrance takes shape that blocks the person in their attempt to reach real spirituality with their vision. They take leave of reality instead of advancing towards it. This destroys all chance of evaluating the supra-sensory world. Someone of this kind may see all manner of things but it will never be guaranteed that what they see corresponds with reality. Only someone capable of discriminating between reality and mere vision will be able to test the veracity of such visions. Only mature discrimination will be able to do this. Without this no vision can be properly tested against reality. Real discernment can only be acquired through working on the physical plane. That is why one remains floating without foundation if one scorns the albeit laborious work of grappling with thinking.

We must really take this to heart. Then the same problems will not arise again and again and those who develop visionary clairvoyance will not remain within their dreams by erecting a barrier against reality. This is synonymous with losing one's way in the physical world or with not being in one's right mind. Sober-mindedness can be achieved by working at the one and only site where sobriety prevails: in clear thinking on the physical plane. In scorning the acquisition of a rigorous mode of thinking, one consigns oneself to drifting around in error. Clarity is what we must actively wrest for ourselves if the anthroposophical movement is not to suffer by being linked with such error. Whoever wishes to exercise blind faith in receiving information from the spiritual worlds on the authority of another without exercising their own rational thinking does something that may be comfortable but which contains a danger. If, instead of independently assessing and thinking through material transmitted by another's vision, one simply takes for granted—on faith—what someone else relates, one potentially harms the anthroposophical movement. Needless to say, nobody should be scared off from becoming involved in this movement. Yet it can indeed happen that people of blind faith can lose themselves and are no longer capable of distinguishing between truth and lies.

Nothing allows mendacity to thrive more than visionary clairvoyance that is not challenged and reined in by thinking. On the contrary, such loose visioning can nurture quite a different tendency, namely a certain high-handed arrogance that can extend to delusions of superiority and megalomania. This is all the more dangerous for going unnoticed. The danger is very great of considering oneself superior on account of seeing things which others do not see. It is not normally apparent just how deep-seated this tendency bordering on megalomania may be rooted in a soul. Much self-importance is concealed behind unconditionally asserted certainties that swear by their authenticity, brooking no argument, so that people can be led to believe the most idiotic things on the basis that they originate in the astral plane. Anything similar claimed on the basis of the physical world would be dismissed out of hand, but because it claims astral origin it is slavishly believed. In breaking with this habit, one can save oneself from falling for every sort of swindle or deceit. Yet this does happen when one fails—by only seeking cosy opinions—to nurture an instinct for rigorous scrutiny. We should not make light of this. We must recognize that it is one of humanity's most sacred privileges to come to our own conclusions. If we appreciate this, we will spare no effort in really working at this capacity instead of just listening to sensational communications. There is a wealth of communication from the spiritual world but it is essential we develop the appropriate attitude—the right means of visualizing—and behave accordingly.

This is what I wished to express today, not just to exhort you in the manner of a sermon but to express it with due reasoning. That is why it may have been rather more taxing on our thinking, on our ability to think in parallel, alongside. I always try, through my methods, to adhere to what is rightly to be expected of a spiritual movement. Many would prefer soothing exhortations. I refrain from supplying these. I try to present things so that they are capable of being clothed in real thought. When issues of a physical nature are expounded, as so often today, it can be hard mental work because they are not as sensational nor as pleasant as those of higher worlds and yet they are incredibly important. You will not underestimate the importance of this hard mental work if you tell yourself: if what must happen in future really does take place—that in their next incarnation sufficiently large numbers of people incarnate who remember this present incarnation—then provision must be made in advance of such times. So do develop your powers of discrimination and you will be candidates for self-remembrance in your future incarnation. Make sure that you are able to follow world events with clarity of thought. Because, however much you may see of a visionary nature, it will be of no help to you in looking back to the present in future incarnations. Anthroposophy is here to help prepare for all necessary eventualities: that there are sufficient numbers of people who are capable of looking back at this incarnation on the basis of their own knowledge.

How many do in fact—in this incarnation—accompany their understanding of spiritual science with any clairvoyant ability? This is a matter of individual karma. Undoubtedly, many are sitting here whose karma it is not to penetrate clairvoyantly beyond this world. But everyone who is prepared to secure what is offered by genuine spiritual science—as presented in the form of thinking—will, in their next incarnation, reap the fruits of having secured a sound basis for their thinking now. Human beings can, as it were, be seers without being aware of this and those who study anthroposophy methodically *have* this potential and in that sense can wait until such time as karma allows them to see through to reality.

Lecture 7

STUTTGART, 14 NOVEMBER 1909

THE GOSPELS

Today we will speak about some aspects of themes that have played a part in the development of our spiritual movement in Germany. You will know—and some of you took part in this—what was last said about the spiritual-scientific truths and knowledge relating to the Gospels. We conveyed in various towns what could be said in connection with St John's Gospel. We also shared some aspects of St Luke's Gospel. Not all of you were able to participate in hearing this. What we will be speaking of today will not presuppose familiarity with what has gone before but instead we will bring you some general perspectives from this spiritual-scientific field that should prove valuable for you.

Christianity and all that appertains to it made a deep incision in the whole evolution of humanity, as has often been mentioned here in Stuttgart. All that takes place around us and all that the human soul is able to experience today can scarcely be understood without taking into account the magnitude of the Christ event in Earth history. This needs to be borne in mind. It is of boundless importance for each individual human soul that they realize the significance of this event.

You are aware that this Christ event is portrayed for humanity in the form of four documents, which we know as the four Gospels and with which you are undoubtedly familiar, having read them in various forms. These four Gospels—those according to Matthew, to Mark, to Luke and to John—have fared variously during human evolution since the founding of Christianity. Great changes have taken place in the human stance towards—and appraisal of—these four records. If we initially ask ourselves how these four documents appear to modern people, even to modern theologians, the answer lies nearby. Firstly, we can say, there are the three texts of the Matthew, Mark and Luke Gospels. They at least agree—according to common modern opinion—in some respects. But the fourth, that of St John, is quite different from the other three. This Gospel of St John has the effect on people of posing the following dilemma: if we take the first three Gospels as historical documents, as depictions of the life of Christ Jesus, the fourth contradicts these three so fundamentally that this fourth Gospel can surely not be appraised as a depiction reflecting historical fact. The resulting opinion is that this fourth manuscript is the declaration of a man faithful to the mission of Christ Jesus, a kind of hymn springing from the heart of one ardently proclaiming his message. The other three Gospels are called canonical in that they appear—and are believed—to offer a historical depiction of historical events. Staying for a moment with contradictions, which seek their explanation in external, physically-bound reasoning, one will actually find that the other three Gospels do also contain contradictions. Is it no contradiction that in Matthew's Gospel the birth of Jesus in Bethlehem is related, the flight to Egypt too, the appearance of the Magi from the Orient, while in Luke's Gospel the journey to Bethlehem is reported yet there is complete silence on St Matthew's Magi, silence on the flight to Egypt, and so on? And this is not even to go into the three years of Christ Jesus' ministry, where discrepancy after discrepancy is to be found.

We could pose the following question: how did contemporary views on the Gospels evolve over the course of Christian times? Has it always been the case that people have seen the Gospels in ways that focused primarily on these contradictory elements? We need to be clear how this evaluation of the Gospels evolved. It is only recently that people have had the Gospels so readily available, that they are so widespread among humanity, confined as they were within the hands of very few before the advent of the printing press; and even then they were not found among the illiterate masses but sequestered among the most educated, the select few who had made them the focal point of their lives. It is certainly not the case that the further back in time one looks, the more people voiced their awareness of such contradictions; the opposite is the case. The further back one observes, the less it appears that any discrepancies were felt to be present and that the four Gospels could be viewed alongside each other without any sense of disparity. The attitude towards the Gospels was quite different in the first centuries of Christianity. Were we to characterize this attitude, we would have to point to the immense reverence with which people were filled, the devotion they brought towards depictions in the Gospels during those early Christian centuries. Their entire mood was affected by their gaze being directed aloft to the majestic figure of Christ Jesus.

How were the Gospels experienced? How did people feel about the stories they heard from Matthew and from Luke being so different? They felt rather like someone today might feel—I used this comparison in lectures held here and there lately—when photographing a tree from one angle. A photo such as this shows a single side of the tree. If one wanted to elicit in other people any real sense of what a tree is, this would be extremely one-sided. One could hope to engender a more comprehensive view of that tree by seeing four photographs of it, taken from four angles; four pictures of the self-same tree. These would not correspond to any significant degree with each other; they would differ considerably. Nevertheless, nobody would be under the impression that these four photographs were not of a single tree. Each would say: by seeing four sides of this tree, I gain a fairly complete picture of it. This is something like the impression created by the Gospels in the early Christian centuries. People felt: this whole mighty event is simply depicted from four perspectives and we can gain an all-embracing view by gathering together these four pictures and creating our own composite picture. The one thing we need to be clear about is *how* these four depictions relate to one another. This great event is indeed shown from four differing viewpoints. If one wishes to be quite clear about each viewpoint, the following has to be taken into account.

Before us we behold the towering individuality of Christ Jesus, an individuality of whom we know from the descriptions previously given here that he descended from spiritual worlds and appeared in Palestine at the beginning of our calculated era. The individuality who descended represents for each human being a great and all-encompassing ideal. Each person strives upwards, as it were, towards those vast distances on high in which they divine unique perfection contained within one individuality—as expressed through Christ Jesus—and they strive towards this ideal. Initially, people see this striving in their own intellectual or moral terms, et cetera. But they perceive even more when they join what we know as this spiritual-scientific movement. There they can follow evolution right into the spiritual world. They know that each person can grow beyond their habitual self, that they can grow towards vision into spiritual realms, that they can develop their senses so as to live within spiritual worlds. Such people recognize this. In the treatise *Knowledge of Higher Worlds—How is it attained?*[14] you encounter one aspect of this upward trajectory, this entry into spiritual realms, and there you will also find a description of what has been called 'the splitting or separation of the personality'. When people develop spiritually and gradually grow towards and into the spiritual world, perhaps becoming visionary, then something akin to a separation of the elements of their personality does indeed take place. Three forces within a personality we know as thinking, feeling and willing. In the normal person, these three are more or less integrated and work in concert. Thinking, feeling and willing act together. You go out into a field and you see a flower; put differently, you had an image of a flower and you thought: I like that flower. You call it beautiful; in other words, you had a feeling. A feeling joined a thought. You pick the flower and take it home; in other words, you wanted, you desired that flower. This is how human life generally proceeds. People imagine, think, feel and act and these three elements interact with each other. Imagination calls forth feelings, these cause willing—action or abstention from a deed—and so forth. If a person now self-develops into the spiritual world, to clairvoyance and to participation in that spiritual world, a separation in these forces takes place. In someone who has arrived at a certain stage of development, each thought no longer elicits a feeling but that thought appears in isolation; feelings can equally appear in isolation, willing likewise. And because the person has now, as it were, divided into three separate beings—whereas thinking, feeling and willing were previously forces that merely coexisted within a whole—they have to be all the stronger in their personality. They not only need to balance out these three forces but become master of each one: master of willing, master of feeling and master of thinking, master of all three forces. They have to be archon or leader of a horde in the form of these three beings, creating order and subordination lest other, primary forces of evil assume dominance, tearing the person asunder: thinking to one side, feeling in another direction and willing in a third direction. That person is then sundered once more into three parts, but such that they can no longer ever be united again, can never find their way back to their rightful entity. This is why human beings need to strengthen themselves inwardly, becoming strong in ruling over—and becoming master of—the forces that have become of their thinking, their feeling and their willing. When human beings develop themselves upwards into spiritual realms, they split apart into three separate beings. When these beings approach us from above, from spiritual regions, and one sees them in their essential nature—something that can only be accomplished through seership—they appear sharply delineated and separate in the form of a thinking being, a feeling being and a willing being. There they are, in the state to which that particular person has advanced them.

This was so to an exceptional degree in the mightiest individuality to descend to us: the Christ being. This is why those who first described the Christ did so by saying: Christ cannot be described just by taking a single viewpoint into account. He has to be pictured as if seeing a wisdom-filled, thinking being, then as if seeing a being of will and then as if describing a feeling being. One has to describe him from the standpoint of wisdom, of willing and of feeling. This is how he should be described, said the people. They were well prepared for such views by the education that was traditional in those ancient days. If someone in those times was to be cultivated for spiritual knowledge—nowadays the first steps towards higher knowledge are necessarily different—if someone was mature enough to be guided in becoming, as it were, a citizen of higher worlds, it would then have been said: Well, yes, this person is indeed ready to be led upwards into higher worlds. But let us look at him in more detail! What should we nurture primarily in this person? Should it be wisdom—the power of thinking—or that of willing?

In the ancient schooling centres, shrouded from general view, not all human forces were progressed in equal measure but—according to the karma of each pupil—in one pupil clairvoyance would be cultivated via thinking, in another intuitive feeling would be advanced while in a third magical power would be nurtured through willing. This is the reason why, in the ancient mystery schools, three classes of advancing powers were developed in pupils. In some the capacity to see into the spiritual world, illumined and filled with wisdom, was nurtured—these were the people to whom one went when needing to know how facts in the spiritual world were contextually related. In trivial parlance, these were the knowledge specialists, the knowledge experts, within the mysteries. There was another class of acolyte in whom feelings were cultivated above all else. In order that feeling could evolve in predominance, attention was given neither to nurturing thinking nor to willing but feelings alone were the focus of their training. This being so, such an acolyte would become something barely acknowledged nowadays: they became healers and doctors. For doctors in ancient times exercised a far more spiritual influence on receptive souls, who were healed by forces originating in a sphere of feeling more highly evolved than is the case today. These formed the second class of initiates. They refined their feelings to a point of such dedication, of such devotion and self-sacrifice, even to the extremity of surrendering all their own forces. Work here was divided among specialists. If one wanted to know what was lacking in someone, one would go to those whose wisdom was most highly evolved. They would ascertain what this lack might be and how it was to be remedied. Then there were those who could not determine what a patient lacked because thinking was not their specialized faculty; instead they would come and offer their forces because they had refined the power of their feeling. These were the same people who had other functions such as caring for those in accidents or mishaps with their highly evolved powers of sacrifice. A third category of initiate comprised the mages, those magicians who had trained their powers of will and who had to fulfil the most exacting conditions. These magi had cultivated their powers of will and would carry out whatever was required of them. So there were three categories of initiate: those of thinking, those initiated into feeling and others initiated into willing. A fourth class or category of initiate consisted of those in whom the attempt was made to develop components of the other three qualities: elements of thinking, elements of feeling and elements of willing. For this reason they did not advance to as high a level as the other more specialized initiates but they were nevertheless initiated such that forces of all three spheres, as it were, overlapped within them. So, there were mighty initiates of wisdom, great initiates of sacrificial service, powerful magus-initiates and a fourth grouping of those possessing some measure of the other three capacities.

The being of Christ Jesus was to be described from all aspects, from all perspectives—and we will go into this in more detail another time; today we can only sketch it out in large brush-strokes—when there appeared four people, each of whom possessed one of the four characteristics naturally combined in Christ, and who were able to depict him from their particular angle. One of them was specially initiated into the mystery of thinking, who could describe in Christ Jesus those faculties he was best qualified to understand, being an initiate of wisdom. He excluded aspects other than this. Another of these four was an initiate into feeling and he it was who depicted Christ Jesus in terms of feeling, as it were from the perspective of a doctor, of a healer. A third was initiated into will as a magus and he describes the forces Christ could unfold for the ordering of humanity as a whole. A fourth individual was initiated into what we have called a fourth category, in whom the forces of the other three initiates interacted and wove harmoniously: in the main he described the humanitarian work undertaken by Christ Jesus. He did not encompass all the power of wisdom, nor that of sacrificial service, neither did he attempt to speak of the magical force of will to be found in Christ Jesus. Yet he saw how harmoniously the three forces of thinking, feeling and willing were united within Christ Jesus and described him in terms of Christ, the human being.

This is how we have descriptions of Christ Jesus from the pens of four initiates. The initiate who describes Christ Jesus from the point of view of an initiate of wisdom was the writer of St John's Gospel; the one describing him in his capacity as an initiate of feeling was the writer of St Luke's Gospel and the individual describing him in terms of his magic will forces wrote St Mark's Gospel. The initiate who describes the harmonious interweaving of the three lower elements constituting the human being wrote St Matthew's Gospel. In this way, each writer describes the particular aspect of Christ Jesus into which they have been initiated.

In like manner, we can encompass a more fully rounded picture of Christ Jesus in that each Gospel writer speaks out of qualities closest to their own. Anyone filled with the requisite awe in face of such a mighty individuality as Christ will say: I am enabled to gain a more comprehensive picture of Christ Jesus precisely because each Gospel writer gives of their best capacities. For this reason it is essential that you do not keep taking what is said here on the basis of spiritual science in relation to the four Gospels—be it the fourth, the third, the second or the first—as if each chapter contained the sum total of truths about Christ Jesus. The notion could easily take hold—with regard to lectures given here or there—that Christ Jesus has been described, and would it not be amazingly fascinating to see how he is connected with a different Gospel? No, it is not like that. In receiving depictions of Christ Jesus through a Gospel, one receives it from one aspect alone. You will have to await such time, in the course of our spiritual movement, as Christ Jesus is eventually described in the context of all four Gospels. Only then will you have heard the combined mysteries about which we can speak.

Now it behoves us to proceed from an albeit rather one-dimensional account in order to create more of a composite picture of Christ Jesus in such a way that really requires of you that you bear in mind what has just been said. You cannot leave today's lecture and say: Well, now we have got to the truth of these matters. No. You should say to yourself: we have been hearing about just one aspect, and further elaboration is needed to shed light on what can be said from other perspectives.

The figure of Christ Jesus does indeed represent a confluence of all earlier spiritual streams in humanity and, simultaneously, we see a rebirth of those streams. All previous streams flow together in Christ Jesus and are reborn, reborn in heightened stature. We could refer to any number of spiritual streams existing in pre-Christian times, and with which we are faced when observing the four Gospels from a spiritual-scientific perspective. However, we only wish to draw attention to three of these streams.

Firstly, we have a powerful stream that has been active since ancient times in Asia. This is the stream of Zarathustrianism. A second stream once blossomed in India and reached a certain zenith in the appearance of Gautama Buddha some six hundred years before our era. A third spiritual stream came to expression in the ancient Hebrew people. Thus in Christ Jesus we see a confluence of the ancient Hebrew spirituality with that in which Gautama Buddha lived his life and the stream synonymous with Zarathustra. We could mention many other spiritual streams but the matter in hand would become too wide-ranging.

Everything that took place in Palestine at the beginning of our era now emerges—if we are to understand it rightly—in the four Gospels. It is not the task of spiritual science to dredge from the Gospels what they intend to say. Nothing said by me has been trawled on the basis of the Gospels. The only source for the spiritual researcher is what is called the Akashic Chronicle or Record and this can be clairvoyantly observed. Were all the Gospels to be lost through some catastrophe, what spiritual science has to say about Christ would nevertheless remain because it rests firmly upon spiritual research. Only subsequently can what spiritual research yields be compared with what is written in the Gospels. It is this which elicits such objective reverence and awe towards all that we encounter in the Gospels. You must never allow this perspective to slip your attention. For nothing is being drawn from the Gospels and, for this reason, neither does what I am about to relate originate from that source. Later we can compare what I am about to say with what is written in the Gospels and we will find both to be entirely congruent.

One of those spiritual streams which flowed into Christianity is that which reached its zenith in the personality of Gautama Buddha, who was incarnated in India some six hundred years before the time of our reckoning. What manner of individuality is this? We will understand this personality if we bear the following in mind: everything that gradually emerges in the history of humanity is a product of evolution that has—little by little, as it were—settled. You would go astray if you imagined that modern humanity's faculties have always been as they are today. For instance, today we are familiar with what we call the voice of conscience. This has not always existed. We can practically seize upon the very moment when conscience arose in the course of human history. If you go back to Aeschylus, you will find in his writings no trace of a description of conscience. Only when you reach Euripides is conscience described. Between the times of these two Greeks, the concept of conscience emerges. What the modern person calls an inner voice has only relatively recently developed. Before the advent of conscience we can say that human consciousness could be characterized as a sort of clairvoyance. If a person did something they should not have done, something akin to a spirit of revenge would appear to follow them. The Greeks called these the Furies. A person would really see the fruits of their evil deeds in the avenging Furies all around them. This manifestation—external to the person—was gradually internalized in the human soul as the voice of conscience. This is how other human faculties evolve over time and it is just human myopia not to see farther than their noses—much as external science does so copiously—if one believes that human beings have always been just as they are today.

People were therefore unfamiliar with the teaching of compassion and love. We must imagine that teachings of compassion and love in those distant times were transmitted quite differently from today's methods. Nowadays, people are able to immerse themselves inwardly. When something or other happens in the outside world, people can generate a feeling of compassion and love and they know this to be good. They can locate the principles of compassion and love within themselves. In ages gone this was not possible. In olden times those charged with caring for humanity would—purely through suggestion—instruct people how they should behave. Humanity had to be guided. There were isolated leaders of humanity who directed them in their conduct. These leaders and forerunners of humanity would evoke in human beings such deeds of charity and love as were to be carried out. These guiding leaders in the field of compassion and love in turn stood under the leadership of higher beings who, together with all those below them, acted under the influence of one called the Bodhisattva of love and compassion himself. His mission was to bring to Earth the teachings of love, compassion and mercy. But this Bodhisattva, compassion-and-love guide of humanity though he was, was not a normally incarnated soul but rather one whose incarnation did not extend completely into his physical body and thereby retaining something of a bridge to the spiritual world.

The Bodhisattva of compassion and love lived only partially as a physical human being while part of his being extended into spiritual realms, from whence he brought to Earth those influences and impulses which had been instilled in him for transmission to humanity. If we wished to depict this in spiritual terms we would say: the seer sees a representation of a human form, in which the Bodhisattva is partially incarnated, and behind this a mighty spiritual-astral figure extending upwards into spiritual realms with only a portion tethered in a physical body. This is how the Bodhisattva appears. This Bodhisattva is the self-same individuality who is later reincarnated in India as the king's son,

Gautama Buddha. This incarnation represents an upward step for this Bodhisattva, an enhanced and heightened state of virtue. He had earlier allowed himself to be guided from above, receiving inspiration and passing this onwards. However, in the incarnation falling six hundred or so years BCE, he was elevated to Buddha-hood at the age of twenty-nine, signifying that in this incarnation he experienced full immersion in his physical body. Whereas, as a Bodhisattva, he was formerly obliged to remain partly outside his physical body so as to create the spiritual bridge mentioned, his progress to Buddha-existence entailed being able to incarnate fully into his body. By this means he was able not only to receive the teaching of love and compassion through Inspiration but could now look within himself and receive these principles as the voice of his own heart. This was Buddha's enlightenment under the Bodhi tree at the age of twenty-nine. This was the moment when the doctrine of love and compassion arose within him— independently of his co-dependence on the spiritual world—in the form of human soul riches so that he was now able to think what he had previously expounded in the Eightfold Path. His sermon on this, the mighty teaching of love and compassion, is the first to emerge from a human heart.

This is what must happen with all human capacities. An individuality must appear for the first time in human evolution who brings to expression—and in whom is manifest—a new capability. Only then can this new capacity gradually start to develop among wider populations, who in turn make it their own. The teaching of love and compassion could only be experienced as something inherent and accessible in each individual once it had been introduced by an individuality and this is known as 'turning the wheel' in oriental philosophy, that is, the wheel of dharma, of compassion and love. This took place through the all-embracing individuality of the Bodhisattva descending into the king's son, Gautama Buddha. From then onwards it became possible for individuals—of themselves—to discover the doctrine of love and compassion. This is how it progresses. More and more people will uncover within themselves the teaching of compassion and love and, some three thousand years into our era, there will be a sufficient number of people on Earth who will be able to evolve in their own hearts what Buddha initiated. In this respect, Buddha's earthly mission will have been fulfilled. For when the Bodhisattva descended to become a Buddha, another being took over the virtue of the Bodhisattva. Until that point, the being we today call Buddha was a Bodhisattva. The stage following Bodhisattva is Buddha. From being a Bodhisattva, the ascending being becomes a Buddha.

Oriental philosophy expresses this as follows: when the Bodhisattva descended to Earth he gave the Bodhisattva crown to the being who followed him. This subsequent being still lives nowadays as a Bodhisattva and will only rise to full Buddha righteousness in some three thousand years hence, and is the individuality known to oriental philosophy as the Maitreya Buddha; today he is a Bodhisattva and he will become Maitreya Buddha in some three thousand years' time. He has a mission which, unlike Gautama Buddha's, is connected with faculties not yet to be independently found within human beings. This is a progressive trajectory such that we can say: the Bodhisattva—who embodies the teaching of compassion and love—has indeed progressed to full Buddhahood and through this he gave his mission colossal impetus. Through the fact that, having immersed his entire being into a human body six hundred years before our era, he merited the right no longer to be incarnated in a physical body on Earth. And indeed this was the last time that a Bodhisattva descended to incarnation. He no longer needed to incarnate in a physical body but thenceforth only to descend to an ether body. All following incarnations of the Buddha are not such that he is visible on the physical plane but can only be seen through the forces that allow human beings to see on an etheric level. And so, in all subsequent incarnations, Buddha only descended as far as an ether body. All that the Buddha wished to bring to humankind he now caused to flow into events heralding the advent of Christianity on Earth, six hundred years after his last presence on Earth. He brought his sacrificial offering towards Christianity, newly establishing itself, as a parallel spiritual stream and allowed this offering to flow into the great combined streams of spirituality. This stream finds its zenith in the Buddha. That is one stream.

Another stream came into existence in the following way. We can picture this if we look into human evolution as a whole. You will remember that, after the catastrophic flooding of Atlantis, human beings did not possess the same faculties as they do today. In post-diluvian times they retained the remnants of a dimming clairvoyance. Logical thinking only emerged gradually. The culture we know as that of ancient India was emerging from a state of etheric clairvoyance. Zarathustrian culture was in a similar state, as were those of Chaldea and Egypt, in all of which thinking was not as it is today. Everything was Inspired—received more or less through inspired Imagination—and not suffused with logic; this also applied to Chaldean astrology and Hermetic wisdom, which then saw the light of day. Human thinking along logical lines had not yet surfaced in these cultures, and was reserved for quite different streams, later to be characterized as logical, thought-based cultures. The first post-Atlantean culture emerged entirely on foundations of etheric clairvoyance. The Zarathustrian culture following this was similarly clairvoyant, but to a less marked degree, while Egypto-Chaldean culture was likewise based upon Inspiration. Thinking in those times was not yet pervaded with logic; it was still permeated throughout with Imaginations that came to expression in the wondrous images in the astrology of the Chaldeans and in the Hermetic wisdom of the Egyptians.

Post-Atlantean cultures proceeded from two sources. Apart from the stream flowing westwards, which populates modern America, two streams of migrating peoples under the guidance of their leaders wandered to the East, one flow heading northwards, the other in a southerly direction.

The northern migration, which left elements behind in Europe, pressed onwards into Asia. While new cultures were being established, the European population lived for centuries as if in waiting. Their strengths were being deferred for all that was to come later. The main traits of their culture were moulded in the main by the great initiate known as Scythianos, who had chosen the expanses extending to the Siberian wastes as his particular area. The leaders of the primal European cultures were inspired by him and their abilities were based not upon the thinking later to enter humanity but rather upon a receptivity to sounds midway between rhythmic-recitative language and a kind of singing, accompanied by highly distinctive music, no longer heard today and consisting of consorting flute-like instruments. This was a most extraordinary feature, the remnants of which resounded among the Bards and Skalds. All that is told in the Greek myths of Apollo and Orpheus has its origin in this culture. Alongside this, the practical skills of settlement and building and so on were being practised in Europe.

The other mass migrations, led by the great Sun initiate, moved onwards into Asia. The farthermost of these created the first post-Atlantean culture under the leadership of the Rishis. In the Middle East the oldest Zarathustrian culture evolved—and here we are not speaking about the historical Zarathustra. What he elicited in some ways contrasts with ancient Indian culture, which was entirely built on etheric clairvoyance. Zarathustra turned his gaze towards the Sun. He beheld the Spirit of the Sun, the 'Great Aura' that was Ahura Mazdao. It was Zarathustra who first brought the unique characteristics of Northern culture to expression here. Everything that followed was to build upon this feature.

The other branch of migration to have traversed across, the Southern branch, created the foundations of Egypto-Chaldean culture, a growing blend that arose between the two cultures. This can be schematically illustrated: Indian culture represents the elaboration of the human ether body, that of Persia saw the evolution of the sentient body; Egypto-Chaldean culture gave rise to the sentient soul, being an inward-looking culture, a culture on an interior evolutionary path. Just as sentient body and sentient soul amalgamate—as they do in all humanity—this process is especially represented in the cultures of Egypt and Chaldea. The same will also come to pass as regards the consciousness soul and spirit-self. This can only take place through what will have occurred in terms of transition in that area where spirituality has hitherto been held back, held in abeyance: this can only happen in Europe. This is the region where the development towards the intellectual- and consciousness souls had been postponed or deferred and where it could only progress after the Christ event. Here, too, will the future melding with qualities of spirit-self be able to take place, and can only come to pass in a spiritual stream such as spiritual science. This will herald the sixth cultural epoch.

While the two streams already mentioned existed under conditions of dim, ancient clairvoyance, the third stream—which later combined with the first two—and which prepared for the advent of the Christ event, was joined by a fourth cultural current, which can in turn be characterized as one of logic and thought, of logical thinking. So that we understand each other quite clearly, please bear in mind that all clairvoyance arises from an ether body working, to a certain extent, independently, and in particular the etheric surrounding of the brain. Where an ether body is tightly conjoined with a brain, the physical tool of logical thinking, clairvoyance cannot emerge. Only when an ether body is slightly detached, retaining an independent element, can seership ensue. If an ether body is comprehensively enmeshed with a physical brain, the person concerned will elaborate their brain in fine detail and their physical brain will be similarly elaborated, leaving no surplus forces to cultivate clairvoyance. Yet it was essential that precisely this facility for brain-bound thinking—that very ability to synthesize world phenomena through brain activity—held its course in human progress. Something now had to be added to this human faculty—something essential to onward evolution, something of a selection process—that can be characterized as follows. Let us take an individual in whom old clairvoyance was least present but in whom the physical instrument of the brain was most incised, was most, as it were, chiselled out. This individual was capable of synthesizing the outer world in terms of measure, number, order and harmony while seeking unity among the phenomena laid out before them. Where adherents of earlier cultures derived their knowledge of the spiritual world from inside outwards, as it were, this individual had to extend his gaze to the very periphery of world phenomena, had to unite these phenomena and weigh them up, reflecting: out there are the phenomena of the external world and everything is harmoniously ordered when observed as a single image of unity. What appears as a united external reality—external unity—once appeared as the Godhead behind such appearances of the physical world. This was a departure from other views of the divine. These latter devotees of the divine expressed it thus: our image of the divine wells up from within. This individual, however, turned his gaze in every direction, evaluating and deciphering the phenomena, looking at the various kingdoms of nature, trying to unify them, in short, he was the great designator of world marvels in terms of number and measure, was selected as such from the entirety of humankind. This individual, chosen to survey the entire external, physical world and to find unity within its calculable diversity was Abraham. Abraham or Abram was the individual selected by divine-spiritual powers to receive a unique mission: to deliver humanity into the world of physical phenomena, to those forces bound up with measure and number. His background was Chaldean culture, a culture which had derived its astrology from clairvoyance. Abraham, primal father of arithmetic, proceeded to seek out everything calculable, to synthesize everything on the basis of calculation, finding in the process that the physical brain had undergone an exceptional degree of etching or incising. A unique mission was allocated to him in this way.

Now we need to consider how this mission was to unfold, because it was not his alone but was to become a common asset for all humankind. As thinking was bound to the individual brain, how could it become a talent common to all? It could only really become an attribute of all humanity through physical heredity. This means that an entire people had to stem from this one individual. It follows that this people had to inherit a singular feature for as long as it was this feature's mission to be dispersed among humanity. An entire people needed to go forth from its origins. A people had to be established—not just a culture—in which teachings could be perpetuated: what was once received through clairvoyance could now be taught. What humanity was now to receive would be transferred to descendants through heredity so that it could be integrated in every detail. What was to be integrated?

That system of orderliness first introduced by Abraham was to be integrated by means of human permutation and combination. By looking upwards to the celestial ordering of the stars, human orderliness through combination can be deduced. The wise men of Chaldea reflected the thoughts of the Gods in their astrology. Now it was a matter of discovering this unique transition to combining, to a logical perception of phenomena found in the external world. A physical attribute had to be inherited—derived from the physical work of thinking itself—that itself yielded an order mirroring the order dispersed in the surrounding world. This is beautifully expressed by the one who gave Abraham his mission: 'Your descendants shall be as the number of stars', which the Bible nonsensically translates as 'Your descendants shall be as the sands of the sea.' What is meant is that the descendants of Abraham shall be disposed in a definite way, structured so as to reflect an after-image of the starry heavens. This is also expressed in relation to the twelve sons of Jacob, who reflect an imprint of the twelve constellations of the Zodiac. Here we see the number processes that are prefigured in the heavens. The sequence of the generations was to reflect this celestial enumeration. Just as starry ciphers are emblazoned across the heavens, so are these to be inscribed as numbers ordering the sequence of generations. Such is the profound wisdom contained in the foolishly translated words: 'Your descendants shall be as the sands of the sea.'

So we gain a sense of Abraham's mission. Other manifestations, too, symbolize this whole mission of Abraham in a wondrous way as reflecting all the mysteries of the world. Let us first reflect: It is the ancient twilight clairvoyance that is to be sacrificed here. Everything established over millennia in humanity was to be sacrificed. The innermost ethos of this entire mission was that everything was to be received as a bequest, as a gift from the external world. Whatever was to arise was to take its course through physical succession; it was in this form that the mission was to make its entrance into world history. Abraham himself had to receive his task as a gift from God. He was initially challenged to sacrifice his son, Isaac, but was then prevented from carrying it out. What did he actually receive from the hand of God? He was given his task. Had he actually sacrificed Isaac, he would have been sacrificing his entire mission. In having Isaac returned to him, all his people are also returned to him. What he was intended to bequeath to the world he then receives as a gift from a divine world order in the form of his son, Isaac. Hence, everything that ensued—and was dependent on Abraham—is itself a gift from God. The last remnants of clairvoyance—and you will soon see what the individual gifts of clairvoyance express, each of which can be connected with one of the Zodiac constellations—the last remains of this clairvoyance, voluntarily sacrificed, is associated with the constellation of Aries the ram. This is why we encounter a ram at the sacrifice of Isaac, a symbol expressing the renunciation of the last gifts of seership in exchange for the new gifts of being able to appraise world phenomena in terms of number and measure. This task was assigned to Abraham.

How does this task proceed? The last remains of clairvoyance are forfeited, ejected from his mission and, where they still emerged through heredity, not tolerated within Abraham's direct line of descent. Joseph was one such regression. He had dreams and clairvoyant abilities. His brothers cast him out. This shows just how strictly Abraham's mission was enacted: Joseph is banished, rejected. He wanders to Egypt to make those very connections with another branch of our common cultural evolution, namely with Egyptian culture. Joseph unifies within himself the universal characteristics inherent in this task with the remains of ancient clairvoyance. In Egypt he caused a complete revolution by importing clairvoyance into a declining Egyptian culture, thereby correcting its course. This is the basis for Joseph's own cultural mission.

Now we witness a unique drama. We see how the missionaries of external thinking—thinking in terms of measure and number—are not on their earlier trajectory. They now seek outer connections—as did Joseph—because the afterglow of what they could no longer elicit from within could still be found in Egypt. The descendants of Abraham journey to Egypt and absorb there what they need. It can approach them from that quarter. That is why they travel to Egypt.

What is needed for the furtherance of this mission—because it is no longer accessible from within—is endowed externally through Egyptian initiation. Moses is able to convey this to them from the periphery, thus uniting Egyptian culture with Abraham's mission. We then see how this human knowledge, this conception of the outer world in terms of number, weight and measure, is propagated from generation to generation through blood kinship and can only be passed on in this way because it is bound to all that must be inherited. This, then, is the second stream.

The third stream is that connected with Zarathustra and which came to expression in ancient Persia and spread into the Near and Middle East, as we have learnt in several lectures. These are the three streams that flow together in Christ Jesus, the individuality who was to be allied with all three of these streams. They had to unite within him. How was this to take place? It took place in the following complex way. Let us first remind ourselves that one of the streams to flow into this worldwide confluence had played its main part in India some six hundred years before that event. At around the same time an event was taking place in ancient Babylonian-Chaldean culture in the form of Zarathustra reappearing under the name of Zaratos or Nazarathos. He lived and taught in Chaldea at the very time when the greatest and most highly acclaimed teachers and leaders of the ancient Jewish-Hebrew people had been led into Babylonian captivity.[15] So you see that this is the first time contact was established between the Hebrew people and Zaratos and how members of that people lived under the direct personal influence of the reincarnated Zarathustra or Zoroaster. Here we see the events described in the Bible being played out.

Here we also encounter the following. At the start of our calendar reckoning, there were two sets of parents, both called Mary and Joseph. The one couple lived in Nazareth, the other in Bethlehem. The husband in one of the married couples was descended from the Solomon line in the house of David, and he was the husband in the Bethlehem couple. The other couple in Nazareth were descended from the Nathan line of the house of David. Solomon and Nathan are both sons of David; both these couples gave birth to a son: to the

Nazarene couple a Jesus child is born—as described by St Luke—and to the Bethlehem couple a Bethlehem Jesus child is born—as described in St Matthew's Gospel. Thus we have two Jesus children at the start of our calendar era.

Let us follow the Jesus child from Bethlehem! How did he come into being as a physical child? We see his lineage as a physical child, which is described as far as Abraham by the writer of Matthew's Gospel. We need to imagine a trail from Ur in Chaldea over to the land of Canaan, thence to Egypt and back again to Canaan. This would approximately replicate the path taken by the Israelites from Chaldea to Palestine, onward to Egypt and returning to Palestine. These were the ancestors of the Bethlehem Jesus child. In that he shared the blood of these ancestors he, as it were, co-experienced this flight into other lands. The individuality who now wanted to incarnate in the Bethlehem Jesus child made this journey—albeit swiftly and in compressed form—and this was the individuality who had taught, as Zarathustra, in ancient Chaldea. Thus, at the moment when the Bethlehem Jesus child was born, a spiritual individuality retraced the same journey as Abraham himself had made from Chaldea to Canaan—only now on a spiritual level—and this individuality was then incarnated in the Bethlehem Jesus child. Shortly after this, the flight to Egypt was indeed re-enacted, as also the return from Egypt to Nazareth, where the family of this being could settle. And here we see the individuality who, so to speak, repeated in spiritual form all the travels of the Israelites. You can retrace all these journeys yourself in the Bible, where you will find that all the descriptions do indeed tally with this. The Bible is the best descriptive document among all records. What can be seen by the seer in the Akashic Chronicle is covered in the Bible: the Israelites' journey from Chaldea to Canaan, onward to Egypt and back to Palestine. Wonderful indeed are the parallels in all this. Who leads the Jews to Egypt? The dreams of one Joseph inspire this. Who inspires the flight of the Bethlehem Jesus child to Egypt? The dreams of another Joseph, his father. The parallels align to this level of detail. It is indeed an exceptional gift of persisting clairvoyance that creates such correlations.

So, born into this Bethlehem Jesus child—having received the element that entered humanity through heredity via Abraham—was the individuality of Zarathustra. Those who were connected with Zarathustra in the Mystery schools of Chaldea now follow the trail. In the spiritual world, their star leads them: Zoroaster himself, who moves towards Bethlehem in order to be born. The three Magi can follow him, they too appear in the Bible. They know the individuality living in the Jesus child in Bethlehem.

This is the one Jesus child, the child of Bethlehem. In the other Jesus child, who was only born in Bethlehem as a result of a journey, there lived a different being whose advent was announced, in all his qualities, as being quite different from the Bethlehem child. The Bethlehem Jesus child is described, from birth onwards, as being exceptionally gifted beyond all human measure, and this is because in him lived a mighty individuality. He was gifted in all that humanity had hitherto conquered culturally. He was exceptionally able to encompass all that could be learnt from his surroundings. The other child, the Nazarene Jesus child, was not in the least gifted in the externals of culture. He had only a deeply, deeply soulful inwardness. Precisely this characteristic of inner, soul-filled quietude was an especial gift in him. He was, however, not talented in taking in his surrounding culture and had little inclination to do so. He did possess a faculty for distinguishing between good and evil, an ability of which people cannot gain the slightest idea. All earthly culture was foreign to him. It was all foreign to him because in him was born an element which the entire span of human evolution had not undergone.

We will understand this if we consider the following. In ancient Lemurian times what we call the luciferic influence came to be within humanity. These luciferic forces slid into human astral bodies and humanity thus became what it did become. The principal powers then had to withhold a portion of the human ether body to prevent this part becoming infected with the luciferic content of the astral body. A part of the ether body was preserved, separated from the influence of the astral body, due to the fact that human beings held sway only over those parts of their ether body to do with being a feeling and a willing entity, but not over the part concerned with thinking activity. This thinking element was held back and was guided from above by the divine-spiritual world. This is why human beings, from the very beginnings of their earthly evolution, each have their individual desires and their personal feelings but they could not have their personal thoughts nor that expression of personal thought, speech. Thinking was such that, through an all-pervading spirituality, it was guided and led equally in all humans. Hence every person thought the same. Speech was also guided for most by folk-Gods such that not every person had their own language. That element expressed by the spirit of speech was—in relation to ether bodies—removed from the arbitrary control of individual personalities and was held in reserve. What was held back in Lemurian times is recounted in the myths about Paradise: human beings ate from the Tree of Knowledge but not from the Tree of Life; they gained power over their own will. But what humanity had not been given was now, by mysterious processes, transferred to this Jesus boy, to the Nazarene Jesus child, whose ether body this was. It was this that had been removed, detached from humanity at its inception and this prevented the Nazarene Jesus child from taking an interest in a culture wrought by humankind. In him was contained something far more originally pristine and primal, reminiscent of the time when humanity had not yet fallen into the sin of individual impiety, of decadence. The writer of St Luke's Gospel expresses this by enumerating the entire family tree back to Adam, thereby showing that in the Nazarene Jesus child an element is manifest that had sunk into Adam but that was withdrawn and preserved from all luciferic influence. Humanity in the state it had existed before any luciferic influence: this was now contained within the Jesus child of Nazareth.

These two Jesus boys lived next to each other. When they were both twelve years old, the following occurred: Zarathustra residing in the Bethlehem Jesus boy took the decision to transfer his individuality to the Jesus boy from Nazareth. This is hinted at in the Bible in an event referred to as the loss of the twelve-year-old and his parents' amazement at finding him again. The Nazarene Jesus boy is quite changed from his former character. Suddenly he is interested in his surroundings and culture, a characteristic attributable to the individuality of Zarathustra dwelling in him. This is the moment described in the Bible as the twelve-year-old Jesus being lost. Something else was also taking place. At the birth of the Jesus child of Nazareth what we can call the later incarnation of Buddha sank down, descending into his astral body. In his reincarnation, Buddha's ether body was now bound, from birth onwards, with the Nazarene Jesus boy such that we see Buddha in the astral body within the aura of Jesus of Nazareth. This is profoundly intimated in Luke's Gospel. Indian legend tells us that there was a remarkable wise man, who was to become a Buddha, at the time when the king's son Gautama Buddha was born. Asita it was who had lived then. He had perceived clairvoyantly that the Bodhisattva had now been born. He saw the child in the king's palace and was filled with enthusiasm. He began to weep. 'Why are you weeping?' asked the king. 'O king, nothing unfortunate lies ahead; on the contrary. The boy who has been born is the Bodhisattva and he will become Buddha. I weep only because I am an old man who will not live to see him as Buddha.' And with that Asita dies. The Bodhisattva does become Buddha. Buddha descends and unites himself with the aura of the Nazarene Jesus child, contributing his humble mite to the great event in Palestine. Simultaneously, through karmic nexus, the once-Asita is reborn. He becomes old Simeon who sees the Buddha who has now evolved from a Bodhisattva. What he could not see in India six hundred years earlier—the unfolding Buddhahood of the Bodhisattva—he now sees in the aura of the Nazarene Jesus child he was cradling, while to Buddha, hovering aloft, he says those wonderful words: 'Lord, now lettest thou thy servant depart in peace, according to thy word. For mine eyes have seen thy salvation'—the Buddha in the aura of the Jesus child.

So we see how these three streams flow together: through blood lineage down from Abraham, the Zarathustra line through the individuality of the Bethlehem Jesus child and the third stream through the fact that the Buddha, in his ether body or Nirmanakaya, drifts downwards and is seen by the shepherds. In this way we see the three streams converging. How these three live onwards within Christianity, how the stream of the Nazarene Jesus child, who is endowed with the individuality of Zarathustra, lives onward can only be presented another time.

It remains to be said that, after the Zarathustra individuality had moved over into the personality inhabiting the body of the Nazareth Jesus boy, the Bethlehem Jesus boy gradually wasted away and soon died.

The important thing for you to understand is the process by which the Zarathustra individuality was led over into the boy Jesus. You know that human development proceeds such that from birth to age seven the physical body is maturing, between seven and fourteen the ether body is being elaborated and unfolding and that the astral body is then born. A unique I or ego-entity, born to humans in Lemurian times, was not present in the Nazarene Jesus boy. Had he developed further without Zarathustra transferring to him, no ego or I could have come to birth. He had the three holy members of his being as they were before the Fall from Paradise: physical body, ether body and astral body and was only endowed with his I through Zarathustra. These all melded together in a wonderful way. These facts are recounted in the Bible and they are a mirror of what can be found in the Akashic Chronicle.

I have only been able to give you sketchy outlines of the confluence of these three mighty spiritual streams: that of Buddha, that of Zarathustra and the ancient Hebrew stream in the Near East where, at the beginning of our calculated era, these three streams were reborn in Christianity. These few lines we can continue another time.

Lecture 8

ZURICH, 19 NOVEMBER 1909

THE MATTHEW GOSPEL AND THE ENIGMA OF CHRIST

In Switzerland, over the last few years, it has been possible to speak about an exceptionally important spiritual-scientific subject, fundamentally the loftiest there is in spiritual science: the enigma of Christ. And if large numbers of today's population outside this spiritual-scientific movement think this the simplest of themes to be discussed, those modern people are in one sense right. What constitutes the greatest factor for Earth—and human evolution—Christ's power, Christ's impetus—has certainly had the effect that the simplest, most naïve of souls can in some way come to an understanding of it. On the other hand, this impulse has had such an effect that no earthly wisdom can suffice, truly to understand the events of Palestine at the start of our calculated era, to comprehend what took place for humanity and, actually, for the entire cosmos.

This mystery of Christ has recently been our subject and I may perhaps be permitted a few words to mention how the German section has just completed its first seven-year cycle. Founded seven years ago, there were few branches in existence, barely ten. This number has now grown to over forty. The number seven is often referred to amongst anthroposophical insights and world conceptions, and it expresses a certain principle: that evolution often takes place in successive seven-year periods. We only need to remind ourselves of what has been touched upon: the evolution of our Earth and how it goes through seven planetary conditions. Also, on a smaller scale, for every single fact of world evolution just as for a movement such as our spiritual-scientific one, the law of the number seven pertains. Those who see deeper into our movement appreciate how in a certain sense this seven-year cycle has played out and how we are now at a decisive point where what gave an initial impetus is repeated at a higher level and can return, like circulation, to its beginnings; this could only happen by working methodically, by working in a truly spiritual mode and not randomly nor haphazardly.

You will also remember that in the human being we distinguish seven elements or components: initially a physical body, an ether body, an astral body and an I or ego. If an astral body is transformed by an I, Spirit Self or Manas arises. If this ego or I transmutes an ether body, Life Spirit or Buddhi arises. If it ultimately transforms its physical body, the highest element of all can arise: Spirit Man or Atma. In this way we can distinguish four components and then a further three that result from a transformation of the initial three.

If one now wishes to accomplish something in the world that incorporates such spiritual lawfulness, this great principle must be followed. If you now, as a young anthroposophical branch,[16] wish to settle into this life in a correspondingly spiritual manner, as it were, it will be beneficial to determine how the organization of this work has progressed; because a young branch such as yours will appreciate how essential it is to reprise—and to adhere to—a developmental law such as this. We have kept to this rhythm in the German movement: the first four years were devoted to gathering everything necessary for acquiring world concepts that originate in spiritual science. We first set out the sevenfold nature of the human being, the teaching of karma and reincarnation, the great cosmic laws, Saturn-, Sun- and Moon-evolutions, the laws of human evolution and this is now in our literature and is being worked on in the various branches. This took place in the first four years.

In the last three years we have not systematically extended this but have instead, as it were, planted loftier wisdom into the material of the first four years' subjects, and then ascended to a conception of the very highest individuality ever to have walked the Earth: the individuality of Christ Jesus—substance we could not have broached had we done so with a collection of unfamiliar concepts. We could only speak of Christ after having communicated the nature of the human being in general. We could only grasp what this deed of Christ's signifies once we had understood human nature in all its stages. Those of you who heard the Basel lectures on St Luke's Gospel—and others who heard something here or there—will know what extremely complex processes took place. For instance, how could we have understood that during the twelfth year of his life something highly significant befell one of the Jesus boys, had we not been aware of what takes place between the ages of twelve and fifteen? Systematic preparations were made before we—with the deepest reverence—attempted to comprehend the mightiest truths of our earthly epoch inherent in the name of Christ Jesus. It was like an ascent to ever higher heights. In this way it became possible to observe Christ Jesus in connection with the Gospels of St John and St Luke. As was emphasized last time in Basel, nobody should believe they know much about the nature or essence of that lofty being on the basis of having heard all the truths connected with these two Gospels. They will only have experienced a single aspect. It is definitely not to be thought superfluous—nor does it merely constitute some kind of renewal—to hear of such realities from other angles, too. The Gospels relate to each other as varying images of the one mighty event that took place in Palestine, each Evangelist describing it from a particular vantage point.

The day before yesterday, in Bern[17], I outlined what was happening in the various branches. For certain reasons, I tried to allude in sketch form—and on the basis of the Luke Gospel—to Christ. This was done for quite specific reasons. Spiritual science is intended to be an outlook on life and not a theory nor a doctrine; it is intended to transform our innermost life of soul. We need to learn to view the world in a completely fresh way. There is one attribute that we need to acquire, one which a person should increasingly absorb through the insights brought by anthroposophy. There is no apposite word for this trait in any language but spiritual science will find a word for this new heart-sensing, this heart-perception. Until then we can only use words that do exist for this new trait: it is *humble modesty*. It is this that must take root ever more ardently in our souls, particularly in face of records such as the Gospels, which bring us tidings of the most significant event in Earth evolution. Here we learn that, fundamentally, we can only draw closer very slowly to the truths and insights essential for fathoming the Christ conundrum. We learn to cultivate a completely new feeling within ourselves, one quite foreign to modern people, who tend to be so hasty in their appraisal of this event. We learn to be circumspect in our portrayal of such truths and we know that, once we have focused on one aspect, we have only viewed that single aspect and never the whole event at once.

This is connected with something else—and we will only very gradually gain any understanding of it—and that is: why are there actually four Gospels? The fact is that even theology is relatively materialistic as far as understanding is concerned and the premises upon which comparisons are made between the four Gospels are superficial. And here contradictions are noticed. We initially looked at one of these, St John's Gospel. What is outwardly presented for our understanding—say such people—contradicts so starkly what the other three Gospels describe that one can only approach any concept of this Gospel if one maintains that the writer had no intention of describing actual situations but was instead writing some kind of hymn, some kind of witness avowal that reflected his sentient perceptions. Some see a great and comprehensive poem in St John's Gospel and in doing so they reduce its stature as a record. Only a superficial, materialistic view does this; for we have also focused on the other three Gospels. Even in those, paradoxes are found; but these are explained by the Gospels being written at differing times. In short, people nowadays are well on their way to tearing these mighty events to shreds to an extent that they no longer have significance for humanity. Spiritual science is directly called upon to reveal why we have four testimonies about the events in Palestine and challenged to reclaim these testaments for spiritual science. Why do four Gospels exist?

People's thinking has not always been as it is today. There was a time when the Gospels were not in the hands of populations but were confined to the very few, that minority tasked with leading spiritual life in the first centuries of Christianity. Why does nobody today ask whether those early leaders were not complete fools not to notice that the Gospels contradicted each other? Were they so mentally befogged that they simply did not see these paradoxes? Did those paragons of their age just accept these documents by humbly turning their gaze aloft and rejoicing that four Gospels exist, of which today's humanity can only say that they are no genuine testament because they contain contradictions?

Now, without allowing this to deter us, let us turn our attention to how, in the first centuries of Christianity, the Gospels were received and how they should be received. They were received in those distant times in a way that can be evaluated as follows: If we take this bunch of flowers here and photograph it from four angles, the result will be four photographs. Seen singly, in isolation, these four will look different from each other. Yet, seeing one such photo, one can nevertheless gain *an* idea of a bouquet. Now someone comes along and picks up a photo of a different angle. The two are compared and it is agreed that they are different pictures that are not of the same subject. And yet: a more rounded picture has been gained. Only when all four photos of the bouquet—taken from all four angles—are compared will one have a fairly complete concept of the actual bouquet. This is how the four Gospels are to be understood, characterizing as they do the same facts as seen from multiple aspects.

Why is a single fact described from four differing angles? Because it was known that each Evangelist, having written one of these Gospels, was imbued with great self-effacing humility, a humility that spoke to each writer: this is the greatest event in Earth evolution; you may not attempt to describe this comprehensively but may only endeavour to portray it to the extent that your own experience and knowledge make possible. In true humility did the writer of Luke's Gospel refrain from depicting any aspect other than the one with which he was familiar by virtue of his special spiritual abilities, which prompted him to say: Christ Jesus was the individuality in whom was manifest the highest revelation of love, a love extending to self-sacrifice. How did this love manifest itself? The writer of Luke's Gospel said of himself: I am not capable of describing the entire phenomenon and I will therefore confine myself to describing one aspect, the aspect of love.

You will understand this restriction to a single facet by the writers of the Gospels if we look into initiation methods in service of the ancient Mysteries. The actions of the Evangelists can only be understood in this context. As you know, initiation leads human beings into higher, supra-sensory worlds, enabling them to dwell within and penetrate these higher, super-sensible spheres by raising soul forces, elevating those forces and capabilities usually concealed and dormant in human souls. Initiations such as these have always existed. In pre-Christian times they existed in Egypt and Chaldea, leading those sufficiently mature in soul into higher realms. This took place in unique manner by working in a way no longer fully possible today. The modern human being has, as you know, three soul forces: thinking, feeling and willing. These three soul forces are used in everyday life such that all three forces, in their relation with the external world, are, as it were, deployed actively, take active part.

An example should illustrate how these three soul forces are active. You are walking across a field. You see a flower. You imagine the flower and you think: I like that flower. You feel that the flower is beautiful. This feeling has now been joined onto your thinking. And then you long to pick the flower, activating your will. Thus thinking, feeling and willing are active in your soul. Now you view human life in its entirety. Inasmuch as life plays out at a soul level, thinking, feeling and willing are intermingled. Human beings go through life with these three forces melded in continual interplay: souls live in thinking, feeling and willing.

Once a person is led into higher worlds their path involves an elaboration of these three soul forces as they existed in ordinary life. Thinking can be developed into spiritual vision. Feeling and willing can also be augmented into spiritual dimensions. This is initiation.

Those among you who have had a look at the book *Knowledge of Higher Worlds—How is it Achieved?* will have read what happens when thinking, feeling and willing are transmuted into spiritual worlds. What then takes place is often referred to as 'the splitting of the personality'. Thinking, feeling and willing are normally bound together organically: the person thinks, feels and wills as a unified personality. However, when developed upwards into spiritual realms, these forces tear apart. Whereas they were previously forces, they now become independent beings once evolved into spirit worlds. Three independent entities now emerge: one thought-like, another feeling-like and a third a will-like being. Therein lies the danger that the individuality's soul could be completely rent asunder. If the right, gradual path of knowledge has not been followed, a person can still raise their thinking into higher worlds. They will see into those realms but they will remain transfixed. They can subdue their will or it can stray onto divergent paths. What is setting in nowadays is that the human I can stride beyond itself, that the I can become a ruler, can reign as king over all three soul forces, over thinking, feeling and willing.

This was not the case in ancient times. In pre-Christian Mystery centres the axiom of division of labour pertained. For instance, someone admitted to a Mystery centre might be told: you are particularly suited to the work of developing your thinking. Their thinking was then the focus for expansion and, by raising it to higher levels, eventually resulting in a sage or magus who could penetrate the spiritual connections behind sense-perceptible events. This was one category of initiate from the ancient Mystery centres: Sages or Magi.

Other neophytes were trained in these Mystery centres to awaken the dormant forces primarily of feeling, leaving their thinking and willing in abeyance in their original states. Feeling was elevated. When feeling is principally elevated in an individual, they attain certain special characteristics. There is a significant difference between someone whose feeling was trained in a Mystery centre of old and a person of today. The soul-psychic reach or influence of a person thus schooled was far greater than would be the case today. The developed forces of such a soul could exert a powerful influence over the soul of their surrounding region. For this reason, those especially initiated into the sphere of feeling became the healers of their peers. Having evolved through the sacrificial service of feeling they were called to work therapeutically, bringing health to their fellow humans.

A third category of initiate consisted of those whose will was especially cultivated. These were the Magicians or Magi of will. Thus there were three kinds of initiate: Magicians, Healers and Sages, all of whom received their initiations in the Mystery centres of yore. Nowadays it would not be possible to cultivate just one element of a person's character because it is no longer possible to create such a high degree of harmony among modern individuals as held sway in ancient Mystery centres. The individual who became a sage in one such Mystery centre would, as it were, renounce this harmony. That is how things were conducted. Whoever became a healer would carry out—with the greatest deference—a sage's directions, forgoing the sage's lofty wisdom and placing their power of feeling at the disposal of the wise man.

Alongside these three groupings within the Mystery centres there was an essential fourth group. Situations arose where no single group of initiates could reach the right perspective to effectively affect the outer world. Some things could be affected by initiates of any one of the specialized cohorts named only because an additional fourth grouping of individuals existed. This consisted of individuals who were suited for initiation by virtue of their gifts, and who were told that the high level of initiation attained by the sages, the healers and the magicians, was not possible for those in this fourth category. Yet it was possible to advance each of the three soul forces of the other categories to a certain level in this group. No single soul force was developed to as high a degree as was the case in the one-sided initiates: the sages, the healers and the magi of will. Yet a certain harmony of all three combined traits existed in this fourth group. An initiate of this group inwardly presented a harmonious synthesis of all three soul faculties trained by the more specialized initiates. Now, in certain circumstances it was necessary to set aside one's individuality and to resort to advice from someone on a, as it were, lower level. There were times in those ancient Mystery centres when neither sages nor healers nor indeed magicians made decisions but instead placed their forces at the disposal of this fourth group of initiates, less highly developed though they were. Nevertheless, it was in their service that they placed their forces. The outcome of this was invariably that world evolution took a greater forward step as a result of those higher initiates listening to those 'beneath' them.

Such was the case in Eastern Mystery centres. Those more highly initiated placed their forces at the disposal of the fourth category, were advised by them and obeyed them unquestioningly. In European Mystery centres councils of twelve initiates existed, at the head of which stood a thirteenth, uninitiated individual to whom they deferred. He it was who decided what should happen, relying on his instinctive will, while those higher placed than him would carry out his instructions. You will only understand this by looking back at those times when great trust was still placed in a being in the world who was not bound to human thinking and willing. Nowadays people consider themselves the cleverest in the world. This has not always been so. There were times when people said to themselves: yes, it is true that I can progress to higher levels. I am capable of this. But to say that I am already the most advanced creature in the world cannot be a presumption I can make.

The veracity of this can be illustrated by another example. Let us remember that it was only over the course of human history that paper was gradually devised, an activity through which various substances were amalgamated to create the fabric of paper. Wasps have long been able to do this! Now people ought to reflect: I had to acquire my knowledge relatively recently. The wasp cannot have learnt its skill from humans. Divine artistry holds sway in the wasp's ability. Wasps' creativity is suffused with divine wisdom.

In similar manner were those councils of twelve initiates ensouled when they would assemble in pre-Christian times and reflect of themselves: we have certainly evolved higher faculties in ourselves but, for all our forces and aptitudes, we can only really attain to a level ordained by divine beings in individuals of lower capacity. They looked towards a thirteenth who, by comparison with them, had remained at a naïve and childlike stage. They said: unlike us, he contains no great human wisdom but yet he is steeped in divine sagacity, in heavenly wisdom. Similarly, the Eastern sages, healers and magicians would say: we follow one who is not yet as advanced as us, but one who is at a level where they are still saturated with divine wisdom. This renunciation, this forbearance, lay unfurled like a magical breath or pall across the Mystery centres that possessed this knowledge.

Now, you will remember the poem by Goethe called 'The Mysteries'[18], where a thirteenth individual, a Brother Markus, is introduced into the circle of momentous men. Here we see an occurrence deeply grounded in human nature—albeit a nature far removed from modern humans—which consists of an initiate of the fourth grouping who has not advanced through the power of his own effort to a level as high as the others and yet who is regarded with such reverence that he leads the other twelve.

We therefore have four kinds of initiate: healers, sages, magicians and a fourth kind who were given the designation 'human being' in this unique sense. Four such initiates set about depicting the greatest event in Earth evolution: a wise sage, a healer, a magus and a human being in the sense of the fourth category of initiates. One of them describes this from the standpoint of the common person, one is the magus who focuses primarily on the will-nature of Christ and who covertly brings these forces into his Gospel; also the healer who wrote the Luke Gospel and is the source of the tradition that St Luke was a physician, which corresponds with his self-sacrificing love of his fellow human beings. Then there is the sage who writes about Christ's wisdom-filled nature.

These are the four initiates who, refraining from describing a totality, reflected: we can only depict the aspect closest to our own soul. The reverent modesty of these four human beings, each of whom has relinquished describing Christ in all his aspects and has restricted themselves to describing the being whom they can see—in terms of their own individuality—as a mighty and exalted being: all this stands as a stance in contrast to modern consciousness, which has no doubt that it can comprehensively encompass the highest phenomena with its reason.

Having shed light on two sides of this immense event during the Basel lectures on the Gospels of Luke and John, today I will say something about Matthew's Gospel. We could just as well have spoken about the Gospel according to Mark but there are reasons why, having taken on to describe a little of this vast event from the standpoint of spiritual science, I now choose to consider St Matthew's Gospel after the Luke and John Gospels. The reason for this is that one must gain a feeling as to how one can draw closer to an understanding of this world event in all self-effacing humility. In the Gospels of St Luke and St John we learn of great truths. What we face in Mark's Gospel, however, is in part so shattering that, if one has not previously heard the various facts relating to Matthew's Gospel, one might well believe that there are profoundly irreconcilable differences between Mark's Gospel and the other Gospels. One would not be able to cope with Mark's Gospel because there we are told the most momentous and shocking truths in the world, albeit not the loftiest, which are to be found in St John's Gospel. This is why today I will speak about St Matthew's Gospel.

We saw in our studies of the Luke Gospel how the most diverse spiritual streams present in the world poured themselves into forming a single, communal stream at the time in which the Christ events came to pass. It was shown how, one the one hand, the teaching of love and compassion streamed into Christianity from the Buddha. On the other hand, the teachings of Zarathustra were also shown to have flowed into Christianity. All the other pre-Christian spiritual streams likewise converged within this momentous phenomenon. In Matthew's Gospel we see particularly how the ancient Hebrew spiritual stream, the spiritual stream of ancient Jewry, joined the confluence so that, in order to understand Matthew's Gospel, we have to speak about the true mission of the ancient Jewish people.

As you know, spiritual research does not only draw on the Gospels as its source but also on the spiritual world, on the eternal Akashic Chronicle. Were all the Gospels to perish, through some catastrophe on Earth, spiritual research into the events in Palestine would still be in a position to recount those events. If we compare what the purest sources make available to spiritual research with the great testimonies of the Evangelists, the most wonderful congruity—eliciting deep awe in face of the Gospels—becomes manifest. This congruity makes clear to us from which high source the Gospels must originate. For the writers of the Gospels tell us what we can only understand once we are schooled in the glimpses afforded us by spiritual science.

What, then, is the mission of the Hebrew people? In order to understand this, we need to look back at the course of human evolution. You know that present human faculties have evolved. That these human faculties have evolved all by themselves is a belief to which only materialistic science subscribes, and it sees no farther than the end of its nose. At best it still believes mankind evolved from animals yet is in no position to retrace this route to actual soul faculties. Spiritual science knows that these soul aptitudes are not the same as today's. In olden times humanity possessed what we could call dim, twilight clairvoyance. Only later did present consciousness gradually emerge from this clairvoyance. There was a definite starting point, a moment at which this way of imagining interposed itself into humanity.

If we turn our gaze back to ancient Indian culture we find a sort of clairvoyance. Modern people have to look at their surroundings and see the things they wish to get to know. The way in which the ancient Indians looked, they did not get to know the things surrounding them. Science, even as taught to children today, did not then exist. A wise man in ancient India acquired his wisdom through inner Intuition, turning away from the outer world and reposing within himself or within his higher being. This he would call his union with Brahma. He received his knowledge through inner Intuition. This was knowledge entirely based on inner clairvoyant Intuition. Outer knowledge for him was, by contrast, Maya or illusion.

This clairvoyance receded ever further. By the time of proto-Persian culture outer observation had become firmly blended with the inner knowledge that was still prevalent. Similarly, inner intuition was present in the third cultural epoch, even though people had progressed in their grasp of outer matters. In ancient Chaldea what we would today call astrology—a kind of stellar science—existed. Today's external science knows nothing about the essence of astrology. However closely you interrogate the stone records, you will uncover nothing about the actual nature of astrology. Nobody today can elicit the feeling the ancient Chaldeans had for astrology. This was no knowledge garnered from observation of the starry heavens. Ancient Chaldeans did not study the physical planet Mars by turning their gaze towards it but what could be learnt of Mars arose inwardly by allowing in-pouring clairvoyant knowledge to radiate within.

This was no external calculating and no awareness existed of the tidings such knowledge could bring about external space. The first concepts of familiarity with the stellar world were to be found in the ancient centres of initiation. Of all that was taught there about the evolution of the Earth and the connection of Earth with Mars we still retain a certain knowing that emanates from within. Similarly, Egyptian geometry was knowledge that emanated from within and was only used for surveying purposes. The Chaldeans of yore were the first who should have been able to unfold other forces enabling them to acquire outer knowledge. The mission to lead humanity towards externally consolidated knowledge was allocated to the Hebrew peoples by the spiritual leaders of world evolution. The combined knowledge of the ancient Indians, Persians, Chaldeans and Egyptians—significant though it was—did not require a physical brain. Such knowledge was not based in the physical brain but in freely functioning ether bodies. When human beings become freely active in their ether bodies, images arise that account for the knowledge possessed by those ancient peoples, just as today all clairvoyant knowledge arises at the point when a person is able to lift their ether body out of their physical body, no longer needing to make use of their physical brain.

Humanity had to acquire the ability to perceive via their brains. To this end, a personality now had to be selected for the suitability of its brain: those least susceptible to clairvoyant vision yet able to use their brains. Here we have another point on which reading the Akashic Record confirms facts in the Bible. What is written in the Bible is to the letter correct. It is true that people were chosen who, on the basis of their physical configuration, had the most suitable attributes for carrying out spiritual work by means of their brains. Just such a person was Abraham. He it was who was chosen to fulfil the mission of enabling his fellow human beings to reach a stage where they perceived the outer world by means of their brains. His was a personality least suited to receiving visions, one who thought logically, investigating external phenomena in terms of weight, measure and number. An older tradition credits Abraham with being the inventor of mathematics and this has more truth than today's material world can imagine. It was now a matter of introducing this mission into the world in the right way. Let us consider how a mission entrusted to a personality would in ancient times have been discharged, transferred into humanity for posterity. It was transmitted from teacher to pupil. Whoever had a vision or intuition would share it with their followers or descendants. But what was entrusted to the old Hebrew peoples was linked to a physical instrument which could not simply be handed on to descendants if they did not possess brains fitted to the task. For this reason it had to be bound to physical heritage and had to be inheritable through the generations. Abraham had to be surrounded not by pupils but by a people through whose generations such a brain could be inherited. In this sense Abraham became the original ancestor, the father-progenitor, of his people.

It is wonderful to see in the Bible how Abraham is entrusted with his mission by leading spiritual powers. What was to be given humankind through Abraham's mission? What had previously been endowed through vision was now to be rediscovered; it was to be won at a new level through calculation. And what was won through calculation was to reflect the laws and commandments. This is why Jehovah said: This mission shall be an image of the highest lawfulness known to us. He said: Your progeny shall be ordered like the stars in the heavens. It is totally incorrect when the Bible is translated as if Jehovah had said that Abraham's descendants should be as *numerous* as the stars in the heavens. Instead he said that they should procreate according to laws such that their propagation should be an expression of the same lawfulness to which the stars in the firmament are also subject.

Abraham had a son, Isaac, and a grandson, Jacob. We see how the twelve tribes of the Israelites stem from these two. These twelve tribes replicate the lawfulness of the twelve signs of the Zodiac. From Abraham a new order was to originate among peoples in emulation of the order of the stars. So we see how spiritual science is able to extract the true sense of what the Bible records and we in turn gain the right picture of humanity's most profound document. Atavistic clairvoyance was to be excluded; no longer was humanity to avert its gaze from external existence; thenceforth humanity was to penetrate and delve into this outer world. This mission was a gift in the form of what humanity was to become. Abraham's task was to hand down to his descendants aptitudes of the brain. This was intended as a gift and we see how Abraham receives the entire Jewish people as a gift. What could a spiritual power have given to Zarathustra? A teaching, something one-sidedly spiritual. But Abraham had to be endowed with his entire people, a very real present that was founded upon the proliferation of a certain physical brain. How was this people gifted to him? In that he was willing to sacrifice his son. Had he carried out this sacrifice, there would be no Jewish people. In receiving his son back he also received the entire Jewish people, given to him as a gift by outside agency. At the moment when Abraham was to sacrifice his son, he received Isaac back, and in this he is given the entire Jewish people, all his descendants, as a reward. This is a gift from Yahweh-Jehovah to Abraham. With this the last of the visionary talents was given away. Individual gifts of clairvoyance are sub-divided such that there are twelve of them, each designated with a sign of the Zodiac, because these are gifts from heaven. The last of these clairvoyant aptitudes was sacrificed by Abraham in return for the Israelite people. The ram that was to be sacrificed by Abraham in place of his son represents the last of these clairvoyant gifts. In this way the Jewish people received their mission to become familiar with the external world by evolving the faculties of calculation within their brains and—by means of their own capabilities—to investigate world phenomena, right down into a certain unity, which they imagined as Yahweh. This mission is taken so literally that all trace of the old, inherited means of perception—clairvoyance—was banished from the Jewish people. Joseph had dreams of the old, clairvoyant kind; he is cast out of the community because the task of the Hebrew peoples is to exclude this ancient faculty from their development. Joseph is therefore banished. However, he is then able to become the mediator between the Jewish people and what it had to absorb in fulfilment of its cultural mission. The sons of Abraham had renounced visions from within; thus they had to receive from without what they would have received thanks these visions. When they are led into Egypt, they receive this from Moses—they, who are the missionaries of external, physical thinking. What others still obtained in the form of inner visions, the Israelites were now given in the form of Commandments. It is indeed so that what we call the Ten Commandments is the same as what other people were receiving as inner inspiration. The Jewish people accepted their Commandments from Egypt—by way of Moses and in external form—Commandments that are actually celestial inspiration.

Having been endowed with inspiration from Egypt, this people settled in Palestine, appointed as they were to give birth to one of the bearers of the Christ. Their aptitudes, passed down from generation to generation, were to give rise to the physical embodiment of Jesus. For this reason all the faculties present in Abraham had to accrue, to accumulate here. All Jewry had to mature and evolve such that what was present in Abraham as latent predisposition had to emerge in a descendant at its highest pinnacle. In order to understand this we need to draw a comparison with the development of an individual person. In the first seven years of life it is primarily the physical body that undergoes development. Between seven and fourteen or fifteen—the second phase of life—it is the ether body that unfolds and thereafter the astral body. Only then does the I or ego emerge. What initially exists as a predisposition only emerges once these three bodies have matured. This also applies to whole peoples. The nascent Abraham first had to be integrated into the physical, etheric and astral bodies before it could be inhabited by an I. The evolution of the Hebrew peoples can be divided into three epochs: what takes place at age seven in an individual person can be extended to seven generations of a nation. You know how often—as regards inherited features—a son can resemble a grandfather rather than a father. In this way, two times seven—in other words fourteen—generations may be necessary in order to replicate what in the individual takes place between birth and the change of teeth. Fourteen generations evolved the characteristics latent in the physical body of Abraham; fourteen further generations were required for the ether body and another fourteen for the astral body. Only then did it become possible for one to reach the level of maturity needed by an entity such as the Christ being.

Matthew describes this in the first chapter of his Gospel by saying that from Abraham to David there were fourteen constituent elements, from David to the Babylonian Captivity another fourteen and thereafter until Jesus another fourteen, three times fourteen or six times seven in all had to pass. The writer of Matthew's Gospel laid out this deep wisdom as the foundation of his book. What constituted Abraham's ordained mission was also to flow into the body of Christ Jesus, but this could come to pass only through the lawful procession of the generations. In this way the Jesus child, descended after forty-two generations from Abraham, could fulfil the mission of his original ancestor. Matthew depicts the wonderful lawfulness within which this takes place.

Once a given cycle of evolution is completed a short repetition of the earlier facts has to take place at a higher level, and we do indeed find one such in St Matthew's Gospel that is marvellously described. Abraham comes from Ur in Chaldea, travels to Canaan and then to Egypt, returning once more to Canaan. This is his journey. The reincarnated Zarathustra, six hundred years before our era, lived as a great teacher in the Chaldean Mystery schools and was incarnated under the name of Zaratos. This was his last incarnation before he was reborn in Jesus. He now takes the same route as Abraham's. Starting in roughly the same place as did Abraham, he travels. In the spiritual world he follows the path that Abraham took to Bethlehem. Thus the route physically covered by Abraham is taken spiritually by Zarathustra. The successors of those who were his pupils six hundred years earlier follow him again in the star that leads them to Bethlehem. They take the path being taken by Zarathustra towards his incarnation. He arrives and is reborn in Canaan.

In the Old Testament we come across a Joseph who, following a dream, is led to Egypt. Now we see a Joseph who, following a dream, is physically led to Egypt. Then the boy is physically guided back to where the Jewish people await the Redeemer. The ancient Jewish people received nourishment from Joseph in Egypt during the famine. Draw the line taken by the Magi on a map; compare, moreover, the route to Egypt taken by Joseph, son of Jacob, with that taken by the Solomon Jesus child and you will find that both these routes are relatively congruent. There are albeit several points of difference but they are caused by other circumstances. This is the level of accuracy with which the writer of the Matthew Gospel describes the route taken.

For just such reasons—of which we could have knowledge even if all the Gospels were to be lost—do we feel such awe and reverence for the Gospels. Humanity could reach ever higher truths and gain ever greater wisdom, the like of which can still hardly be imagined nowadays. Even if we will have far, far more wisdom concerning these monumental events in the coming millions of years, such wisdom can equally be drawn from the Gospels. This is a measure of what can bring us closer to an understanding of the Christ event. Just as the teachings of Buddha and those of Zarathustra, so also has the being of the Hebrew people flowed into the individuality of Christ Jesus. Everything that had hitherto appeared on Earth was reborn in higher guise through Christianity. Everything that constitutes all spiritual cultures that had ever existed on Earth existed for the reason that Christ, the great leader of Earth evolution, sent to Earth those to whom he had given the task of preparing on Earth for what he had to fulfil. While still in the heights of heaven, he sent his emissaries ahead. They, the great founders of religions, were to prepare humankind for his coming. The last of these heralds was Buddha, who brought the teaching of compassion and love. There were other early Bodhisattvas and there will be more in future whose task it will be to build upon all that has been brought to Earth through Christ Jesus.

It will be beneficial for human beings to pay heed to what those later Bodhisattvas have to tell, for they are servants of Christ. Each time a Bodhisattva of the future appears—for example, in around three thousand years—we will be helped, somewhat the better to understand the Christ, who irradiates all things. Christ it is who is the utmost profound of all beings, and the others exist with the sole objective that the Christ be better understood. This is why we say that Christ sent the Bodhisattvas ahead in order to prepare humankind for his coming; and he sends them also after the event so that this greatest of deeds in Earth evolution shall be ever more fully understood. We are only at the very beginning of comprehending this being and we will realize his being ever better the more wise men, sages and Bodhisattvas come to Earth. By dint of all the wisdom thus poured out into Earth existence we will become ever more capable of recognizing the Christ.

We exist on Earth as seeking human beings. We have made a start at struggling towards an understanding of the Christ. What we have recognized about him we have put to use—and will in future be putting to use—whatever those future Bodhisattvas will teach us, with the aim of better comprehending that Master of all Bodhisattvas, the fulcrum, the turning point of all our structures and systems. In this way, humanity will increase in wisdom and will become ever more adept at recognizing the Christ. Humankind will only encompass him when the last of the Bodhisattvas has fulfilled their duty to its very conclusion, having brought the necessary teachings to empower us to conceive of this most profound of beings in all Earth existence: the Christ Jesus.

LECTURE 9

MUNICH, 4 DECEMBER 1909

GROUP SOULS AND INDIVIDUALITY

ToDAY we will concern ourselves with a general theme, namely one that asks the question: What is the meaning and task of anthroposophically orientated spiritual science in the present? On Tuesday we will tackle a more personalized theme concerning individual being and destiny.

As we have often emphasized, anthroposophy has a specific task and significance for humanity at this particular time. Ultimately, every thinking person who engages with anthroposophy has to ask themselves: What exactly are the aims being pursued by this spiritual movement? How are these related to other challenges of our time? As we have often done, we can throw light on these tasks from a number of standpoints. Today we want to try to encapsulate our own times and look at those of the near future in the context of human evolution by asking ourselves: What is anthroposophy's mission in terms of human evolution and our present time?

We know that, ever since the great Atlantean cataclysm, when the orb of the Earth—dwelling place of humanity—completely metamorphosed, five cultural epochs can be differentiated before present times. These cultural epochs have often been designated ancient Indian, ancient Persian, Egypto-Chaldean, Greco-Latin eras and then the present age, the fifth cultural epoch—in the middle of which we find ourselves—in preparation, let's say, since the eighth, ninth and tenth centuries. We need to be clear that these time designations are not intended to imply abrupt endings and new beginnings between developmental ages but rather that what was new was gradually prepared for before an age had really run its course. This we can say of our fifth post-Atlantean era: that it is already in meaningful preparation for what will be characteristic of the sixth cultural age. The humanity of today will basically—and in general—be divided into two: into those who cannot conceive of a sixth epoch being prepared, who, as it were, live blindly into each day and those who sense or imagine that a new age is in preparation and who also realize that innovation will take place through—and be prepared for by—human beings. One can either imagine a future where things are done as usual, just as our forefathers and others have always done them or one can be more aware by saying: if you wish to be a conscious member of humanity's continuity, you need to work either on yourself or on your environs so that you contribute to the coming sixth cultural epoch and realize how much depends upon you. We will only understand how to prepare for what is approaching by going into the character of our own times a little; this will offer us the best means of comparison.

We know that the cultural epochs differ intrinsically from one another and many examples have been brought over the years of our anthroposophical movement as to what those differences are. We referred to the ancient Indian culture and showed in which ways the constitution of human souls differed from later times, how they were highly gifted in clairvoyant consciousness, how evolution in the following epochs involved a gradual loss of clairvoyance while an ability to perceive and to reason were increasingly restricted to their physical environment. We saw how the fourth cultural age slowly emerged and how humanity stepped, as it were, right onto the physical plane so that the being whom we call Christ Jesus could be embodied as a physical human being. We then saw how in subsequent times, throughout certain streams, the following emerged: human faculties all became more robust in physical terms, noted the materialistic cast of our time and how all the pressure on human beings to validate what is present in the physical world is connected with a wider descent into the physical plane. But we will certainly not remain here as far as evolution is concerned. Humanity must ascend once more into spiritual worlds, but must ascend together with all the achievements and fruits wrested from physical existence. This is precisely where anthroposophy can offer the potential to re-ascend to spiritual realms.

We can only say: Just after the great Atlantean disaster there were numerous people who knew from their immediate ability to perceive that they were surrounded by a spiritual world and that they lived within it. Those who knew this became fewer and fewer as faculties became increasingly restricted to physical perception. Whilst, on the one hand, supra-sensory knowledge of higher worlds is now at its lowest conceivable ebb, on the other hand preparations are afoot for something so momentous that, for a large number of people, capabilities quite unlike those we have at present will exist in the incarnation following their present one. Just as human faculties have metamorphosed throughout the five cultural epochs, so they will also evolve into the sixth epoch and a large number of today's individuals will then—through the whole nature of their souls—clearly show that their capacities have changed. And this is where we would like to create some clarity today: just how different the souls of tomorrow—in a considerable portion of humanity—will be by the time of their next or subsequent incarnation.

We can also view human evolution over ages that have long flowed by in another way. We would then see how, the farther back we go towards clairvoyance, the more did human souls resemble what we can call group souls. Whoever felt, consciously felt, themselves to be part of the ancient Hebrew people would have said—and this is to be well noted: as an individual person, I am a fleeting transience but within me lives a direct connection with all the soul essence that has flowed down to me since our progenitor, Abraham. This is what a member of the ancient Hebrew people would have felt. In esoteric terms, we can even call what the ancient Hebrews felt a spiritual manifestation. We will understand this better if we focus on the following.

Take a Hebrew initiate. Though initiation was less widespread than among other peoples, we cannot characterize one such properly initiated person—not just one inducted into theories and laws, but one who could genuinely see into spiritual realms—without taking account of the singularity of their people. Modern science, cluelessly casting around for physical documentation, is in the habit of seeking to confirm everything in the Old Testament against physical records, which it can then not find. We will have occasion to point to the fact that the Old Testament is truer to the facts than recorded history can credit. Spiritual science shows that in the Hebrew peoples a blood relationship with Abraham, their ancestor, can be shown to exist and that presumption of Abraham as progenitor is justifiable. This was something known primarily in ancient Hebrew Mystery schools: an individuality—a soul being—such as Abraham was not only incarnated as Abraham but remains as an eternal spiritual being of enduring presence. And in truth he was a genuine initiate, inspired by the same spirit as inspired Abraham, and who adjured Abraham as his own and who was pervaded by the same soulfulness as Abraham. Thus there was a real connection between every initiate and the original forebear, Abraham. We need to hold onto this because in it is expressed that feeling of belonging to the entire ancient Hebrew folk, which was a sense of belonging to a communal or group soul. What was expressed in Abraham was felt to be the group soul of the people. Group soul qualities were also felt in this way among wider humanity.

Humanity as a whole can be traced back to soul groupings. The further back we go in human evolution the less distinct does the individual become. Just as in the animal kingdom group souls still pertain, so the further we retrace our steps into the antiquity of human evolution, the more widely do we find human group souls. Groups of people belong together and any one group soul was far stronger than the individual souls existing singly within it.

We can say that, even now, the tendency to group souls among humanity is by no means overcome, and whoever thinks this to be past is not focusing on certain more subtle phenomena in life. However, anyone bearing this in mind will soon see that in fact some people not only resemble each other in their physiognomy but that soul qualities among groups of people show kinship, that they can, as it were, be classified into groups. Everyone nowadays still thinks themselves to be included in some category or other. As regards this or that characteristic one might feel one belongs to several of these, but there still remains a certain group soul quality not only through the fact that peoples still exist but in other regards, too. The boundaries drawn between nations are increasingly falling away, yet other groupings are still observable. Certain fundamental characteristics in individuals may form clusters and are visible to anyone who can see that the last remnants of a group soul quality still persist.

We are living through times that are transitional to an exceptional degree. All group soul tendencies are gradually being sloughed off. Just as the gulf between nations disappears the more individual nations learn to understand each other ever better, so will all other group soul characteristics vanish and the individual human being will increasingly come to the fore.

In this way we have illustrated something quite fundamental in evolution. If we wish to approach this from another perspective we can say that—over the course of human evolution—the concept within which group soul qualities are most often expressed, the notion of race, loses its significance. If we look back beyond the great Atlantean catastrophe we can trace how human races were being prepared. In ancient Atlantis human beings were grouped much more on the basis of physically perceptible attributes and build than is now the case. What we today think of as race is merely a remnant of those substantial differences between people as they existed in ancient Atlantis. Concepts of race are only really applicable to ancient Atlantis. Here we are using a concept—as regards genuine human evolution and post-Atlantean epochs—a notion of race that is in no way used in any flagrant sense. We do not speak of an Indian race, a Persian race and so on because that is no longer true; we speak of an Indian cultural epoch, an ancient Persian cultural era and so on.

It would be totally senseless were we to suggest that a sixth *race* were in preparation in our times. Even though remnants of ancient Atlantean differentiation and group soul qualities may still be discernible—to the extent that one can speak of division into races as a residual after-chime of Atlantis—but what is being prepared for in advance of the sixth epoch consists precisely in the fact that racial characteristics are to be stripped away. That is the whole point. And that is why the fundamental nature of a movement such as anthroposophy, intended as it is to prepare for the sixth cultural era, must exemplify the drive to be rid of all racial connotations by seeking to unite people of all nations, all races, by bridging all remaining differentiation, all gulfs, all distinctions between human beings and groupings. What once constituted an ethnic viewpoint retained a certain physicality that will be transformed into a far more spiritual quality, which will find fulfilment in future.

This is why it is so crucial that we understand our anthroposophical movement to be a spiritual movement that looks towards what is spiritual and overcomes—with all possible vigour—whatever stirs from physical differentiation. It is understandable that all movements have, as it were, their childhood illnesses and that at the start of the theosophical movement the subject was presented as if Earth evolution could simply be divided into seven time spans—termed primal or root races at the time—and each of these seven was further subdivided into seven subsidiary races; it was said that these are recapitulated such that one would always be speaking of seven races and seven subsidiary races. However, one has to go beyond childhood illnesses and be quite clear that the concept of race ceases to have any relevance precisely in our time.

Something else is being prepared, something eminently connected with the individual, which has to do with the process of ever increasing individualization among human beings. It is just a matter of each individual becoming more and more individual in the right sense—and anthroposophy should be aiding this process whereby individuals become more individual in an appropriate way. How can it do that?

Here we need to look at the most prominent and recent soul faculty under development. The question is often asked: If reincarnation is a fact, why is it that people cannot remember their previous incarnations? I have often answered this question in following mien: It is tantamount to saying to a four-year-old child—on the basis that they can't do arithmetic but they are nevertheless human—that human beings can't do arithmetic. Just leave it a few years until they are aged ten and they will surely be able to do arithmetic. It is similar with human souls. If they cannot today remember, the time will come when they will be able to remember, a time when they will have the same faculties as an initiate of today. It is now that this transformation is taking place. There are numerous souls nowadays who are on the brink of recalling at least their last incarnation, if not those further in the past. Many people are as if at the very point when the portal opens onto memory that can fully encompass not only life between birth and death but previous incarnations, or at least the most recent of those lives. And if after their present incarnation a number of people are reborn, they may indeed remember their present life. It is just a matter of *how* they remember it. To this end anthroposophical development indicates the right direction and the positive means by which one will be enabled to remember.

Characterizing the anthroposophical movement from this perspective, one would have to say: anthroposophy is disposed to help people to comprehend the human I, that inmost element of each person's being, in its truest sense. I have often mentioned the fact that Fichte[19] says, quite rightly, that most people would prefer to imagine themselves as a lump of Moon lava than as an I. If you think how many people nowadays even wonder what an I is, in other words who they actually are, you will come to a very sad conclusion.

Whenever this question crops up I have to recall a peer of over thirty years ago who was then a young chap totally infected with a materialistic outlook. Today this outlook goes by the more modern name of monistic. Despite his young age he was completely captivated by materialism. He would laugh whenever it was suggested that humans might have a spiritual component, something one could call a spiritual nature because he was of the opinion that what is alive in us by way of thoughts are just a result of mechanical or chemical processes in the brain. I often said: Look, if you seriously believe this is the sum total of life, why do you carry on lying? He was indeed lying because he never said: My brain feels, my brain thinks. Instead he would say: I think, I feel, I know this or that. He was subscribing to a theory contradicted by his every word and this is something everyone does because it is impossible to uphold an imagined materialistic theory. One cannot remain truthful if one thinks materialistically. In saying: my brain loves you—one should really not say you but: my brain loves your brain. People fail to make this consequence clear to themselves. This is not just funny but it reveals what untruthfulness underlies our spiritual culture nowadays.

Most people would really seem to prefer to self-identify as a piece of Moon lava or some such amalgamation than what we call the I or ego. Least of all does one arrive at a conception of an I through the methods of external science, which are bound to materialistic thought forms. How is one to reach a concept of an I? How can we gradually form an idea, a conception, of what we instinctively feel when we say: I think? Only and exclusively by means of what can be learnt from anthroposophy as to how the human being is constituted of Saturnine physical body, Sun-derived ether body, Moon-natured astral body and Earth-related I. Once we focus on all these ideas, gleaned from the entire cosmos, we will understand how the I works as the real foreman of all the other elements. Then we will gradually arrive at a concept of the entity for which we substitute the word 'I'.

We will be exerting ourselves in gradual pursuit of the highest possible understanding of this 'I' if we learn to understand the word. Not only do we experience ourselves to be a spiritual being when we become aware within one such I but we can also reflect: in our individuality lives something that predates Abraham, that arch-ancestor. We need not only say to ourselves: I and Father Abraham are one, but rather: I and Father Abraham are the spiritual element weaving throughout and enlivening the entire world. What inhabits the I is of the same spiritual substance as interweaves and vivifies the world, the cosmos. In this way we are gradually toiling towards an understanding of this I, this bearer of human individuality that persists and endures from incarnation to incarnation.

In which manner do we grasp the I—conceive, in fact, of the world—through an anthroposophical understanding? An anthroposophical world outlook takes shape through the most individual means possible, yet it is simultaneously the most non-individual and universal view that can be imagined. It can only be arrived at by the most individual means because the mysteries of the universe are revealed within a human soul, in that mighty beings of the cosmos stream into it. World content must be experienced in the most uniquely individual way yet must simultaneously be experienced as possessing a character of complete non-personality. Whoever longs to experience the true nature of cosmic mysteries must fully inhabit a standpoint from which they can say: anyone who still heeds their own opinion can never attain to truth. This is what is peculiar to anthroposophical wisdom, that an observer cannot retain their own opinion or preference for this or that theory—as a result of their own particular, individual idiosyncrasy—but that they must show no preference for one or another viewpoint. As long as they take a partial stance, true world mysteries will be unable to reveal themselves. A person must acknowledge on an individual basis; but their individuality needs to extend so widely that it retains no trace of anything personal, neither by way of sympathy nor antipathy. This needs to be taken seriously, wholeheartedly and stringently. Anyone maintaining partiality in relation to particular definitions, concepts or opinions, whether through their education, temperament or other leaning, one way or another, will never be in a position to recognize objective truth.

This summer we tried to conceive of Eastern wisdom from a perspective of Western teaching.[20] We tried to be equitable in relation to Oriental wisdom and presented it in a way that fully honoured it. It must be strongly underlined that one cannot profess a preference for either an Eastern or a Western world outlook at a time such as ours when spiritual knowledge is to be sought independently. Whoever says, according to temperament, that they like the uniqueness or the lawfulness of the world as it is expressed in Oriental or Occidental form has not fully understood the nature of the issue. For example, one should not decide in favour of the greater significance of, say, Christ as opposed to all that Eastern traditions offer on the basis of one's Western upbringing or because one is temperamentally inclined towards Christ. One is only called upon to resolve the question: How does Christ compare with the East? when one is, from a personal point of view, equally disinterested as to whether Christ or Orient is the answer. As long as one has a preference for this or that, one is not called upon to make a decision. One only starts to become objective when one allows the facts to speak for themselves, when one pays no heed to any reasoning out of one's own opinion but merely allows the facts to speak on the subject in hand.

For just such reasons does what we encounter in anthroposophy —when perceived in its true form—approach us as if inwardly interwoven with human individuality because it must issue from the power of the I, must spring forth from individuality while, on the other hand, remaining independent so that individuality returns again to a state of even-handed equilibrium. Anyone in whom anthroposophical insight dawns has to be the most dispassionate of them all; insight must not be dependent on anything. What it must rely on, though, is that the person imposes no personal colouring onto it. People will have to exercise their individuality because what is spiritual can emerge—neither by starlight nor moonshine—but only in the human soul, within the individuality. This faculty will in turn have to have been developed to a sufficient level that it can switch itself off when facing the advent of such world wisdom.

The same applies to anthroposophy and what it can offer humanity: on the one hand it is something every person can access, regardless of their background in terms of nation, race and so on, because it addresses only new humanity, the human being per se, not the abstraction called 'person' but each human being individually. This is what matters. Just as it issues from the very fount of human reality, it speaks to the deepest core of the human *being* itself; this is how anthroposophy seizes the very essence of human beings. In the way that we speak person to person we are really only speaking surface to surface; our inmost core is not bound to it. Understanding between human and human—complete understanding—is hardly possible today except when what we generate issues from the centre of our human being and when, rightly received by the other person, it in turn speaks to their deepest core. This is why what anthroposophy transmits is in a certain sense a new language. Even though we are still obliged to communicate in diverse foreign languages, the substance of what is communicated is a new language that speaks of anthroposophy.

The language spoken in the world at large is actually only valid for a very limited field. In antiquity, when humans still gazed into the spiritual with their archaic nascent clairvoyance, words represented realities residing in the spiritual world. Even as late as Greek times, words retained a significance that differs from ours today. Plato's use of the word 'idea' is different from the word 'idea' as used by today's philosophers, who can no longer fathom Plato because they have no comparable outlook onto what he termed 'idea' and they therefore mistake it for an abstract concept. Plato still had the spiritual before him, albeit in somewhat distilled form; it was still, as it were, 'somewhat completely real'. Words still contained—if we may express it thus—the sap of spirituality. You can discern this in words. Anyone using the word 'wind' or 'air' today will have in mind something of an external, physical nature. For example, if one said in ancient Hebrew the word for wind—'*ruach*'—one had in mind not something external or physical but something spiritual that coursed through space. If someone breathes in, natural science today states simply that physical air is being inhaled. In antiquity it was not thought that physical air was inhaled; it was quite clear that one was inhaling something spiritual, or at least something possessing soul qualities.

Words in their totality represented spirit and soul. This has ceased and today language is restricted to externalities; even those wishing to keep up with the times, making an effort to see soul-spiritual derivation behind the palpable, only use words in a materialistic context. Physics speaks of 'force' applied to bodies, forgetting that this derives from living forces and that when two living beings come into contact it is a result of animate beings causing this themselves. The original meaning of the simplest words is thus forgotten.

Language has become capable only of expressing material effects, materiality—and this is especially pronounced in scientific language. What is contained in our souls while we are speaking is only comprehensible to those soul faculties that are bound to—and use as their instrument—our physical brains. As a consequence, our souls understand nothing of all that words signify once it is disembodied. Once our souls have gone through the portal of death they make no further use of our brains and all today's scientific disquisition becomes mere figment, unintelligible to the discarnate soul. It hears none of the talk, understands nothing expressed in the speech of our times. It can derive no sense from what only makes sense in physical life.

It is even more important to be alert to material tendencies in what we can call our mode of imagining, our way of thinking. Here it is far more important to be really awake—not just theoretically, because it concerns life, not theory—that such traits can even be observed in theosophical circles: materialism has been slinking in. Because it is in current vogue, this has insinuated itself widely into theosophical attitudes so that, even in theosophy itself, real materialism holds sway when, for instance, describing the ether- or life body. Even though every effort must be made in striving for what is spiritual, this is generally couched in terms merely of a finer, more subtle materiality, including even such phenomena as the astral body. Usually taking the physical body as their starting point and proceeding to the ether- or life body, they assert: this ether body is based on the configuration of the physical body, but just more subtly so—and off it strides towards Nirvana. Descriptive images can be found that originate from nothing more than physical phenomena. I have experienced how, when describing the good mood among those in a room, no simple phrase was used but it was framed thus: There are some fine and rarefied vibrations in this room. What is spiritual in a mood is ignored and materialized by picturing a room as being filled with a fine pea-souper fog through which vibrations are coursing.

You see, this is what I wanted to illustrate: conceptually materialistic thought forms. Materialism even has those who wish to think spiritually by the collar. This is only by way of highlighting a contemporary tendency. But it is important that we are awake to it for precisely the reason just mentioned: our language is still a sort of tyrant over human thinking, that our language brings a bias towards materialism into our thinking. Many who would very much like to be idealists today—seduced by the tyranny of language—express them-selves in materialistic terms. This is a language no longer understood by a soul as soon as it is not bound to the human brain.

There is something else, believe it or not. For anyone who knows genuine spiritual vision, real seership, today's prevalent manner of depiction, and all theosophical-scientific writings, represent an actual pain because it seems to them nonsensical once they have started to think with their soul—now detached from its brain and fully alive in spiritual realms—rather than with their physical brain. As long as thinking is bound to the physical brain the world will continue to be described in physical terms. But as soon as spiritual thinking is achieved, describing the world in these terms becomes meaningless. At that point it becomes truly painful to hear: There are good vibra-tions in this room instead of: People here are in good spirits. This causes pain to someone able to see things clearly, spiritually, because thoughts are a reality. That room does in fact become a dark pea-souper fog when filled with thoughts such as: 'the room is full of good vibrations' instead of 'people are in good spirits'.

It is the task of spiritual-scientific pictorial representation—more important than theorizing—that we learn to speak a language not only understood by human souls while embedded in a physical body but also comprehensible when that soul is independent of its physi-cal instrument, either in seership or when beyond the portal of death. That is the essential thing! When we set forth concepts explaining the world and the human being our language must be capable of explaining this both to those present physically and to those living between death and a future birth. Yes, indeed, what is spoken upon our very ground of anthroposophy is heard and understood by the so-called dead. They stand upon the same ground where a common language is being spoken. We are then really speaking to all human beings. It is then to a certain extent of little consequence whether a person is physically incarnated or in another state between death and a new birth. In anthroposophy we learn a language capable of being understood by all humans, regardless of whether in this or that state of being. Within the field of anthroposophy we speak a language aimed equally at the dead. In this we touch upon what might seem abstract but which in anthroposophical iteration tends the inmost being of humanity. We penetrate into each soul itself. In this way we are freeing human beings from any group-soul tendencies or qualities and each individual can become ever more empowered to take hold of their own unique I-ness.

That is the peculiar thing: that those who find anthroposophy today, who take it up energetically, can be distinguished from those who remain distant from it, as if—through anthroposophical thoughts—their I were to crystallize as a spiritual entity and accompany the individual through the gates of death. In place of the I-being that can remain intact—after life in a body—beyond the portal of death, in others there remains a hollow space, an absence. Everything else in terms of concepts absorbable today will become increasingly superfluous and irrelevant to the actual core of the individual, to the essential kernel of their being. This central being of each person will be held, gripped by what it can apprehend of anthroposophical thinking. This in turn crystallizes a spiritual substance, which individuals can take with them and through which they are able to perceive their spiritual surroundings, seeing and hearing in a world otherwise cloaked in darkness. This is how it comes about that, when a person develops their I within through anthroposophical concepts and anthroposophical means of imagining, they now have a connection with all the wisdom of the world to be garnered—once this I is developed—and which can be transferred into their ensuing incarnation. They will then be reborn with an evolved I and will remember their previously evolved I. That is the deeper task of the anthroposophical world movement: to send into their next incarnation a number of individuals possessing an I which can remember its own individual self. These will be the people who will shape the seed-like beginnings of the next cultural epoch.

Those human beings well prepared—through the spiritual movement of anthroposophy—to remember their individual I will be distributed throughout the world. The essential feature of the coming cultural period will be that such people will not be limited by geographical locality but will be scattered across the entire world. Thus across Earth existence will be dispersed the core of a future humanity crucial to the creation of a sixth cultural epoch. Amongst these will be those who can remember and recognize the I towards whose advance they themselves strove in their last incarnation.

This is the right soul cultivation of which we were speaking. Such soul faculties will not only be present in those individuals just described but others will also be able to remember. More and more people will, despite not having developed their I, be able to remember their previous life. They will, however, not remember a personal I so much as a group identity in which they have remained. There will thus be people who have ensured that they developed their individual I and who remember that I. They will remember their self—as an independent entity—and will be able to look back and say: You were this or that person in those days. Those who have not advanced their I individuality will be unable to remember their present identity.

Please do not believe that by attaining visionary clairvoyance alone one will be able to recall one's previous I-identity. Human beings were all once clairvoyant. Were this sufficient, everyone would be able to remember, as everyone was clairvoyant in the past. It is beside the point whether or not someone was clairvoyant because we will all be clairvoyant in future. It is a question of whether one has tended one's I-individuality in this incarnation. Unattended, it is not present as an inward, human entity. In looking back, it will be remembered as part of a group ego, as a member of a communal identity. Humans will say: Yes, I was there but I did not liberate myself. This will be experienced as a new feeling among humanity: that of having reverted back to a conscious blending with—or subsuming into—a group soul. This will be something terrible for the sixth cultural epoch: the inability to sense oneself as an individual in retrospect but instead being stunted and confined within a group soul beyond whose bounds one is unable to escape. To express this crassly, one could say: Those individuals who now tend their I-individuality will inherit the Earth and all that it brings forth—speaking pictorially—and those who fail to penetrate and shape their individuality will be dependent on connecting them-selves with a certain group by whom they will allow themselves to be instructed as to how they should think, feel and act. This will be experienced as a descent, a deterioration, as a Fall by a future humanity.

We may regard all that constitutes the spiritual life of the anthroposophical movement not merely as theory but as something given to us in the present because it prepares in us qualities vital for the future of humanity. When we really take stock of where we have now arrived by way of the past and look into the future a little we will have to say: Now is the time when we start to nurture the faculty of recall. It is only a matter of doing so in the right way, and this depends on whether we have forged an individual I for ourselves. We will only be able to recall what we have ourselves fashioned in our souls. Not having forged any such identity, all that will be left to us is a compulsive memory of group entity which will be experienced as a retrogressive fall into a group of higher animality. Though human group souls are more refined and elevated than those of animals, they are nevertheless group souls. The humanity of antiquity did not experience this as a fall because they were engaged in extricating themselves from everything resembling groupness and into individuality of soul. If souls are now arrested in their development, this will be consciously the case, and it will be the oppressive experience of those who—either now or in a future incarnation—fail to make the right connections that they experience a fall into a group soul existence.

The real task of anthroposophy consists in providing these very connections and they must be grasped within the span of human life. If we focus on the fact that the sixth cultural era will represent the first—the total—overcoming of all racial notions, we need to be clear that it would be fantastical to imagine that races of the sixth epoch will issue from any one place and take shape in the manner of the ancient races. That is the nature of progress: that ever new forms of progression in life arise, that concepts once valid lose their relevance in later times. Otherwise, in failing to understand this, we will also have failed to grasp the very idea of what advance signifies. We will always revert to making the mistake of saying: this or that number of rotations, so and so many races, circles, laps, round and round it revolves, always the same[21]. One cannot fathom why this wheel of revolutions, circles, globes, races would need to continue. So the word 'race' is a designation only applicable to a particular time. Around the time of the sixth era that term will have lost all but residual significance. Race will have retained only those elements applicable in ancient Atlantis.

In the future what speaks to the deepest levels of the human soul will increasingly be expressed in the external appearance of people. What each person has, on the one hand, conquered individually or, on the other, experienced in a non-individual, universal way will in future be etched into human countenances. Human individuality will be graven into faces, group-soul features not. Humanity's manifold nature will be on display. Everything will be individually earned, yet won through conquest over individuality. We will not find those fired by their I among groups yet their individuality will be expressed in their appearance. This is what will cause differences between people. There will be those who have striven to gain their I-individuality. They will be dispersed across the Earth and have the most varied features, but in this multifarious diversity it will still be discernible—even down to their gestures—how each individual I is manifest. Whereas in those who have not developed their individuality, the resulting group-soul attributes will likewise be expressed; they will show group-soul characteristics in their outer features. In other words, they will fall back into groupings bearing similarities. Such will be the external physiognomy of our Earth: that the potential is in preparation for bearing one's I-individuality as an external emblem and also for bearing one's group-soul nature as an external emblem.

This is the purpose of earthly evolution: that human beings ever increasingly achieve the capacity to express externally what lives within. There is an ancient text in which the highest ideal for the development of the human I—Christ Jesus—is characterized thus: When two are one, when outer reflects inner, human beings will have attained to Christ-likeness within themselves. That is the gist in part of the so-called Gospel of the Egyptians.[22] Passages such as this can be understood in light of anthroposophical insight.

Having tried to gain an understanding of anthroposophy's task on the basis of our deepest knowledge, on Tuesday we will tackle a spiritual conundrum that will lead us to a particular issue of humanity relating to its destiny and to its very being.

LECTURE 10

MUNICH, 7 DECEMBER 1909

THE I, THE GOD WITHIN AND THE GOD OF OUTER MANIFESTATION

From the whole spirit of our anthroposophical work over the course of the year, you will have noticed that the purpose of this work lies not in creating something instantly sensational but rather in calmly following the facts of spiritual events; such knowledge can also be valuable for our lives. The day is not well served by always speaking about immediate matters; spiritually, the day is better served by acquiring knowledge of the wider connections of life. Basically, our own individual life is dependent on the great events of existence and we can only rightly judge our own lives by gauging them against the greatest phenomena of life. This is why, having over the seven years that the German Section has existed spent four years laying the foundations of our outlook and knowledge, we made efforts over the last three years to deepen this fundamental knowledge in relation to world-encompassing issues. In what you have gleaned from considerations shared in the various lecture cycles, you will have seen that this includes the recent contemplations of the Gospels. This was not only because the contents of the Gospels bring much home to us but also because, in considering them, we learn vitally applicable aspects of human nature. For these reasons, let us today speak about the Gospels and their wide applicability to individual human lives.

The Gospels are ever less considered by science to be historic documents about the greatest individuality ever to have acted upon human evolution—Christ Jesus. The attitudes towards the Gospels were quite different in the first Christian centuries and throughout the Middle Ages from those prevailing nowadays. The Gospels are now considered four contradictory documents and nothing seems more obvious than the view that queries: how can four documents constitute a historical record when they contradict one another to the extent that the four Gospels do in attempting to convey to us what took place in Palestine at the beginning of our era?

Were human thinking not so intent on disregarding the most salient facts, something might occur to it. One could, for instance, reflect: It doesn't take much to recognize that the Gospels are contradictory in the sense of how they are conceived today. Any child could do so, one would like to suggest. One could, however, say: Now that the Gospels are largely available to all, everyone can engage with them. There was a time, before the invention of the printing press, when these records were not freely obtainable and were only read by a minority—and this minority was precisely those at the pinnacle of spiritual life. They brought the contents closer to the populace in a form comprehensible to them. One might ask: Was this spiritual and educated elite really so foolish that they could not see what every child could understand, i.e. that the Gospels are indeed—in terms of today's outlook—contradictory?

Were we to follow this question, we would immediately notice something else, namely that people's entire realm of feeling towards the Gospels was then quite differently attuned from today's critical reason, whose modus operandi it is to think as inculcated by external reality. It is this thinking that seeks to opine about the Gospels and it will be easy for such thinking to identify contradictions. It is childishly easy to do so.

How did the cultural-spiritual elite, who had access to the Bible, reconcile what are today called contradictions? Those people of old had developed an extraordinary—and today barely imaginable—sense of awe when reading of the great Christ event recounted in the four Gospels. Strangely enough, because they had the Bible, they felt all the more moved to honour and value accounts of this event. How is that possible? It comes about because those old arbiters of the

Gospels focused on something quite different from today's readers. The critics of today are no more clever than someone, let's say, who takes a single-aspect photo of a bouquet of flowers. They go about the world with their photo. People note what they see on the photo and think they have an exact image of a bunch of flowers. Then someone else comes along and shows them a photo of the other side of the bouquet. This changes the picture and, when shown to the same people, they say: This cannot be the same bunch; the pictures are contradictory. Even when photographed from four angles, each photo is quite different from the next. Yet they all illustrate the bouquet. This is how observers of the Gospels used to feel. They would say: the four Gospels are four depictions of the same events and, because this is so, we are given a more complete impression of a single life. Though they are dissimilar, once we are in a position to see this from four perspectives, we will have gained a more complete picture of events in Palestine. These people felt impelled to say: We must look aloft with all the more humility in face of the events in Palestine on hearing of them from four quarters because this event is so mighty that it cannot be fathomed on the basis of a single portrayal. We must be grateful that the four Gospels are available to us and that we can view this lofty event from four angles. Yet we need to understand how these four views arose and, once we know this, we can form a view of the four Gospels that is also available to every single person.

What we call the Christ event is an immeasurable occurrence in the spiritual evolution of humankind. How can we place what took its course in Palestine into the context of the entire evolution of humankind? We can place it in that we say: All spiritual development and human experience preceding this event flowed together, flowed into the event in Palestine in order to flow onwards as a combined tide.

As part of this we have—to name but the few—the ancient Hebrew teachings, as imparted to us in the Old Testament. This is one tributary stream. It was flowing while the event of Palestine was in progress. Then there was another spiritual stream, that originating in Zarathustra. This also flowed into the great stream of Christianity, the primary combined current flowing throughout the world.

Then there is what we can call the Eastern or Oriental spiritual stream that found its greatest representative in Gautama Buddha. This also flowed into that vast confluence and onwards into the future. These individual streams are now combined within Christianity.

This will not reveal to you what Buddhism is today, a Buddhism that re-heats Buddha's teachings of six hundred years before the Christian era. It joined in flowing into Christianity. Likewise, what is today taken from ancient Persian records and from that point onwards tries to show the being of Zarathustra will not demonstrate to you what Zarathustrianism really is, because he who taught in ancient Persia—as recorded in contemporary documents—has evolved further and has offered up his contribution to pass into the spiritual life of humanity, the stream of Christianity. We must seek Zarathustrianism within the onward stream of Christianity.

In seeking to imagine the core circumstances of our subject, we must ask ourselves: How exactly did these three tributaries—Buddhism, Zarathustrianism and ancient Hebrew lore—converge within Christianity?

If we wish to understand how Zarathustrianism joined this spiritual current we need to remember that the individual we refer to as Zarathustra was the great teacher of the second post-Atlantean cultural epoch who first taught the so-called original Persian people* and who was repeatedly incarnated. Rising ever higher with each incarnation, he reappeared some six hundred years before our era as a contemporary of the great Buddha within the Mystery schools of ancient Chaldean-Babylonian culture. Here he was reincarnated as the teacher of Pythagoras, who went to Chaldea in search of just such spiritual enlightenment. This Zarathustra who, some six hundred years before our times, appeared under the name of Zaratos or Nazarathos, was then reborn at the beginning of our calculated era in the form of a child born to parents called Mary and Joseph, as told to us in the Matthew Gospel. We call this child of Mary and Joseph— the so-called Bethlehem parents—one of two Jesus children born at this same time. In this way we have transplanted the individuality who was the bearer of Zarathustrianism into a significant spiritual stream.

---

* Steiner uses the term 'urpersischen Volk'.

This was not the only stream to re-emerge into life and to flow onwards in a new Christian form. There were other spiritual currents and several of these had to join at that time. For instance, it had to transpire that Zarathustra was born into a body offering the physical configuration that would enable him—as a being so highly evolved over many incarnations—to develop the qualities essential to this particular incarnation. For we must always remember the axiom that, however lofty the individual descending to incarnation, were no suitable body to be found, those highly developed faculties would find no fitting instrument through which their individuality could be expressed. A specially structured brain was essential for Zarathustra to fully exercise his faculties, and this entailed being born into a body, inherited from forebears, which could furnish him with an instrument matched in its attributes with his individuality. Not only did it have to be ensured that the Jesus child incarnating—as described in the Matthew Gospel—had such a highly evolved soul-spiritual configuration that it could perform the mighty deeds ordained to be carried out but also that this soul would be born into a physical body made perfect for it through inheritance. Just such a physical brain had to be available to Zarathustra.

That a perfectly suited physical body could be elaborated was due to the ancient Hebrew peoples and constitutes their contribution to Christianity. A body with characteristics most perfectly suited as a physical instrument was to be elaborated through purely physical heredity. For this to succeed, many earlier generations had to be prepared so that the salient characteristics could be inherited in a body at the beginning of our calculated era.

Now we should like to create a picture as to how this life flowed into the main stream of our present spiritual life. Just as we saw the mission of Zarathustra within Christianity, let us now look at the mission of the ancient Hebrew people within the total culture of our Earth. It has to be said that, the further spiritual research advances, the more does it confer ever greater validity on the Bible than does present-day cultural history. What is excavated in the latter appears slightly childish in comparison with what is recounted in the Bible, which only has to be read in the right light to be understood.

In the eyes of genuine spiritual research it is the more correct version. Among other things, it is also correct to say that later Jewry stems from one ancestor-progenitor, Abraham or Abram. Behind this fact lies something thoroughly rightful: that when we go back over the generations we arrive at an original ancestor to whom the spiritual world granted quite exceptional qualities. What were these qualities? If we want to understand with which exceptional capabilities he was endowed by the spiritual world we will briefly have to remind ourselves about what was recently said here.

Going back into ancient times, we see that human beings had different soul qualities, qualities we would now describe as dimly clairvoyant in contrast with today's consciousness. People were unable to see the world with the reasoned self-consciousness of today, but they still retained the ability to see what was spiritual—what manifested as spiritual facts and beings—in their surroundings. This vision—because it occurred within subdued, dampened consciousness—was more akin to a living dream, albeit a dream vitally linked with reality. This ancient clairvoyance was to become ever weaker and weaker to the end that human beings would gradually connect with outwardly-orientated perspectives and reasoning such as ours today.

All human evolution is a kind of education. Individual capacities are mastered gradually over time. The modern way of observing, say, a flower with normal consciousness, does not perceive the astral body weaving around the plant, whereas an observer from antiquity would have seen this astral body shimmering around it. Humanity had to be brought up so as to arrive gradually at our modern perception of sharply contoured objects, and this entailed loss of clairvoyance. A definitive axiom pertains in spiritual development: every developmental step in humankind must originate in an individuality. Capacities that are to become common to a great number of people must, shall we say, be inaugurated within one individual. Faculties connected with turning away from clairvoyant vision to judging the world in terms of measure, number and weight—specifically those not concerned with seeing into spiritual realms but with calculating the sensory world—were implanted by the spiritual world into the individuality known as Abraham or Abram. He was chosen to be the first to cultivate characteristics bound in the most inward sense with the physical brain. Not for nothing was Abraham called the inventor of arithmetic, that facility to order and evaluate the world in terms of measure and number. He was one of the first to extinguish the old, dim clairvoyance while his brain predisposed him towards such faculties as require a brain, and these faculties came to the fore. Such was the crucial and potent mission allocated specifically to Abraham.

This faculty, laid upon Abraham from out of the spiritual world as potential—just as all potential must be—was to be ever more perfected. You can easily understand that everything appearing in the world must evolve. In just such a way was the potential to view the world through a physical brain to evolve gradually. The evolution of this faculty took place through ensuing generations in that what was bequeathed to Abraham was transmitted to following generations down the years. But something additional had to occur that was different from the old transferral of a mission from an older to a younger generation, because other mission transferrals were not bound to a physical instrument. Those greatest of missions were not bound to a physical attribute. Let us take Zarathustra: what he offered his pupils was an enhanced clairvoyant vision of a far higher order than that possessed by other humans of the time. This was not bound to a physical instrument but was transferred from teacher to pupil. That pupil would become a teacher and in turn transfer their knowledge to subsequent pupils, and so on. Here, on the other hand, it is not a case of teachings or a means to clairvoyant vision but of something inherently brain-based. A capability such as this can only be transplanted into later times through heredity. This is why it fell to Abraham to pass on what could only be handed down through heredity; in other words, the excellence of Abraham's physical brain configuration was intended to be inherited by subsequent generations. Because his mission consisted in evolving a physical brain to ever greater perfection, it follows that each generation improved it to an ever more refined state of perfection.

Thus Abraham's mission is concerned with the propagation of ever more perfected brain attributes over the course of physical evolution. Something else is connected with this contribution by the culture of the ancient Hebrew folk, something we will understand by setting out the following.

If we take other human beings in antique cultures with their dim clairvoyance, we will say: How did they receive their most valuable gift, what did they venerate most highly in the world? They would receive this in the form of inspiration that lit up within them. Unlike today, research was not required. Today scientific knowledge is advanced by external research and experimentation and its laws are based on a synthesis of observable facts. This is not how the archaic human reached knowledge necessary to them; no, it would light up within in the form of a vision. Their soul had to give birth to it inwardly; their gaze would turn inwards, away from the outer world, when they wished to allow the highest truths to inspire them, to illumine them inwardly.

This was to become different in the people deriving their mission from Abraham. Abraham was to bring humanity precisely what was observable and calculable. When a follower of another culture built on clairvoyance would look to their highest divinity they would say: I am thankful to God who manifests within me. I turn my gaze away from outer things and God is most often present within me when I—without turning to the outer world— allow the inspiration of the Godhead to irradiate my inner being. By contrast, the people of Abraham were to express it thus: I will renounce the inspiration that merely emanates from within; instead I will prepare myself to direct my gaze towards my environment. I wish to observe what is manifested in air and water, in mountain and plain, in the starry heavens—this is where my gaze will be directed and, thereafter, I will be in a position to consider all these as they exist in relation to each other. I want to be able to combine those outer phenomena in pursuit of a comprehensive thought. Once I have gathered what is observable in the outer world and have compressed it into a single thought, then I will call everything that the outer world tells me 'Yahweh' or 'Jehovah'. I will receive what is highest via a manifestation, a revelation speaking through and throughout the external world.

Such was the mission of the Abrahamic peoples: to bequeath to humanity what it received as revelation from the outer world, in contrast to all that other cultures could proffer. That is why this instrument of spiritual life—corresponding in its configuration with external revelation—had to be inheritable, just as earlier soul qualities corresponded with the revelations they received from within.

Now we may ask ourselves: What transpired when the ancient seers gave themselves up to inner revelation? They turned their gaze away from all things exterior because nothing existing in that external world could tell them about spiritual realms. They even turned away from Sun and Moon, listening only to their inwardness, as the great mysteries of the world were disclosed to them; visions would arise within revealing how the wide universe is formed. What they knew of the stars and their movements, of spiritual worlds—all this was not acquired through outer observation by those adherents to ancient cultures. In this way, too, they knew of Mars, Saturn and so on, as the nature of these stars was revealed to their inner vision. The laws of the cosmos that were written in the stars, so to speak, were simultaneously written into the inner souls of those human beings, revealed within through Inspiration. As these cosmic laws, ruled by starry throngs, had been revealed through inward vision, so were the laws governing the outer world now to be won through calculation and manifest in the people of Abraham. To this end, heredity had to be guided in pursuit of cerebral qualities capable of calculating the world aright. As wonderful lawfulness implanted as an aptitude in Abraham, these attributes were to be transmitted and perfected through the generations in a way corresponding with the great laws of the cosmos. Brains and their internal configuration had to be inherited which were formed such that they reflected those mighty numeric stellar laws found above in the cosmos. This is why Jehovah says to Abraham: You will see the generations of your descendants who are arrayed as the numbers of stars in the heavens. As the stars on high are arrayed in harmonious numeric relationship, so shall the generations be deployed down the ages according to numerically calculable laws. That is: these generations shall inherently bear such laws within, just as the laws of the stars reign in the heavens.

There are twelve constellations. A reflected image of these was to arise within each of the twelve tribes of Abraham so that the corresponding faculties—implanted as aptitudes in Abraham—could flow down through the generations. Through the organic onward evolution of these peoples an image of celestial proportion and number was to be created. This has been translated by one translator of the Bible as: Your descendants shall be a numerous as the stars in heaven, whereas this passage should in all truth mean: Your descendants shall be well ordered in their blood relations such that they form a reflected image of the laws governing the stars in the heavens. Oh, the Bible is profound! What we find in the Bible today is coloured by later world views, so that 'Your descendants shall be as numerous as the stars in heaven' should in truth be translated somewhat as: All will be regulated in your descendants so that, for instance, twelve tribes will issue forth that reflect the twelvefold constellations of the Zodiac in the heavens.

Individual traits were to come to the fore and continually express Abraham's mission, within which they existed: I receive my mission as a gift from my surroundings—not as something lighting up within. What I have to contribute to the world is given to me from without. It is wonderfully depicted in the Bible how Abraham's task is intended to be bequeathed him from the external world in contrast to ancient revelations received from within. What is the task of Abraham to be? Abraham's mission it is to furnish through bloodlines what flows down to Christ Jesus. Into this the entire spirituality of a certain stream is to be transferred, intended to have the effect of an external gift, as if donated from without. Abraham was to give the world the ancient Hebrew people. That is his mission.

If this is to represent the whole nature of his mission, the gift of this people itself—being his mission—needed to be expressly given to him from an external source. Abraham had a son, Isaac. He was to be sacrificed, as is related in the Bible. As Abraham was about to sacrifice Isaac, his son was re-bequeathed him, restored to him, by Yahweh. What is bequeathed him in that moment? The whole people stems from Isaac. Had Isaac been sacrificed, there would be no Hebrew people. This entire people was therefore given to

Abraham as a gift. His offering of Isaac expresses beautifully the nature of this gift. The people as a whole is itself Abraham's mission, and with the return of Isaac he also receives the entire Hebrew people as a gift from Yahweh.

Such is the depth of the depictions in the Bible, each corresponding in their every detail with the great and majestic inner nature of the onward course of human evolution. Piece by piece did the ancient Hebrew people have to discard what other cultures still espoused: their old, atavistic clairvoyance. This ancient clairvoyance was bound to faculties originating in spiritual worlds and these visionary faculties were each designated according to their nature with terms taken from the constellations. The last of the faculties relinquished in exchange for the ancient Hebrews being donated to Abraham was that connected with the constellation of Aries the Ram. This is the reason for a ram being sacrificed in place of Isaac. It is the outer expression of the last of the clairvoyant faculties being sacrificed so that Abraham could be given the Hebrew people. This is how the people were chosen to develop especially those capacities based on observing the external world. Among all these, remnants of the atavistic vision of old would emerge, necessitating those ancient Hebrews to ever and again exclude what was not pure in their blood, what did not contribute to outward-directed observation, anything reminiscent of atavism. Anything inherited from other cultures constantly had to be expelled.

Here we touch upon a subject that is hard to describe nowadays because it contains a truth as foreign to modern thinking as it is possible to be. Yet it is a truth and as such it is fair to challenge those who have been involved in our Branches for some time: they should be able to bear facts from which habitual thinking slightly retreats.

We should be clear that certain groups of people of old retained into later times antiquated faculties for knowledge, contained in their souls as visionary traits and connecting them closely with spiritual beings. These would reveal themselves to their inner sight. This would be expressed in certain people—those who retained declining attributes from remote times—in that they represented a lower form of the connection with the spirituality of the external world. Whereas genuine seers usually connect with the wide universe through spiritual Intuition and Inspiration, those lesser human beings were enthralled in decline, in the decadence of this ancient bond with the outer world. They were not independent, the power of their I was not able to assert itself, but neither was their clairvoyance of an order as high as that of old. Human beings of this kind would always surface and an affinity between their physical organs and old organs of clairvoyance would persist. And now follows the fact that will sound so strange. What we could term ancient clairvoyance—that inward lighting up of world mysteries—must in some way have found entry into souls. We need to imagine that human beings were subject to inward-streaming radiations. Humans of old were unaware of this inward-bound radiating yet, once the radiation had taken place and had irradiated their inner vision, it was perceived as their ancient inspiration. Certain radiating emanations flowed into human beings from their surroundings; these later metamorphosed within the person.

In antiquity these radiating forces were purely spiritual, perceptible to the genuine seer as pure astral-etheric rays. Later, however, this pure spiritual radiation, as it were, dried out, became increasingly dense to the point where it became etheric-physical radiation. What then became of them? Hair is what they became. Hair is a result of ancient centripetal radiation. What is now human hair was once spiritual radiation, raying inwards from the periphery. Today's hair is the desiccated astral-etheric radiation of ancient times. Such facts are only preserved where purely external scriptural transmission of ancient truths have persisted. In Hebrew the words for 'hair' and 'light' are designated by practically the same script character because an awareness of the connection between the astral-instreaming of light and of hair used to persist. Altogether, archaic Hebrew script contains the greatest truths in the words themselves.

We can confirm that the onward evolution of humanity is a reality. In people possessing the declining atavistic capacities these radiations were transformed, became desiccated, so that no fresh abilities were evolved for them. They were connected in ancient fashion with what was new, and yet not really connected, due to the 'dryness' of the inward-flowing radiation. These people were robustly hirsute whilst those having evolved onwards tended to be less so because new capacities arose in those faculties which later consolidated into hair.

Science will only arrive at such significant conclusions long ages hence. They exist in the Bible. The Bible is far more erudite and wise than present-day science, which is still at something of a pre-literate, childlike stage. Just read the story of Jacob and Esau! Jacob has moved slightly ahead in terms of his more modern faculties. Esau has remained at a previous stage and, compared with Jacob, is something of a dunce. When brought before their father Isaac, their mother has, with false hair, exchanged the brothers so that Isaac will confuse his younger son with Esau. This is intended to show that those ancient Hebrew people still inheriting something of other cultures were to be expelled. Esau is banished. Through Jacob the necessary facility for external synthesis was disseminated down the generations.

Just as the slightly retarded faculties and figure of Esau had to be expelled, in Joseph likewise there remained a legacy of atavistic clairvoyance, and he was banished to Egypt by his brothers. He had dreams and could descry world events, abilities not to be included in Abraham's mission. He was therefore exiled to Egyptian lands.

So we see how a stream works its way among ancient Hebrew peoples, a stream grounded in generational bloodlines and how, gradually, archaic inheritance is ejected. This was the legacy of the ancient Hebrew people: inheritance down the generations was to be increasingly perfected, creating an instrument from which could evolve a body to be yielded up for that individuality to be reincarnated. Where once this people could receive direct inspiration from within, it now had to receive it from without. Even direct revelations, received inwardly by other peoples, now had to be sought from external sources. This entailed the Jewish people—led by Joseph—travelling to another nation still receptive to inner illumination. Here Joseph was initiated into the Egyptian Mysteries and this enabled the people—by external means—to gain the knowledge they needed about the singularities of spiritual worlds.

Even their moral laws were obtained externally in this way and not as illumination from within. Such was the mission of the ancient Hebrews. Having acquired all they needed from this external source, they travelled back to Palestine.

Now, having undergone what they had, the ancient Hebrew people were to show how all that had evolved through the generations was ultimately to give birth to what would become the body of Jesus at the very confluence of the ancient Hebrew stream with that of Christianity.

Remember how we discussed the evolution of capacities within the individual, whose life can be viewed in seven-year periods. The first of these is between birth and the change of teeth at around age seven, when the physical body is simply building its structures. The second seven-year period, to sexual maturity, sees the ether body actively cultivating growth of these structures. Their structure is determined to age seven, then their predetermined structures merely grow. Between fourteen and twenty-one the astral body is the main element under development. We see how the actual human I is only born—and becomes independent—at twenty-one. So we see how, through definite time spans within the individual, the birth of the I itself comes about.

This is also how elements gradually evolved within a people, one that would—as a people—provide a body for the most perfected I. Evolution had to proceed in such a way that what takes place in the individual over years here had to evolve from generation to generation. Each successive generation had to further unfold what it inherited from an earlier generation. Nothing can suddenly unfold within a generation. To explore why this is the case for occult reasons would take us too far. But we can recall quite a simple phenomenon. Remember that heredity can work in such a way that certain traits are not directly inherited but can jump a generation; a grandchild may resemble their grandfather in some aspect. In certain respects this was the case with the continuing inheritance of attributes within the ancient Hebrew people; a generation would be missed. A single developmental phase in the individual would correspond with two in terms of generation. We can therefore say that the people had to evolve over generations in a way similar to an enormous individual: from birth to the change of teeth would take twice seven generations, fourteen generations. A second time span was to follow in which twice seven generations correspond with the period from change of teeth to reproductive maturity. A third such span of twice seven generations followed, representing ages fourteen to twenty-one, when the astral body is particularly prominent. Only then can an I come to birth. The I could only be born in the ancient Hebrews once three times twice seven—which is three times fourteen generations—had passed.

Anyone wanting to describe to us the body granted to Zarathustra as an instrument would have to show how, over the course of three times twice seven generations, the potentialities bestowed on Abraham had evolved in a way that—after three times fourteen generations—an I could be born into his threefold embodiment. This is what the writer of St Matthew's Gospel does. He describes three times fourteen generations: from David to the Babylonian captivity and those from Babylon to the birth of Jesus. In the Matthew Gospel we have something from the depths of knowledge that points to the mission of the old Hebrew people, how over time the forces were evolved that made it possible that a body from among this people could be host to a perfected I such as Zarathustra had attained.

If we now look at the destiny of these archaic Hebrew peoples, we will find that the captivity affecting an entire people corresponds with the time after age fourteen that prepares an individual for life itself, when what will later be carried out between fourteen and twenty-one wells up in the form of youthful hopes: this captivity represents the time when the astral body of the Hebrew peoples came to the fore, where what had been implanted over fourteen previous generations gave impetus to their mission. This is the reason why the Israelites were led into captivity in Babylon, the very place where—six hundred years before our era—Zaratos or Nazarathos, then in incarnation, was a teacher in the occult schools of Babylon. The main leading Israelites came into contact with these occult schools and with Zaratos, that great teacher of archaic times.

He became their teacher, was allied with them, and this is where they took up the mighty impulses he propounded which had the effect that this people was prepared over fourteen generations for the birth of Jesus.

Events then followed about which you are aware. Then we see something remarkable. We see in Matthew's Gospel a law of the spiritual realm being observed that will increasingly be recognized as an important law applicable to all life. That is the law that what takes place earlier is later recapitulated at a higher level. Modern science reiterates this in somewhat distorted form by maintaining that individual entities repeat in short order what has befallen lower species over longer time spans. The writer of Matthew's Gospel demonstrates this in a wonderful manner by saying: the I-individuality of Zarathustra was to be incarnated in a body prepared over ages within the people of Abraham. Abraham went forth from Ur in Chaldea, from the original source of Babylonian culture, making his way through Asia Minor to Palestine. His descendants were led southwards following Joseph's dreams and, having there absorbed many an Egyptian cultural impetus, returned to Canaan.

This represents the destiny of an entire people. The whole population is led through Canaan, over to Egypt and finally returns to Canaan. This folk destiny is to be repeated in short form. In the place where an I-individuality is to be born, for whom a corporeal vessel is being prepared following potentialities laid down in Abraham, that particular I takes its start from Chaldea. It was in Chaldea that Zarathustra, in his previous incarnation, had been a Mystery school leader; his spirit was bound to Chaldea.

Which route does the soul of Zarathustra take when approaching incarnation in Bethlehem? Zarathustra remained connected with those Magi who were initiated in the Mystery centres of Chaldea. They will have recalled how they heard from their teacher that he would see them again, that to the soul of the once-Zarathustra would be ascribed that golden star which, at the appointed time, was to take its course towards Bethlehem. As the time approached, they followed the route taken by that soul, thereby reprising the path taken by the old Hebrew peoples. Just as Abraham took the path to Canaan, so did the star: in other words the soul of Zarathustra followed that path to Canaan. The three Magi followed the star-Zarathustra to the place where he would be born into the body predestined him from out of the Abrahamic people. Zarathustra— the I-individuality of Zarathustra—thus repeated in spirit the path taken by Abraham to its destination in Palestine. Thereafter, the Hebrew people were to seek a path over to Egypt, directed by the dreams of the older Joseph. Now the I born into the Jesus child of Bethlehem—again prompted by the dreams of another Joseph— is directed to flee to Egypt by the same path taken by the Abrahamic peoples, through the dreams of the older Joseph. The I of Zarathustra repeats in spirit the entire destiny undergone by the ancient Hebrews, now in the body of Jesus, fleeing to Egypt and returning again to Palestine. In this we see the spiritual recapitulation of the path taken by the soul of Zarathustra and this reflects the archaic Hebrew folk's destiny.

All this is reliably described in the Gospel of St Matthew on the basis of knowledge of the law that what appears at a more advanced stage is a brief recapitulation of what has gone before. Oh, these Gospels depict most profoundly the event at the start of our calculated era. This event is of such mighty import that the writers of the four Gospels will have said: each of us is only capable of depicting such an immense event from our own perspective. Each of these four describes this one event according to their limited abilities. Just as we would describe a being from four perspectives yet only achieve one image—relying on a composite image of contradictory accounts to achieve an understanding of an overarching being—just so did the writer of the Matthew Gospel, as an initiate, rely on what he had understood of the law of three times twice seven in the preparations—within the mission of the ancient Hebrew peoples—for the body that would host the vast I of Jesus of Nazareth.

With consciousness of his initiation, the writer of the Luke Gospel wrote how, by other means, the stream of Buddhism flowed into Christianity in order to continue into the future within it. The other Evangelists wrote on the basis of knowledge gleaned from the conditions of their respective initiations. The events they describe are so vast that we must be grateful that we can approach them from four perspectives, through the results of four initiations.

Just a few observations on the spiritual genesis of Christianity were to be mentioned today to indicate how our knowledge of the world increases once we begin to comprehend this greatest of all events in human history. The intention was to awaken a mere inkling as to just how deeply this event is to be approached and how profound are the Gospels, once we learn to read and understand them.

LECTURE 11

BERLIN, 21 DECEMBER 1909

THE CHRISTMAS TREE—A SYMBOL

ON this day, which ought be a festival of consecration for us, it is only fitting that we vary our practice to the extent that we pause in our quest for knowledge and truth and instead contemplate the realm of feeling and empathy which is awakened and illumined by the light we receive from spiritual science.

The festival now approaching once more is, for countless people, a festival of ensoulment—in the most wonderful sense of the word and in the context of our anthroposophical worldview—and is not a very ancient festival. What we call the Christian festival of Christmas was not celebrated in the years when Christianity was first making its appearance in the world. The first Christians did not celebrate any such Christmas; they did not celebrate the birth of Christ. Almost three centuries were to pass before a celebration of Christ's birth was marked within Christendom.

In those first centuries when Christianity was coursing through the world, those experiencing the Christ impetus in their souls felt an inwardness that corresponded with their withdrawal from much that was taking place in external life around them in forms it had taken since ancient times and since the Christ impetus. A dark inkling arose in the souls of those early Christians that they should act to transform earthly matters, instigate new forms in a world transfused with new feeling, new sentience and, above all, new hope and confidence in human evolution. What was to surge forth to the very horizons of world existence was to take its starting point—we can even say 'literally'—from a spiritual seed or kernel in Earth's interior.

We have often imagined the Roman catacombs where, sequestered from daily life, the first Christians celebrated the festivals of their hearts and souls. We placed ourselves spiritually in these places of devotion. Festivals of birth were not initially celebrated apart from weekly Sunday festivals in remembrance of the event on Golgotha. Also celebrated in those early times were the deaths of those who had—with deep feeling and exceptional enthusiasm—spoken of Golgotha or who had taken significant and incisive action in the course of humanity's evolution to the extent that they were persecuted by a world grown old. The death days of these martyrs, departed into spiritual life, were celebrated as humanity's birth days by Christians in those early centuries.

In those days the birth of Christ was likewise not celebrated. But the genesis of this festival of Christ's birth can show us how today we can rightly state: Christianity was not suddenly founded with this doctrine or another, this procedure or another, to be perpetuated from generation to generation, but we may rightly recall Christ's saying that he is with us, that he fills all our days with his spirit. When we feel ourselves filled with his spirit, we may feel called upon to perpetuate a never-ending onward evolution of this Christian spirit. We are not called—especially through anthroposophical spiritual development—to preserve a rigidly unresponsive Christianity but to generate a continually regenerating Christianity into the future, a Christianity that brings forth ever new wisdom and knowledge. We never speak of the once-existent Christ but always of the eternally living Christ. And we may bring to mind the ever-living, ever-active Christ working within us especially when speaking of the festival of Christ's birth. The Christians of the first centuries could feel newness impressing itself upon the whole organism of Christian evolution and that they could themselves contribute what flowed into them out of Christ's spirit.

A Christmas festival was first inaugurated in the fourth century. We can say that this first Christmas festival took place in the year 354 in Rome. This shows us particularly how, in a time less critical than ours, those confessing to Christianity were suffused with the justly-divined knowledge that they should elicit ever new fruits from the great Christian tree of life. For this reason we may honour one of the outer symbols of Christmas—the Christmas tree—such as we have here before us. In the coming days countless people will place a tree in their midst, the significance of which spiritual science feels called upon to impress ever more deeply on the hearts and souls of human beings.

We might almost come to contradict temporal evolution were we simply to become attached to this symbol. It would be wrong to believe that this symbol is an ancient one and the belief might easily lodge in the modern mind that the graceful midwinter fir tree was a custom established in antiquity. There is a picture showing a Christmas tree in Luther's living room. Drawn only in the nineteenth century, this gives the impression that Christmas trees were widespread in Luther's day. This is a completely false impression because, across German territories, as elsewhere in Europe, Christmas trees were not yet part of the festival in Luther's time. It is a later emblem yet it points to something remarkable. Could we not also think of the Christmas tree as a portent of the future, something future-boding? Might people not, over time, come to see in a Christmas tree an image of something far more meaningful and important?

Let us turn our gaze to the Christmas tree here, having dispelled all illusion as to its historical origins, and call to mind what has often been brought before us: the holy legend, as it is called. This tells us that, when Adam was expelled from Paradise—the legend comes in many guises, but we will retell it as briefly as possible—he is said to have brought with him three seeds from the Tree of Life, whereof human beings were not to eat, having eaten of good and evil from the Tree of Knowledge. When Adam died Seth took these three seeds and planted them on Adam's grave. A tree grew from those seeds on Adam's grave. It is said in the legend that, from the wood of this tree, several things were made: Moses fashioned his rod from its wood and, later, wood from this tree was used to make the cross on Golgotha.

One legend, then, reminds us evocatively of that second tree also standing in Paradise. Humans had eaten of the Tree of Knowledge and enjoyment of the Tree of Life was denied them. But a longing for—an urge towards—this tree remained forever in human hearts. Banished from spiritual worlds—designated as 'Paradise'—into the world of external phenomena, human beings felt in their hearts a desire towards the Tree of Life. What they were not allowed to have without having earned it—without having evolved towards it—they could gradually attain with the aid of knowledge, reaping the rewards of labouring on the physical plane, working for the maturity and merit to receive the fruits of the Tree of Life.

The three seeds represent for us our longing for the fruits of the Tree of Life. The legend tells us that the wood of the cross contained elements stemming from the Tree of Life. Throughout evolution an awareness has persisted that the brittle wood of the cross contained the germ of a new spiritual life and that—rightly gloried in—from it would grow what can unite human beings with their souls as the fruit of the Tree of Life, bestowing immortality in the truest sense of the word and kindling the light of soul to illumine their path out of the dark depths of the physical world into the bright heights of spiritual existence, there to partake of immortal life.

Without succumbing to illusion—and as sentient human beings rather than as historians—we may allow ourselves to see the Christmas tree as a symbol of that light which must flare up within our souls and that will vouchsafe immortality in spiritual existence. Looking within, we feel ourselves—through our anthroposophical spiritual stream—to be suffused with that force which allows us to look upwards into spiritual worlds. There we see, in its outer symbolism, the Christmas tree we have before us and we may say: let it be an emblem for the light that should shine and blaze in our souls and bear us up into spiritual worlds!

This tree has also, in a way, sprung from darkest depths. People who disparage a non-historical perspective, such as the one just characterized, simply do not realize that something physically described does nonetheless contain deeper spiritual imperatives. It may elude the outer eye just how remarkable it is that the Christmas tree has embedded itself into the everyday lives of humanity. In a relatively short time it has become a custom bringing soul solace and blessing into worldwide circulation. This may escape our notice. Yet anyone who is aware that outer phenomena reflect spiritual evolution will surely feel that there is possibly a deeper reason for the emergence of the Christmas tree: that it emerges onto the physical plane as if from a deep spiritual source; that the appearance of the Christmas tree hails from a deep impetus invisibly guiding human beings— inspiring even seemingly insensate souls—and inspiring them to allow the light that must shine into world existence to come to outer expression in the form of the beautiful Christmas tree. Once such awareness of wisdom has been awakened, this tree can—through our willing—become an outer emblem of all that is most exalted.

If anthroposophy is intended to be wisdom, it should be active wisdom, should suffuse all with wisdom, gilding external impressions and customs. In this way anthroposophy may perhaps gild the tradition of the Christmas tree, which has become so materialistic and superficial, gradually warming and enlightening hearts and souls by spreading its gold across humanity of the present and the future. Permeated with wisdom, may this tree become one of our most significant symbols, newly emerging into earthly life as if from the dark underground of the soul. If we dig a little deeper and assume that deeper spiritual guidance places its motives into human hearts, it appears—not without reason—that human beings live out the thoughts implanted by those spiritual guides with deep inwardness around the radiant tree.

It has long been the tradition across several European countries that, during Advent—the weeks before Christmas—deciduous twigs and branches were collected which would come into leaf or at least sprout on Christmas Eve. Many are the souls in whom an inkling of ever-unconquering victory would dawn, recalling the invincible life that vanquishes death, as the carefully collected twigs and boughs would unseasonably burst into festive leaf in the warmth of living rooms on the eve of Christ's Mass, at the Sun's darkest nadir. This was an old custom. That of the Christmas tree itself is, however, far younger. Where do we first find the custom of a Christmas tree?

We recall the striking language of our great German mystics, especially that of Johannes Tauler,[23] who worked in Alsace.

Whoever allowed the sermons of Johannes Tauler to affect them with their deep inwardness and boundless reserves of feeling, will say: in the days when Tauler was working for the deepening and spiritualizing—even the heartening—of Christianity, a quite exceptional spirit was circulating, seeking everywhere souls effused with the Mystery of Golgotha. When Tauler gave his sermons in Strasbourg, his fiery words penetrated deeply into the souls of those present, creating lasting impressions that would burgeon later in memory, including his wonderful Christmas sermon. He proclaimed that God would be born for humanity three times over: would be thrice-born. Once, in that we stem from the Father, from the great world-all. Secondly, in that God descended to humanity, assuming the sheaths of human incarnation. And thirdly, that Christ will be born in each human soul able to find the inner potential to unite with divine wisdom and give birth to higher individuality.

In all manner of wondrous, festive turns of phrase did Johannes Tauler express the most profound wisdom in Strasbourg, especially on Christmas day. This wisdom will have sunk into souls, deeply affecting them and remaining as an echo long afterwards. Feelings also have their traditions. What sank into souls long since may work on from century to century. So may those feelings implanted into human souls long ago work onwards—as do all true feelings suffused with spirit—into eye and hand, and may our eyes be inspired through feeling to see in our sensory surroundings the resurrection, the birth of human spirit light. For materialistic thinking it may therefore be a happy coincidence—but for anyone who knows how spiritual guidance throngs our existence it will be no such mere coincidence—when we hear the first tidings of a Christmas tree inside a house reaching us from Strasbourg[24] in the Alsace. This news came in 1642 and reported how a tree had been brought indoors for the blessing of those who wanted to see in sensory externals an image of the light that can be awakened within through the receiving of spiritual wisdom.

We see how badly the German mystics were received by the Church of its day, adhering as it did to external usage, in the example of Meister Eckhart[25], the great forerunner of Johannes Tauler: he was declared a heretic after his death, the Church having neglected to do so during his lifetime. Those fiery words from Johannes Tauler, too, issuing from a truly Christian heart, met with little recognition. In just such a way as superficial Christianity—which does not really believe in the spirit—related to Johannes Tauler and Meister Eckhart, do we likewise hear of a Christmas tree from a spiritual opponent who opined that trees were mere child's play and that people should instead head to places where the correct doctrine could be heard.

Only slowly at first did the Christmas tree custom take hold. We encounter it in isolated places in mid-Germany around the eighteenth century. Only towards the nineteenth century does the Christmas tree become an ever more frequent spiritual enhancement at Christmas, a new-found symbol of something that had been surviving throughout the centuries. For those who could truly feel not merely the sheen of verbose Christianity but the radiance of true spiritual Christianity it had always been the case that the Christmas tree could elicit wondrous human feelings. You will be easily convinced of the Christmas tree's recent emergence when you note that the greatest German-speaking poets wrote nothing about it. Had it been prevalent earlier, Klopstock, for instance, would have waxed poetical about this emblem. Let this Christmas tree, therefore, be a pledge that emblems of the most exalted and mighty may arise anew. Such symbols can emerge in our souls particularly when we feel the spiritual truth of the awakening I within our human souls, that intrinsic I which senses the spiritual bond from soul to soul and feels this to a heightened degree when human beings of noble intent work together.

Just one example will be mentioned here, from which we can see how the light of the Christmas tree shone into the soul of a great leader of humankind. In 1822 Goethe—whom we have so often encountered when studying spiritual life in the light of anthroposophy—felt at the end of his *Faust* that only Christian symbolism could express his poetic intentions; he felt that Christianity must inspire the most noble connections between human souls, that it must found bonds of brotherly love not based on blood but between souls devoted to the spirit. We feel the impetus still inherent in Christianity as potential when we think about the conclusion of the Gospels. From the cross on Golgotha Christ Jesus gazes down upon his mother, she looks to her son, and he bestows community on a humanity previously based only in blood relations. A mother was once given a son, a son a mother, through bonds of blood. These blood relations were not to be abolished through Christianity; they remain. But, in addition, spiritual connections are to be forged, spiritual bonds that irradiate blood relations with spiritual light. This is the reason why Christ Jesus said from the cross: Woman, behold, this is your son! And to the disciple he said: Behold, this is your mother! The bonds formerly only founded in blood were bequeathed from the cross as spiritual ties.

Where spirit was alive among noble-minded spiritual communities, Goethe always felt compelled to seek the true spirit of Christianity. He felt the need to allow this Christian spirit to flow from heart to eye. In 1822 he had cause to do so. The people of the principality, to whose wellbeing Goethe had dedicated so much energy, had come together to found a school for the children of citizens—a Civic or Citizens' School. This was, simultaneously, a present from the people to the Prince of Weimar. Goethe knew no better way to celebrate this small event betokening spiritual progress than—before Christmas—to invite a number of people to contribute individual pieces of poetry, each according to their ability. He gathered these poems, written by townsfolk, into a booklet and wrote an Introduction. Karl Alexander, later to become the Grand Duke, was at the time a three-year-old boy and he was to hand this booklet of collected poems to Prince Karl August under the Christmas tree; by 1822 Christmas trees had already become a constant symbol.

With this humble deed, Goethe showed that the Christmas tree had become for him an emblem of feelings and perceptions towards spiritual progress, both small and large. In the poetic introduction to the little book now in the Weimar library, Goethe sang the praises of the Christmas tree[26] as a symbol in the following way:

Shining trees, radiant trees
All around exuding peace.
Dancing in their gleaming brightness
Spark in every heart a lightness—
Such a joyous celebration!
And such dazzling decoration;
We look up and down amazed,
Our adoring hearts they all are raised.

But, O Prince, if e'er you meet
An evening blessing you so sweet,
Lights and flames and purest ether
Gleaming, gathering all together,
All that you have e'er achieved,
All those present, who in you believe:
Gifted with exalted sight,
May you feel supreme delight.

This poem by our Goethe may be among the first Christmas poems. When speaking in spiritual science about emblems, we may also mention that symbols—rising up from the unconscious or the sub-conscious into human souls—appear over the course of time, gilded and clothed in wisdom.

So we see the first Christian Christmas celebrated in fourth century Rome. We must almost regard it as an act of God that into an ancient festival celebrating the Sun's deepest nadir—when much of Middle- and Northern Europe celebrates the Winter Solstice—came the festival of Christ's Mass, not through exoteric-materialist expediency but inwardly like a mysterious act of God. Do not believe that across Middle and Northern Europe the intention was to align Christmas with the old celebrations simply to placate folk. Christianity gave birth to Christmas. Precisely the acceptance of Christmas in Northern regions shows the deep spiritual association between people, their symbols and Christianity. Whereas in Armenia Christmas did not become a custom—and even in Palestine there has been a certain dismissiveness—it was quickly assimilated among people in Europe.

Let us really try to understand the Christmas festival from an anthroposophical perspective and summarize the Christmas tree as an emblem. Throughout the year, when we gather here, let us feel words clamouring from spiritual sources—words which are not mere words but spiritual forces—acting ever more powerfully upon us, rendering our souls citizens of eternity. All year long we gather here so that words—the logos in its manifold forms—may resound in this room: that Christ is evermore with us and, when we meet, the spirit of Christ nears and moves us so that our words become suffused with the spirit of Christ. When we speak of things and are conscious that our words are like winged bearers of revelation from the spirit to humankind, we allow spirit words to flow into our souls. Yet we know that the spirit word cannot be fully grasped by us and cannot be all that it is intended to be if it is only received as superficial or abstract knowledge. We know that spirit can only be what it is intended to be once it generates warmth, enabling our souls to expand—to experience being extended through warmth—ultimately pouring out into all world phenomena; we learn to feel at one with this spirit drenching all manifestation.

We feel that in us strength must become life, life that throngs our ears with spirit words, so that we—when the time is right—place in our midst a symbol to fortify and appeal to our souls: Let a new spirit-human arise in you that can kindle to warmth and illumine with light the word springing from spiritual sources, welling from spiritual undergrounds towards us—then we will also feel the importance of which spirit word resounds towards us. Let us feel seriously—at a moment such as this—what spiritual science can bring us by way of soul warmth and soul light! Let us feel this in the following way:

Look at the modern, materialistic world with all its commotion of people hurrying to and fro from morning till night, judging and measuring everything in terms of material worth: they do not suspect that, behind all this, the spirit lives and weaves. People go to sleep of an evening, never imagining that they are anything but unconscious and that they will wake to another day on the physical plane. People go to sleep, oblivious, after another rushed working day without considering life's meaning. The spiritual seeker who has heard the word of spirit will know something that is not theory nor doctrine: they know that they are given soul warmth and soul light. They also know that, were they during the day only to take in images of physical life, their lives would become desiccated and barren and any gains would perish. When you lie down to sleep at night you enter a world of spirit, diving down with all your soul powers into a realm of higher spiritual beings, towards whose stature your very being is intended to grow. On waking, you return, newly strengthened from a spiritual world and—consciously or unconsciously—divine spiritual vitality spills out over everything you receive from the physical plane. Out of eternity do you every morning rejuvenate what is temporal in your existence.

We transform the word of the spirit into the feeling we can have at eventide: I am not only departing into unconsciousness but I am immersing myself in a world where the beings of eternity dwell and among whose ranks my own being is intended to belong. I go to sleep with the feeling: Onwards into spiritual worlds! And I awake with the feeling: Forth from the spirit! We will then be filled with the feeling into which spirit word is transformed when tended here from day to day, from week to week, in a life dedicated to spiritual knowledge. Then will the spirit become life in us, then will we go to sleep and wake up differently.

Once we feel connected with the spirit of the cosmos, feel ourselves every morning anew to be emissaries of the spirit, of the cosmos, once we gradually feel connected with the spirit weaving through and pervading all outer phenomena, then we will also feel—when the high Sun of summer radiates its life-giving forces towards Earth—how spirit works into external phenomena and while its outer countenance is turned towards us in the raying of the Sun, its inner being is simultaneously receding.

Where do we see this spirit of cosmic world creation, announced by Zarathustra as dwelling in the Sun, if only the physical rays of the Sun reach us? We see this world-spirit when we recognize where it sees itself. In truth, the spirit of the cosmos creates its sense organs, through which it can see itself, during summer. It creates outer sense organs for itself. We must learn to understand that, in clothing itself in a garment of green from spring onwards, the Earth is creating a new countenance. What is this? It is a mirror for the world spirit of the Sun. While the Sun is sending us its physical rays, the spirit of the cosmos gazes down at Earth. What overflows from all plant growth, blossoms, foliage is nothing other than the counter-imagery of the pure, chaste cosmic spirit, which sees itself reflected in its own creation while causing all growth to burgeon forth from the Earth. The sense organs of the world spirit exist within the Earth's plant cover.

As this plant cover withers in autumn we see how the outer strength of the Sun dwindles and how the world spirit's countenance withdraws. If we are rightly prepared, we feel the spirit pulsing throughout the world and within us, too. We can also follow the world spirit as it withdraws its countenance from our view. We then feel, when we can no longer rest our gaze on the plant covering, how within us the spirit awakens in inverse proportion with the spirit's withdrawal from world phenomena.

This awakening spirit becomes for us a guide to the depths, into which spiritual life retreats, those depths into whose spirit we entrust the seeds for next spring. There we learn to see spiritually and to reflect: As outer life retreats from our physical senses, gradually disappearing from sight, when autumn sadness seeps into our souls, our souls can follow the spirit into dead rock, there to extract forces which will cover the Earth anew with sense organs for the cosmic spirit.

This is how such human beings felt who grasped the spirit—in spirit—and who accompanied the world spirit downwards with the seeds in winter. When the external Sun is at its weakest, radiating least strongly, and when outer gloom is at its darkest, then does the spirit in us—through the spirit from the cosmos, to which it has bound itself—unite below with those forces which are at their most visibly perceptible when they are conveying new life to the seeds.

In this way, like the power of seeds, do we live downwards into the Earth, do we literally penetrate the Earth. Whereas in summer we turned towards the shining expanses of the air, outwards to Earth's germinating, thriving and fruiting, so do we now turn to inanimate rocks, yet knowing: in this inanimate rock slumbers what will reappear as outer existence. In spirit does our own soul follow the sprouting, flourishing forces as they withdraw from outer view and rest through winter in the mineral Earth. Once winter has reached its darkest mid-point and the outer world no longer captivates our attention, we feel spiritually—in the depths, into which we too have retreated—how spirit light surges forth; that same spirit light through which Christ Jesus bestowed upon humanity its most mighty onward impetus. We may echo the feelings of those who in ancient times spoke of the need to follow the seeds to where they rest in their winter seclusion, in darkness and gloom, in order to recognize the spirit by its hidden forces. We feel that we are to seek Christ in seclusion, in the solitude that remains dark and gloomy if we have not illumined our souls, which become radiant and shining once we have received the light of Christ into our souls. We then find that with every Christmas we strengthen and fortify ourselves through the power that flowed into humanity in the Mystery of Golgotha.

In this way we feel, with every passing year, Christ's impetus strengthening us in our striving. We take from this impetus the surety, the pledge that—from year to year—life in us will be fortified and will lead into spiritual worlds, where death—as we know it in the physical world—cannot exist. We can spiritualize and endow with soul what for people of materialistic leaning is no symbol but just an external delight for the senses. We sense reality in this symbol of the tree, we sense the same as Johannes Tauler had in mind when he spoke of Christ being born three times: once into the eternal Father God, who enlivens the world, weaving throughout creation, once as a human being at the start of Christianity and then ever and again in the souls of those who awaken within themselves the world of spirit. Without this last birth, Christianity would be incomplete and anthroposophy would be unable to encompass the spirit of Christ; were it not to understand what it signifies that the word—resounding to us year after year—should remain no mere theory or doctrine but bring us warmth, light and life, so that, through this power, we bring the vitality of spirituality into the world, incorporating it and ourselves into eternity.

Such are the feelings we should engender when standing around this symbol of Christmas, feeling ourselves delving beneath the Earth into the frosty depths of the seemingly dead world, not only boding but knowing that spirit wakens new life from death. At whichever stage we find ourselves, we can echo the feeling—felt by initiates throughout all ages—who really descended on this night of consecration to the place where the Midnight Sun, the Spirit Sun of the sanctified mid-winter is seen and where it calls forth the burgeoning growth and life of spring from the seeming death of rock.

We feel united with the forces reigning throughout the world, even when they have physically withdrawn behind frost and dimness of light. We wish to feel this in common with all those who around Christmastide truly commemorate the Spiritual Sun—the Sun of Christ—behind the physical Sun. Let us reflect that feeling, so that we gradually ascend to an experience—and thence to vision—of what human beings are capable of seeing when they cultivate ever-new forces connecting them with the spirit. Let us close these reflections with the verse we spoke several years ago when celebrating Christmas, filling our souls with the most vital aspect to which we can be open and which can pour into our souls:

Behold the Sun
At the midnight hour.
Build with stones
In the lifeless ground.

Thus in decay
And in the night of death
Find Creation's new beginning,
Young morning's strength.

Glory in the heights
The eternal word of Gods,
Shelter in the depths
The powers of peace.

In darkness dwelling
Create a Sun
In matter weaving
Know the joy of Spirit.[27]

Lecture 12

BERLIN, 26 DECEMBER 1909

CHRISTMAS MOOD

In the days before Christmas we tried to lift the mood to one worthy of being—in an anthroposophical sense—the appropriate mood for Christmas. We tried to conjure for our souls a Christmas celebration which in some respects makes this Christmas mood applicable to vital human experience throughout the year. For those seeking knowledge, especially those present, celebrating Christmas in direct contact with spiritual knowledge must be among our most essential attitudes. Celebrating Christmas in the presence of spirit knowledge: what could this mean other than inwardly, fervently, bringing to mind how we carry out our spiritual duty over the year in the context of present human evolution? By understanding humanity's tasks, we increasingly enrich our souls with spirit-derived content so as to be worthy of being among those who are to carry out the spiritual work essential for the coming epoch.

So let us throughout the year seek to steep our souls in spiritual-scientific content, seek to penetrate anthroposophical wisdom. As the year nears its end, outwardly signifying the waning light of the Sun's rays and allowing an excess of gloom to hold sway, we try to understand how to celebrate this festival in connection with other festivals in the anthroposophical year. Let us ever and again be clear that all anthroposophical truth must be saturated—suffused—with the mighty impetus we call the Christ impulse! If we try to inscribe anthroposophical truths on our hearts and souls as the message itself of Christ, we may say that at Christmas we need to develop an anthroposophical Christmas mood by allowing what we have gathered in our souls over the rest of the year to be illuminated by deeper soul-feelings so that it becomes for us a power, enabling us to feel: we not only know a little of anthroposophical wisdom but it breaks through into our souls, into our hearts, as an all-pervading power of warmth and light. This will enable us in the coming year—in all areas of our lives, wherever we may find ourselves—to fulfil our duties, to bring order to our work. If we then try to transform those sacred spiritual truths into hallowed feelings—into a divine force—in our souls, then will the earthly forces we initially absorb be born in us at a higher level. That is why, at Christmastide, we may ever more vividly call to mind those instances when humanity attempted to advance itself to the spiritual regions where Christ himself is to be found. This is the soul region into which our own German-Christian poet *Novalis* led us this Christmas. Today, too, something of the Christmas mood just mentioned—that feeling of being warmed by beams of warmth—can radiate from a genuinely theosophical[28] poet such as Novalis. If we encounter Novalis in all his gloriously poetical wisdom, we may feel most warmly how—from out of spirit knowledge—we are given the opportunity to fill our lives with a new lustrous gleam.

Outside, life surges on past us and our own work is connected with life's daily bustle. If, within anthroposophy, we have the opportunity to draw down wisdom from spiritual worlds, we will—however prosaic such opportunities may appear to be—be able to gild our lives with the gold of anthroposophical wisdom. This is something we need to learn. Then we will see that we can fill our lives with a new lustrous gleam once we allow the mood of Christmas to infiltrate our souls, when we allow anthroposophy to be reborn within us as a feeling, as a sensitivity towards Christmas. We will then feel how impossible it is—if we wish to remain within the ordinary world—to ascend, however tentatively, to spirituality. Oh, there are plenty of reasons that prevent human beings from unfolding wings to reach the spiritual world! What I am about to tell you may be symbolic of this.

Many among us might say of spiritual science: Well, everything offered by spiritual science is lovely, glorious, would lovingly warm my heart and soul; but I simply cannot believe it! Everything I have learnt from the external world, the opinions I have acquired, holds me in its grip and tells me: These are just dreams, not built on properly solid foundations! This is how some people are trapped in bitter doubt. Were they able to lift themselves out of the prejudice, opinion and the pressures of a relentlessly intrusive culture, they would be free to experience the pure ether of spirit, they would see that they are experiencing the power of the spirit and they would draw this down into the everyday work of their hands. The following small incident typifies the feelings preventing someone in the midst of modern, mundane life from feeling—in free and unfettered ways—what spiritual science offers.

Spanning the eighteenth and nineteenth centuries, there lived a man, the German aristocrat von Hardenberg.[29] He had a son, of whom we can attest—within the limits of our working group—that poetry and wisdom poured from his soul, being as he was the re-embodiment of one of the most significant, mighty and incisive personalities ever to have endowed the Earth. Being under the influence exerted by the external world, how would the father of this soul recognize his son? How could he possibly guess at the spirit to emerge from the soul of his son? On the basis of material opinion, he could recognize him just as little as free himself from co-dependency on physical life, and just as little as today's human being can—amid material prejudice—experience the purity and compelling power of spiritual wisdom contained in anthroposophy.

Old Hardenberg had had to struggle out of raw incomprehension of his son. He had had to hoist himself out of an utterly materialistic life in order, nevertheless, to experience in his Moravian congregation something of its deeply religious spirit, one might almost say towards recognizing a spirit of universal stature, as in days of old. However, he did not succeed in experiencing the power and grandeur of the wisdom issuing from his son's soul. To achieve this—having for so long been in thrall to the rigidly authoritative rules often experienced suggestively within a congregation such as his—he would have had to be fired to the depths of his soul by that truly Christian spirit, which can only be understood when it is suffused with the breath of spirit knowledge.

Strangely enough, Old Hardenberg did once feel that breath of spirit—of Christian spirit—when in the midst of his Moravian congregation a hymn was sung. This song, of whose origins he was ignorant, drifted towards him like a breath of eternity and he was deeply moved by the hymn[30] then beginning:

> What had I been wert Thou not?
> What were I now if Thou wert gone?

He felt something he had never before been able to feel. The celebration came to an end. Old Hardenberg went outside and asked some members of the congregation: Who wrote that glorious poem? Your son wrote it! Liberated from all physical connection, not misled by the prejudices of the physical plane, Old Hardenberg felt the compelling power of spiritual life. His son, however, had already been—as regards his physical body—underground for some months! Old Hardenberg only had this experience a few months after Novalis's death. Such was his state that he was briefly swept aloft to spiritual heights, away from all physical prejudice, where he could experience the undeniable might of spiritual realms—something we should feel when untroubled by all bias of materiality. Let us leave all present bias down below! Let us feel the urgency of spiritual life and allow its strength and warmth to flow into our hearts! If we do this at the right time we will be able to fulfil our duty to present-day humanity.

This example, taken from the actual life of Novalis's father, serves to illustrate what I wished to contribute to today's mood, to whose heights we want to raise ourselves by means of that insistent force contained in Novalis's songs and poetry:

> [At this point Marie von Sivers (Marie Steiner) performed nine of Novalis' *Spiritual Songs*]

During this festive time it is perhaps easiest to feel and to sense—not just to understand and know—what we have been studying over these hours in connection with the Gospels. A good deal of the time we had available over the past year was devoted to these Gospels. So let today's short contemplation, intended as part of our Christmas celebrations, point to some important corollaries to our Gospel studies:[31] the connection with the event that, especially at Christmas, should appear to us in all its vibrancy, the connection with the phenomenon of Christ.

The might and significance of the anthroposophical worldview for the present time and for humanity's evolution can—in several respects—be measured against the Christ event. If we allow the Christ event to elicit as deep a feeling in our souls as it elicited within Novalis, we will always be challenged anew to ask: How can we to an ever greater extent experience the truth of that immense impetus given humankind by the birth of Christ Jesus in Palestine? Within these circles we may bring anthroposophy into especially inward connection with the occurrence of Christ. We showed how the various streams of human spiritual life in antiquity flowed together into the events of Palestine; we also indicated how the enormity of this event is at best faintly divined by large numbers of people today. Only gradually, in the far future, once humanity has deepened its spiritual life, will this be able to be understood in all its towering magnitude and substance. What wisdom will emerge in the course of Earth evolution! The most wonderful deepening of this wisdom will be found in that it—itself—becomes an instrument for the understanding of what this Christ impetus really is.

Today there is, in certain respects, a pressing urgency to speak of Christ's significance from the standpoint of spiritual knowledge. At the time when Christ walked the Earth in human form, humanity received the immensely powerful stimulus to turn once again towards the spirit. Yet this impetus had the effect—an effect persisting into our times—of, as it were, firing only suitable souls with its full import. The rest of humanity, by contrast—as if to exemplify all that needed to be overcome—initially set its course ever deeper into material existence. Human existence is an intensifying descent into matter. Since post-Atlantean times, humanity has been descending ever more deeply into matter. The Christ event signifies the impulsion to re-ascend from these depths. This powerful impetus has only been fulfilled to a very small degree. By contrast, the descent into matter—in these times since Christ, too—has become an ever more earthly process such that in this descent thinking, feeling and human sensibility have also come under attack.

We live in—and face—an era in which materialistic research has encroached on the very idea of the Christ event. In this solemn hour it behoves us to indicate serious matters of our times such as this: materialistic research has infringed even the greatest spiritual event ever to take place on Earth. Just see how materialistic theologians, after the fashion of so-called 'historical theology', claim that there can be no external proof of the existence of a historical Christ! It is theologians[32] who say: Historical research itself is forced to admit that there is no historical proof that any such person existed in Palestine at the beginning of our era; nobody of whom the powerful words of the Gospels foretold and still tell, nor of the mighty impetus granted to—or discharged into—human spiritual life.

Today 'science' seems to feel obliged—on the basis of its methods—to expunge the historical Christ from the world. One therefore has to remember that spiritual science is just beginning to be called upon to prove Christ's existence on the basis of its constituent elements. Human belief does not depend on the obscure veracities of a branch of science. Proof upon proof could be brought for the specious, threadbare results of some disciplines. People can live without taking much notice of any such evidence. In future, too—and this will be the case for a long time yet—ever increasing numbers of people will be inclined towards materialistic thinking, held in the grip of belief in the 'reliable' research of the Historical Method that denies the certainty of a historical Christ Jesus[33]. What we hope to gain here, as has been said many times—a new symbol with the golden gleam of wisdom—will appear to be expunged. The time will certainly come when Christ will be known about in circles such as this, circles where there will be openness to spiritual science and through which there will be an understanding of the words: 'I am with you always, even unto the end of the world' and where those who are able to see into spiritual worlds will know that He, from whom the impulse of Christianity emanates, will always be found in the spiritual world and that certainty about Christ's deeds will be gleaned from the spiritual world. Only within circles professing to such an awareness will there be certainty about the symbol under consideration here. Others outside these circles will not acknowledge that the external Historical Method is itself on shaky ground. Those with chapter and verse on science know from its worn and groundless methods how little is claimed when those qualified say: None of the figures, from Christ to the Apostles, can be historically verified. It will be a long time before people rid themselves of their faith in authority, which they vow is no faith in authority. The worst kind of faith in authority is rife today. People do not realize that the true Redeemer from belief in authority is the individuality who—within each human being—teaches us to build on the power of our own I. He who has shown us what is to be incorporated into our I can also show us how we find the power of truth—the founts of truth—in our inner being. With Christ within we find truth within; with Christ within we find firm ground for free and independent judgement, we find the firm ground extending beyond all authority. But we must allow a grave word at this serious hour so that we learn to feel our calling as anthroposophists.

I would have commented later—comments I feel constrained to make now—in the next lectures, were it not some time before we meet again. But I must allude to something an anthroposophist should recognize as a symptom underlying the times, namely what is not possible for the science of our times. Those who want to believe in the science that discusses away the historical Christ will remain unteachable, incorrigible. Yet there must be some people who understand—on the basis of anthroposophy—how all fields of science will dissipate and how spiritual life alone will be the saviour of a future humanity.

The most important things in current events are not being seen. A court case is taking place in Vienna,[34] watched by the world. The whole of Europe was present in the form of its news representatives, so that news thought to be important could be followed. The crucial thing taking place, however, was probably not noticed by any present.

Those not prepared through anthroposophy would, had they heard about it, have considered this vital feature a figment. There was a historian, famous across Europe, considered an expert by his peers, widely published and a firm adherent of the Historical Method, i.e. 'a good scientist'. This good scientist got hold of some documents from a southern region of Europe, purporting to prove treachery in Southern Austria. Who better than a historian—required to research provenance and sources—to validate such a thing? The whole world relies on documentation! How they are used, compiled and checked provides truth. That alone is supposed to deliver the truth about the great wonders of Christianity!

This particular historian was a pupil of a historian I remember from my youth. There were two such historians, one by method a strictly document-based historical researcher, the other, his colleague, adhered less to those principles, relying more on his students' knowledge of actual historical process. The favourite student of the documentarian presented his doctoral thesis. He was questioned on his knowledge of existing records, upon which documents his contention was based, which physical records supported the veracity of his thesis; for instance, which papal edict contained the first dotted i ?—essential knowledge! The student knew that this took place under a certain Pope Innocent. The second professor then asked the candidate—the latter's dotted-i-knowledge being so extensive—which year that Pope had ascended the papal throne. He did not know. When did that Pope die? He did not know. Tell us something about this Pope: he could not. The first professor, whose favourite the candidate was, then said: Mr. Candidate, it is as if you have a board nailed to your forehead today. The second professor, however, said to his colleague: But Professor, he is your favourite student. So who nailed that board to his forehead?

That historian had not learnt anything particular, but he became an efficient archival researcher, establishing with all means at his disposal the verity of times long gone. Was anyone more called upon to examine what treachery had been perpetrated in documents put his way by the most erudite? He went to work with all available means and, in a public article, accused a swathe of people of serious misconduct.

A court case followed, during which one of the prime pieces of evidence turned out to be a scandalous fake. It was put forward that a certain person in a certain town had presided over a certain union. A simple enquiry would have established that the person in question was—at the time in question—in Berlin.

Here historical research has gone to work strictly on the basis of factual documentation originating in the present and achieving nothing more than being duped by contemporary papers. What I referred to as the most important thing is not that people appeared in court but that the scientific-Historical Method has itself been scrutinized, has itself quite literally been judged! Symbolically, that is the most important totem of a case taking place at present.

We need to seriously ask ourselves: how valuable is a method that wades in to pass judgement on whether or not an event took place some nineteen centuries ago if that method is unfit to track down the most obvious things of the present? 'The Science' was itself on trial here. We need to be alert to that! A science proceeding on the basis of materialistic prejudice will always be in the dock where people are too indolent to hold it to account. This is merely an authority of the present moment—it can only be temporary—the sort of authority to be differentiated from that other authority, which knows who it is. All other authorities are unknown quantities: one never knows who they are, who 'The Science' or this 'Madame Science' may be.

If you investigate what goes by the name of The Science today— duly acknowledging a spiritual world outlook—you will see how it crumbles, how it proves to be built on friable, sandy foundations, toppling when genuinely scrutinized. Yet people will not concede to viewing the present from any such perspective. People—excluding those living with anthroposophy—will not be sufficiently conscientious to scrutinize the methods created to force violent materialistic opinions into human souls.

For this reason it will be a long time before there is any possibility—other than in close circles of anthroposophical work—of seeing in its true light what will bring humanity the greatest salvation. When what took place in Palestine—which we allow to arise anew in our hearts every year as a symbol—is increasingly denied and expunged by outer science, then there will still be a place within anthroposophical spiritual-world streams where the power of the event in Palestine will ray out ever more brightly and from whence will flow out into humanity the life that can issue from this event alone.

What can arise and bear fruit in our souls from genuinely witnessing the event in Palestine? 'I am with you all the days, even unto the end of world epochs'! We can say this is Christ Jesus' prime word to us. This means that Christ Jesus walked the Earth—embodied in Palestine—at the beginning of the Christian era. Since that time he is to be found in the spiritual world because, ever since, he has united with the spiritual atmosphere of the Earth. He has become the Spirit of the Earth. When we seek him, we find him within the spiritual atmosphere of our Earth. Ever more and more does he pervade and suffuse all life on our Earth.

Yet what are human beings to secure through the Christ Spirit ever increasingly inhabiting their souls? If we want to understand clearly how this Christ Spirit comes to rest in human souls in future, then we must attempt what we have been doing for some time in our anthroposophical movement. What we do in the anthroposophical movement does not spring from random caprice, does not originate in some programme founded by this or that person. Spiritual life ultimately leads back to the sources we seek in the individualities we call the Masters of Wisdom and of the Harmony of Feelings. Here, with them, we find—if we seek assiduously—the impetus and momentum guiding how we are to work from epoch to epoch, from age to age.

A great impetus such as this has come from spiritual worlds to humanity in recent times. On this festive Christmas evening, and among kindred circles, this important impetus can be referred to as an intimation, which has flowed towards us by astral means from spiritual worlds over the last years. Our anthroposophical movement in central Europe has evolved under the sign of this momentum. In human words, we could characterize this momentum in the following way: Observe what is happening in the outer world: the words of the Gospels are being ever more misunderstood! People quibble about their meaning, they are analysed with superficial historical methods. All such 'historical' noise has to be silenced for a while by the spiritual researcher. The vital thing is for the Gospels to be understood anew in their literal sense, because in such literal comprehension lies the true foundation of their wisdom.

We have been led by the spiritual world to literally come to know the Gospels anew, to understand what is contained in their words. On the basis of this impetus—on the extension and elaboration of this impetus—we proceeded in our studies of St John's Gospel, those of St Luke and St Matthew, and we will also attempt future studies of St Mark's Gospel. We must try to understand the Gospels literally! So say those, whose impetus we receive from spiritual worlds. This is future Christianity: to follow this stimulus to understand the Gospels in their literal sense. What will transpire if we understand the Gospels verbatim, if we follow the guidance of spiritual forces who have now spoken to us more clearly from astral regions than for a century? This will be something which will have to become essential for us if we wish to make ourselves instruments for the right direction and guidance of humanity in the context of what needs to be directed and guided in spatial existence.

Looking back into primordial times at the way in which humanity evolved, we know that the human I was not yet fully elaborated. Human evolution leads us back to group souls. Just as animals still possess group souls, certain numbers of human beings possessed a common I-soul. This is found among all peoples. So we know that humankind evolved out of a quality of group-soul-ness. At the time when the Christ descended to our Earth, humanity had reached a point where ancient group souls had begun to lose their significance; these archaic group souls had withdrawn. Each human being became reliant on themselves for the development of their own soul, their own I-filled egohood. And who was it who generated what was to pour into each individual human soul? This was caused by the Christ force itself! The more we fill ourselves with this Christ will, the richer will our I-identity become, enabling those truths and wisdom to arise in us which we will need to live into the future.

Right now, in the present, we have reached an important turning point. Today some may ask: What significance do we attach to the fact that we speak about reincarnation and yet we cannot remember our previous incarnations? We certainly do not remember them nowadays. I have mentioned this before. If one points to a four-year-old child and says: This is a human being, but he can't do arithmetic, this does not prove that human beings cannot do arithmetic. One just has to wait until that child has matured sufficiently to do arithmetic. Within ten years the child will be quite capable of arithmetic. In like manner will the human soul mature sufficiently to recall previous lives on Earth. Whether it can recall them correctly is another question.

Now we are at an important turning point. In the fourth post-Atlantean epoch Christ descended as the motivating force for humankind to experience their selfhood as a state of being within themselves. We are now in the fifth epoch, the last in which humans will not be able to remember their past incarnations. In the sixth epoch, following our present times, people will be able to remember their past lives. Whether they remember correctly will depend on whether their souls have acquired the impetus to do so and whether they have made themselves capable of remembering accurately. Only those will in future prove capable of correctly remembering their present lives who have embraced the Christ impulse, the source of true selfhood. Conversely, for those not embracing the true source of their own I, new group souls will take shape.

Look, if you will, at external reality: how people nowadays throng towards loci of group-soul qualities, without needing to do so, whereas they could find sources of truth that allow life to burgeon in their souls. Observe how many people do things the way 'they ought to be done'. They do not seek—within their own souls—for what can uniquely be found there, but we see them looking around to join others in categories and groups, and how they are happiest not when independently seeking truth but when they can have what others also have. In fact, they hate individuality, believing that, in hating individuality, they are forging the strongest weapons against such wisdom as is found in anthroposophy. For anthroposophical wisdom must shine within each human being; it cannot be experimentally fabricated using levers, screws and suchlike implements. We do not encounter what is offered on the part of anthroposophy in levers and screws. Each of us must seek within, because we belong to an invisible world, into which we must penetrate with our thinking, each individually acquiring wisdom without recourse to external tools. We become an individual through anthroposophical wisdom.

If we take this anthroposophical wisdom into our souls in the right individual way, suffused with the Christ impetus, then what will enable us to recall a true I-identity in the sixth cultural epoch— something enclosed within itself, something each person has individually—will descend into our souls. Conversely, the memories of those seeking artificial group souls today will be such that they will again encounter group-soul qualities. In the sixth epoch human beings will remember their present incarnations, but then it will be clear: Your judgement depended on the judgement of others! And it will be felt as an awful shackle to be confined within such bonds of group soul. Group soul adherence threatens those unable to take up the Christ impetus in our times. If we receive the message of the Christ event—that message of human ego-hood—then the potential to reach humanity's goals in the sixth epoch descends into our souls: that we do not look back at qualities relating to group souls but instead at a Christened, Christ-filled I.

In this way, the essential element towards becoming fully human in the sixth epoch infiltrates the souls of those who understand how to grasp the spirit of anthroposophy—to cause it to glow and radiate, to stream throughout—which will enable us to become instruments, working rightfully and truly in the future.

That is the question: Do we decide to look back on our present I-am from our future reincarnations in the sixth epoch as non-individual, dependent and sequestered within group cohesion? Or do we want to recall an I that has embraced the very source of spirituality itself in our earthly evolution, an I that has encompassed the mighty words: 'Before all personality was, before there was anything that could live on Earth' and 'Before Abraham was, was the I-am' [or 'Before Abraham was, I am.']?[35]

What lives in us is closely bound with the Father Spirit. What comes alive in us through an understanding of the Christ impulse can only be consciously bound in us with the source of the world if we understand that Christ impetus. The Christ impulse offers us the opportunity—inasmuch as it descends into our souls—to be resurrected in the sixth epoch as one such I-identity who can look back over the genesis of their independence. If we allow the rightly understood Christ to be born in our own inner souls, then we will be able to reawaken the memory of this rightly understood Christ from the sixth post-Atlantean age.

If we can really celebrate a Christmas festival in this fifth epoch, we will really be able to celebrate Easter in the sixth era. As that lovely song tells us at Christmas: 'Unto us a Saviour is born!' so will we, in remembering back to the Christ born in our souls, ourselves hear tidings of this truly lofty I-being. We will recall this and the memory will be resurrected within us as an Easter festival. Then will we be able to hear the great Easter organ-clarion proclaiming: May the Christ in us arise, firing and illuminating our own godly-divine individuality!

In this way Christmas and Easter are united in the fifth and sixth epoch of our post-Atlantean times. This is the sense in which we can learn to regard what we experienced from the Gospels. We have learnt in part—and we will learn more in future—how the Buddha stream, the Zarathustra stream and the ancient Hebrew stream flowed together into the river of Christianity, how these streams also flowed—in the sense in which the Gospels depict—into the personality of Christ Jesus. The vitality weaving throughout the pre-Christian world must come to life in our own I-identity, must be reborn, suffused with the Christ impetus. Then we will be celebrating the anthroposophical festival of Christmas in our own souls: the birth of Christ in us. And if we bring this known and understood Christ with us through Kamaloka and Devachan[36] regions into a new life on Earth, and from there ever and again into each new earthly existence, right into the sixth epoch, then will we remember what we experienced in this fifth epoch, then will we celebrate the Christian Easter within ourselves.

So may there live symbolically in us—in the form of Christmas—
what we have of late taken into our souls and learnt from the Gospels to be the Christ Mystery. Let these lights, burning here in our
midst, be a challenge to us to live out that imperative, nearing us
from spiritual worlds: to understand the Gospels literally! Let these
outwardly shining lights be an image of the lights we need to ignite
within our souls which, when lit through anthroposophical knowledge of Christ, will continue burning through to the sixth post-Atlantean age.

At this Christmas festival, feel—in the sense outlined—that it
is within your soul's gift to decide to become a worthy instrument
for humanity's evolution into the future! Feel the whole gravity, the
whole weight of this anthroposophical resolution: we should not be
anthroposophists on our own behalf, but rather—in that we take
into consideration what has been said here—we should be anthroposophists with a sense of duty towards humanity, duty towards all
the tasks and missions of humankind. Let the light from the Christmas tree shine, as an emblem, upon us; let this light ignite us for this,
our spiritual mission for humankind. Then we will have understood
something which can give us strength for a new year, for finding our
way ever further into anthroposophical life and into anthroposophical wisdom.

NOTES

Textual Sources

The first two lectures—those of 11 and 18 October 1909—are summarized, the first of which is by Jakob Mühletaler, the second in all likelihood taken from notes by Alice Kinkel. Notes of lectures on 2, 9 and 23 November 1909 are copied from those of Berta Reebstein. Post-lecture notes of lectures on 13, 14 and 19 November are by a person unknown. Lectures of 4 and 7 December were taken down by Camille Wandrey; those of the Christmas lectures on 21 and 26 December 1909 are from Walter Vegelahn. Original shorthand notes are available only for lectures on 2, 9 and 23 November 1909.

('GA' refers to the original edition of Rudolf Steiner's works in German.)

1 *The Gospel of St Luke* [*Das Lukas-Evangelium*], 10 lectures given in Basel between 15–24 September 1909, GA 114.

2 The German Section refers to the Section within the Theosophical Society, of which Steiner was leader at the time.

3 These introductory words, which characterize Rudolf Steiner's preferred method of spiritual-scientific research in work relating to an understanding of the being of Christ, will appear in Volume 251 of the Collected Works. They have already appeared in the Newsletter *Was in der Anthroposophischen Gesellschaft vorgeht* ['What is happening in the Anthroposophical Society'], 11th publication year, No. 44 of 4 November 1934.

4 '…in the Gall Wasp'. The shape and behaviour relate to the Sand Wasp (Ammophila sabulosa, today called *Psammophilia hirsuta*).

5 Aeschylos or Aeschylus, 525–456 BCE, Greek tragedian.

6 *The Gospel of St John and its Relation to the other Gospels* [*Das Johannes- Evangelium im Verhaeltnis zu den drei anderen Evangelien, besonders zu dem Lukas-Evangelium*]: 14 lectures given in Kassel; GA 112, *The Gospel of St Luke [Das Lukas-Evangelium]*. See endnote 1.

[7]   1. Genesis. 22, 17.

[8]   Hebbel: Diary No. 1336: 'In terms of the migration of souls, it is possible that Plato, at his school desk, is again being punished for not understanding Plato.'

[9]   …the words of John the Baptist: Matthew 3: 7-9.

[10]   See *From the Akasha Chronicle* (*Cosmic Memory*) 1904, GA 11.

[11]   Spinoza: 1632 – 1677. *Ethics* 1677.

[12]   *Occult Science, An Outline*, 1910, GA 13.

[13]   Dmitri Ivanovitch Mendelyéyev, 1834–1907, Russian chemist.

[14]   *Knowledge of Higher Words, How is it Achieved?* First published in the magazine *Lucifer Gnosis*, No. 26, 1904, GA 10.

[15]   This is the time of the destruction of Jerusalem in 586 BCE and the exile to Babylon.

[16]   '… as a young … branch': this was inaugurated on 10 October 1908.

[17]   Insufficient notes of this are available.

[18]   Goethe's 'The Mysteries'. Compare Rudolf Steiner: 'The Mysteries, a Christmas and Easter poem by Goethe' in *Die Geheimnisse, ein Wiehnachts- und Ostergedicht von Goethe*, lecture in Cologne on 25 December 1907, Dornach 1963 (in GA 98). English edition *The Mysteries*, SteinerBooks 2014.

[19]   'Fichte says, quite rightly, that … the majority of men could sooner be brought to believe themselves a piece of lava on the Moon than to take themselves for a self.' In *Grundlage der gesamten Wissenschaftslehre*, 1794, *Doctrine of Scientific Knowledge*, note on paragraph 4. (Inspired by his reading of Kant, Fichte developed—during the last decade of the eighteenth century—a radically revised version of transcendental idealism, which he called his *Doctrine of Scientific Knowledge,* representing his effort to ground his entire system upon the bare subject … the pure I—translator's note.)

[20]   Compare Rudolf Steiner, *The East in Light of the West: The Children of Lucifer and the Brothers of Christ*, GA 113.

[21]   '…round and round…' refers to the circular nature of descriptions in books by the Theosophical Society.

[22]   The so-called Gospel of the Egyptians: refers to fragments of an apocryphal Gospel. The phrase referred to (in Hennecke's *New Testament Apocrypha*, 2nd Edition, Tuebingen 1924), is as follows: '… to the query of Salome, as to when the object of her enquiry becomes known, [when] "his kingdom will come", the Lord said: When you have trampled the garment of shame and when the two become one … when the outside [becomes] the inside and the male one with the female, neither male nor female.'

[23]   Johannes Tauler, around 1300–1361, Dominican. Eighty of his sermons are preserved.

24 Earliest Christmas tree indoors: this is placed in Strasbourg in 1539, according to Kluge's Etymological Dictionary, 1934.

25 Meister Eckhart, *c.* 1260–1328. Dominican teaching in Paris and Cologne. 1329, convicted and condemned for 26 stanzas of his didacticism.

26 'Shining trees, radiant trees…'. Goethe's poem appeared under the title of 'Weihnachten' [Christmas] in 1822, written for the occasion of the founding of the Higher Citizens' School.

27 'Die Sonne schaue…'. These words were first spoken in Berlin on 17 December 1906. This text is translated from an entry in a notebook dating from 1906. There are small variations on this in later years, e.g. 1921-22.

28 '… a genuinely theosophical poet': 'theosophical' in the sense described by Rudolf Steiner on 23 October 1909 (Lecture 1 in *A Psychology of Body, Soul and Spirit* [*Anthroposophie, Psychopathie, Pneumatosophie*], GA 115). Novalis wrote to Friedrich Schlegel on 26 December 1797: 'If only we could meet! To exchange papers, mine with yours! You would find much theosophy and alchemy.'

29 '…the German aristocrat Von Hardenberg': Heinrich Ulrich Erasmus, Baron von Hardenberg, 1738–1814.

30 Novalis' *Spiritual Songs*, of which this is the first. (*Was wär' ich ohne dich gewesen?*)

31 See endnote 1.

32 For instance, theologians such as Albert Kalthoff in *The Christ Problem*, Leipzig 1902.

33 For instance, John Mackinnon Robertson in *The Jesus Problem* (1917) or *Christianity and Mythology* (1910) and Prof. Arthur Drews: *The Christ Myth* (1909). On the same subject, Rudolf Steiner in a lecture of 8 May 1910 in *The Christ Impulse and the Evolution of Ego-Consciousness*, GA 116: '… and, lo, I am with you always, even unto the end of the world.' Matthew 28: 20.

34 '… a court case taking place in Vienna.' Heinrich Friedjung, 1851–1920, Austrian historian and political writer, allowed a false document claiming to prove that Serbians were agitating against Austria to substantiate allegations. Compare with this *Masaryk tells his story*, conversations with Karel Capek, Cassirer Verlag, Berlin, 1937, pp. 130-31.

35 Before Abraham was, I am. John 8: 58.

36 Kamaloka and Devachan: 'Soul world' (elemental world) and 'the spiritual world' (spirit land). Compare with Rudolf Steiner *The Theosophy of the Rosicrucian* (*Rosicrucian Wisdom*), 14 lectures 22 May–6 June 1907, GA 99.

Rudolf Steiner's Collected Works

THE German Edition of Rudolf Steiner's Collected Works (the *Gesamtausgabe* [GA] published by Rudolf Steiner Verlag, Dornach, Switzerland) presently runs to 354 titles, organized either by type of work (written or spoken), chronology, audience (public or other), or subject (education, art, etc.). For ease of comparison, the Collected Works in English [CW] follows the German organization exactly. A complete listing of the CWs follows with literal translations of the German titles. Other than in the case of the books published in his lifetime, titles were rarely given by Rudolf Steiner himself, and were often provided by the editors of the German editions. The titles in English are not necessarily the same as the German; and, indeed, over the past 75 years have frequently been different, with the same book sometimes appearing under different titles.

For ease of identification and to avoid confusion, we suggest that readers looking for a title should do so by CW number. Because the work of creating the Collected Works of Rudolf Steiner is an ongoing process, with new titles being published every year, we have not indicated in this listing which books are presently available. To find out what titles in the Collected Works are currently in print, please check our website at www.rudolfsteinerpress.com (or www.steinerbooks.org for US readers).

Written Work

CW 6   Goethe's Worldview
CW 6a   Now in CW 30
CW 7   Mysticism at the Dawn of Modern Spiritual Life and Its Relationship with Modern Worldviews
CW 8   Christianity as Mystical Fact and the Mysteries of Antiquity
CW 9   Theosophy: An Introduction into Supersensible World Knowledge and Human Purpose
CW 10   How Does One Attain Knowledge of Higher Worlds?
CW 11   From the Akasha-Chronicle
CW 12   Levels of Higher Knowledge
CW 13   Occult Science in Outline
CW 14   Four Mystery Dramas
CW 15   The Spiritual Guidance of the Individual and Humanity
CW 16   A Way to Human Self-Knowledge: Eight Meditations
CW 17   The Threshold of the Spiritual World. Aphoristic Comments
CW 18   The Riddles of Philosophy in Their History, Presented as an Outline
CW 19   Contained in CW 24
CW 20   The Riddles of the Human Being: Articulated and Unarticulated in the Thinking, Views and Opinions of a Series of German and Austrian Personalities
CW 21   The Riddles of the Soul
CW 22   Goethe's Spiritual Nature and its Revelation in 'Faust' and through the 'Fairy Tale of the Snake and the Lily'
CW 23   The Central Points of the Social Question in the Necessities of Life in the Present and the Future
CW 24   Essays Concerning the Threefold Division of the Social Organism and the Period 1915-1921
CW 25   Cosmology, Religion and Philosophy
CW 26   Anthroposophical Leading Thoughts
CW 27   Fundamentals for Expansion of the Art of Healing according to Spiritual-Scientific Insights
CW28   The Course of My Life
CW 29   Collected Essays on Dramaturgy, 1889-1900
CW 30   Methodical Foundations of Anthroposophy: Collected Essays on Philosophy, Natural Science, Aesthetics and Psychology, 1884-1901
CW 31   Collected Essays on Culture and Current Events, 1887-1901
CW 32   Collected Essays on Literature, 1884-1902
CW 33   Biographies and Biographical Sketches, 1894-1905
CW 34   Lucifer-Gnosis: Foundational Essays on Anthroposophy and Reports from the Periodicals 'Lucifer' and 'Lucifer-Gnosis,' 1903-1908
CW 35   Philosophy and Anthroposophy: Collected Essays, 1904-1923
CW 36   The Goetheanum-Idea in the Middle of the Cultural Crisis of the Present: Collected Essays from the Periodical 'Das Goetheanum,' 1921-1925

Lectures to the Members of the Anthroposophical Society

SIGNIFICANT EVENTS IN THE LIFE OF
Rudolf Steiner

1829:   June 23: birth of Johann Steiner (1829–1910)—Rudolf Steiner's father—in Geras, Lower Austria.

1834:   May 8: birth of Franciska Blie (1834–1918)—Rudolf Steiner's mother—in Horn, Lower Austria. 'My father and mother were both children of the glorious Lower Austrian forest district north of the Danube.'

1860:   May 16: marriage of Johann Steiner and Franciska Blie.

1861:   February 25: birth of *Rudolf Joseph Lorenz Steiner* in Kraljevec, Croatia, near the border with Hungary, where Johann Steiner works as a telegrapher for the South Austria Railroad. Rudolf Steiner is baptized two days later, February 27, the date usually given as his birthday.

1862:   Summer: the family moves to Modling, Lower Austria.

1863:   The family moves to Pottschach, Lower Austria, near the Styrian border, where Johann Steiner becomes station master. 'The view stretched to the mountains . . . majestic peaks in the distance and the sweet charm of nature in the immediate surroundings.'

1864:   November 15: birth of Rudolf Steiner's sister, Leopoldine (d. November 1, 1927). She will become a seamstress and live with her parents for the rest of her life.

1866:   July 28: birth of Rudolf Steiner's deaf-mute brother, Gustav (d. May 1, 1941).

1867:   Rudolf Steiner enters the village school. Following a disagreement between his father and the schoolmaster, whose wife falsely accused the boy of causing a commotion, Rudolf Steiner is taken out of school and taught at home.

1868:   A critical experience. Unknown to the family, an aunt dies in a distant town. Sitting in the station waiting room, Rudolf Steiner sees her 'form,' which speaks to him, asking for help. 'Beginning with this experience, a new soul life began in the boy, one in which not only the outer trees and mountains spoke to him, but also the worlds that lay behind them. From this moment on, the boy began to live with the spirits of nature . . .'

1869:   The family moves to the peaceful, rural village of Neudorfl, near Wiener Neustadt in present-day Austria. Rudolf Steiner attends the village school. Because of the 'unorthodoxy' of his writing and spelling, he has to do 'extra lessons'.

1870:   Through a book lent to him by his tutor, he discovers geometry: 'To grasp something purely in the spirit brought me inner happiness. I know that I first learned happiness through geometry.' The same tutor allows him to draw, while other students still struggle with their reading and writing. 'An artistic element' thus enters his education.

1871:   Though his parents are not religious, Rudolf Steiner becomes a 'church child,' a favourite of the priest, who was 'an exceptional character.' 'Up to the age of ten or eleven, among those I came to know, he was far and away the most significant.' Among other things, he introduces Steiner to Copernican, heliocentric cosmology. As an altar boy, Rudolf Steiner serves at masses, funerals, and Corpus Christi processions. At year's end, after an incident in which he escapes a thrashing, his father forbids him to go to church.

1872:   Rudolf Steiner transfers to grammar school in Wiener-Neustadt, a five-mile walk from home, which must be done in all weathers.

1873–75:   Through his teachers and on his own, Rudolf Steiner has many wonderful experiences with science and mathematics. Outside school, he teaches himself analytic geometry, trigonometry, differential equations, and calculus.

1876:   Rudolf Steiner begins tutoring other students. He learns bookbinding from his father. He also teaches himself stenography.

1877:   Rudolf Steiner discovers Kant's *Critique of Pure Reason,* which he reads and rereads. He also discovers and reads von Rotteck's *World History.*

1878:   He studies extensively in contemporary psychology and philosophy.

1879:   Rudolf Steiner graduates from high school with honours. His father is transferred to Inzersdorf, near Vienna. He uses his first visit to Vienna 'to purchase a great number of philosophy books'—Kant, Fichte, Schelling, and Hegel, as well as numerous histories of philosophy. His aim: to find a path from the 'I' to nature.

October
1879–1883:   Rudolf Steiner attends the Technical College in Vienna—to study mathematics, chemistry, physics, mineralogy, botany, zoology,

biology, geology, and mechanics—with a scholarship. He also attends lectures in history and literature, while avidly reading philosophy on his own. His two favourite professors are Karl Julius Schröer (German language and literature) and Edmund Reitlinger (physics). He also audits lectures by Robert Zimmermann on aesthetics and Franz Brentano on philosophy. During this year he begins his friendship with Moritz Zitter (1861–1921), who will help support him financially when he is in Berlin.

1880:   Rudolf Steiner attends lectures on Schiller and Goethe by Karl Julius Schröer, who becomes his mentor. Also 'through a remarkable combination of circumstances,' he meets Felix Koguzki, a 'herb gatherer' and healer, who could 'see deeply into the secrets of nature'. Rudolf Steiner will meet and study with this 'emissary of the Master' throughout his time in Vienna.

1881:   January: '... I didn't sleep a wink. I was busy with philosophical problems until about 12:30 a.m. Then, finally, I threw myself down on my couch. All my striving during the previous year had been to research whether the following statement by Schelling was true or not: *Within everyone dwells a secret, marvellous capacity to draw back from the stream of time—out of the self clothed in all that comes to us from outside— into our innermost being and there, in the immutable form of the Eternal, to look into ourselves.* I believe, and I am still quite certain of it, that I discovered this capacity in myself; I had long had an inkling of it. Now the whole of idealist philosophy stood before me in modified form. What's a sleepless night compared to that!'
Rudolf Steiner begins communicating with leading thinkers of the day, who send him books in return, which he reads eagerly.

July: 'I am not one of those who dives into the day like an animal in human form. I pursue a quite specific goal, an idealistic aim— knowledge of the truth! This cannot be done offhandedly. It requires the greatest striving in the world, free of all egotism, and equally of all resignation.'

August: Steiner puts down on paper for the first time thoughts for a 'Philosophy of Freedom.' 'The striving for the absolute: this human yearning is freedom.' He also seeks to outline a 'peasant philosophy,' describing what the worldview of a 'peasant'—one who lives close to the earth and the old ways   really is.

1881–1882: Felix Koguzki, the herb gatherer, reveals himself to be the envoy of another, higher initiatory personality, who instructs Rudolf Steiner to penetrate Fichte's philosophy and to master modern scientific thinking as a preparation for right entry into the spirit. This 'Master' also teaches him the double (evolutionary and involutionary) nature of time.

1882:   Through the offices of Karl Julius Schröer, Rudolf Steiner is asked by Joseph Kürschner to edit Goethe's scientific works for the *Deutschen National-Literatur* edition. He writes 'A Possible Critique of Atomistic Concepts' and sends it to Friedrich Theodor Vischer.

1883:   Rudolf Steiner completes his college studies and begins work on the Goethe project.

1884:   First volume of Goethe's *Scientific Writings* (CW 1) appears (March). He lectures on Goethe and Lessing, and Goethe's approach to science. In July, he enters the household of Ladislaus and Pauline Specht as tutor to the four Specht boys. He will live there until 1890. At this time, he meets Josef Breuer (1842–1925), the co-author with Sigmund Freud of *Studies in Hysteria,* who is the Specht family doctor.

1885:   While continuing to edit Goethe's writings, Rudolf Steiner reads deeply in contemporary philosophy (Eduard von Hartmann, Johannes Volkelt, and Richard Wahle, among others).

1886:   May: Rudolf Steiner sends Kürschner the manuscript of *Outlines of Goethe's Theory of Knowledge* (CW 2), which appears in October, and which he sends out widely. He also meets the poet Marie Eugenie Delle Grazie and writes 'Nature and Our Ideals' for her. He attends her salon, where he meets many priests, theologians, and philosophers, who will become his friends. Meanwhile, the director of the Goethe Archive in Weimar requests his collaboration with the *Sophien* edition of Goethe's works, particularly the writings on colour.

1887:   At the beginning of the year, Rudolf Steiner is very sick. As the year progresses and his health improves, he becomes increasingly 'a man of letters,' lecturing, writing essays, and taking part in Austrian cultural life. In August–September, the second volume of Goethe's *Scientific Writings* appears.

1888:   January–July: Rudolf Steiner assumes editorship of the 'German Weekly' *(Deutsche Wochenschrift)*. He begins lecturing more intensively, giving, for example, a lecture titled 'Goethe as Father of a New Aesthetics.' He meets and becomes soul friends with Friedrich Eckstein (1861–1939), a vegetarian, philosopher of symbolism, alchemist, and musician, who will introduce him to various spiritual currents (including Theosophy) and with whom he will meditate and interpret esoteric and alchemical texts.

1889:   Rudolf Steiner first reads Nietzsche *(Beyond Good and Evil)*. He encounters Theosophy again and learns of Madame Blavatsky in the theosophical circle around Marie Lang (1858–1934). Here he also meets well-known figures of Austrian life, as well as esoteric figures like the occultist Franz Hartmann and Karl Leinigen-Billigen (translator of C.G. Harrison's *The Transcendental Universe*). During this period, Steiner first reads A.P. Sinnett's *Esoteric Buddhism* and Mabel Collins's *Light on the Path*. He also begins travelling, visiting Budapest, Weimar, and Berlin (where he meets philosopher Eduard von Hartmann).

1890: Rudolf Steiner finishes Volume 3 of Goethe's scientific writings. He begins his doctoral dissertation, which will become *Truth and Science* (CW 3). He also meets the poet and feminist Rosa Mayreder (1858–1938), with whom he can exchange his most intimate thoughts. In September, Rudolf Steiner moves to Weimar to work in the Goethe-Schiller Archive.

1891: Volume 3 of the Kürschner edition of Goethe appears. Meanwhile, Rudolf Steiner edits Goethe's studies in mineralogy and scientific writings for the *Sophien* edition. He meets Ludwig Laistner of the Cotta Publishing Company, who asks for a book on the basic question of metaphysics. From this will result, ultimately, *The Philosophy of Freedom* (CW 4), which will be published not by Cotta but by Emil Felber. In October, Rudolf Steiner takes the oral exam for a doctorate in philosophy, mathematics, and mechanics at Rostock University, receiving his doctorate on the twenty-sixth. In November, he gives his first lecture on Goethe's 'Fairy Tale' in Vienna.

1892: Rudolf Steiner continues work at the Goethe-Schiller Archive and on his *Philosophy of Freedom*. *Truth and Science,* his doctoral dissertation, is published. Steiner undertakes to write Introductions to books on Schopenhauer and Jean Paul for Cotta. At year's end, he finds lodging with Anna Eunike, née Schulz (1853–1911), a widow with four daughters and a son. He also develops a friendship with Otto Erich Hartleben (1864–1905) with whom he shares literary interests.

1893: Rudolf Steiner begins his habit of producing many reviews and articles. In March, he gives a lecture titled 'Hypnotism, with Reference to Spiritism.' In September, volume 4 of the Kürschner edition is completed. In November, *The Philosophy of Freedom* appears. This year, too, he meets John Henry Mackay (1864–1933), the anarchist, and Max Stirner, a scholar and biographer.

1894: Rudolf Steiner meets Elisabeth Fürster Nietzsche, the philosopher's sister, and begins to read Nietzsche in earnest, beginning with the as yet unpublished *Antichrist.* He also meets Ernst Haeckel (1834–1919). In the fall, he begins to write *Nietzsche, A Fighter against His Time* (CW 5).

1895: May, *Nietzsche, A Fighter against His Time* appears.

1896: January 22: Rudolf Steiner sees Friedrich Nietzsche for the first and only time. Moves between the Nietzsche and the Goethe-Schiller

Archives, where he completes his work before year's end. He falls out with Elisabeth Förster Nietzsche, thus ending his association with the Nietzsche Archive.

1897: Rudolf Steiner finishes the manuscript of *Goethe's Worldview* (CW 6). He moves to Berlin with Anna Eunike and begins editorship of the *Magazin für Literatur*. From now on, Steiner will write countless reviews, literary and philosophical articles, and so on. He begins lecturing at the 'Free Literary Society.' In September, he attends the Zionist Congress in Basel. He sides with Dreyfus in the Dreyfus affair.

1898: Rudolf Steiner is very active as an editor in the political, artistic, and theatrical life of Berlin. He becomes friendly with John Henry Mackay and poet Ludwig Jacobowski (1868–1900). He joins Jacobowski's circle of writers, artists, and scientists—'The Coming Ones' (*Die Kommenden*)—and contributes lectures to the group until 1903. He also lectures at the 'League for College Pedagogy.' He writes an article for Goethe's sesquicentennial, 'Goethe's Secret Revelation,' on the 'Fairy Tale of the Green Snake and the Beautiful Lily.'

1898–99: 'This was a trying time for my soul as I looked at Christianity. . . . I was able to progress only by contemplating, by means of spiritual perception, the evolution of Christianity. . . . Conscious knowledge of real Christianity began to dawn in me around the turn of the century. This seed continued to develop. My soul trial occurred shortly before the beginning of the twentieth century. It was decisive for my soul's development that I stood spiritually before the Mystery of Golgotha in a deep and solemn celebration of knowledge.'

1899: Rudolf Steiner begins teaching and giving lectures and lecture cycles at the Workers' College, founded by Wilhelm Liebknecht (1826–1900). He will continue to do so until 1904. Writes: *Literature and Spiritual Life in the Nineteenth Century; Individualism in Philosophy; Haeckel and His Opponents; Poetry in the Present;* and begins what will become (fifteen years later) *The Riddles of Philosophy* (CW 18). He also meets many artists and writers, including Kothe Kollwitz, Stefan Zweig, and Rainer Maria Rilke. On October 31, he marries Anna Eunike.

1900: 'I thought that the turn of the century must bring humanity a new light. It seemed to me that the separation of human thinking and willing from the spirit had peaked. A turn or reversal of direction in human evolution seemed to me a necessity.' Rudolf Steiner finishes *World and Life Views in the Nineteenth Century* (the second part of what will become *The Riddles of Philosophy*) and dedicates it to

Ernst Haeckel. It is published in March. He continues lecturing at *Die Kommenden,* whose leadership he assumes after the death of Jacobowski. Also, he gives the Gutenberg Jubilee lecture before 7,000 typesetters and printers. In September, Rudolf Steiner is invited by Count and Countess Brockdorff to lecture in the Theosophical Library. His first lecture is on Nietzsche. His second lecture is titled 'Goethe's Secret Revelation.' October 6, he begins a lecture cycle on the mystics that will become *Mystics after Modernism* (CW 7). November–December: 'Marie von Sivers appears in the audience. . . .' Also in November, Steiner gives his first lecture at the Giordano Bruno Bund (where he will continue to lecture until May, 1905). He speaks on Bruno and modern Rome, focusing on the importance of the philosophy of Thomas Aquinas as monism.

1901: In continual financial straits, Rudolf Steiner's early friends Moritz Zitter and Rosa Mayreder help support him. In October, he begins the lecture cycle *Christianity as Mystical Fact* (CW 8) at the Theosophical Library. In November, he gives his first 'theosophical lecture' on Goethe's 'Fairy Tale' in Hamburg at the invitation of Wilhelm Hubbe-Schleiden. He also attends a gathering to celebrate the founding of the Theosophical Society at Count and Countess Brockdorff's. He gives a lecture cycle, 'From Buddha to Christ,' for the circle of the *Kommenden*. November 17, Marie von Sivers asks Rudolf Steiner if Theosophy needs a Western–Christian spiritual movement (to complement Theosophy's Eastern emphasis). 'The question was posed. Now, following spiritual laws, I could begin to give an answer. . . .' In December, Rudolf Steiner writes his first article for a theosophical publication. At year's end, the Brockdorffs and possibly Wilhelm Hubbe-Schleiden ask Rudolf Steiner to join the Theosophical Society and undertake the leadership of the German section. Rudolf Steiner agrees, on the condition that Marie von Sivers (then in Italy) work with him.

1902: Beginning in January, Rudolf Steiner attends the opening of the Workers' School in Spandau with Rosa Luxemberg (1870–1919). January 17, Rudolf Steiner joins the Theosophical Society. In April, he is asked to become general secretary of the German Section of the theosophical Society, and works on preparations for its founding. In July, he visits London for a theosophical congress. He meets Bertram Keightly, G.R.S. Mead, A.P. Sinnett, and Annie Besant, among others. In September, *Christianity as Mystical Fact* appears. In October, Rudolf Steiner gives his first public lecture on Theosophy ('Monism and Theosophy') to about three hundred people at the Giordano Bruno Bund. On October 19–21, the

German Section of the Theosophical Society has its first meeting; Rudolf Steiner is the general secretary, and Annie Besant attends. Steiner lectures on practical karma studies. On October 23, Annie Besant inducts Rudolf Steiner into the Esoteric School of the Theosophical Society. On October 25, Steiner begins a weekly series of lectures: 'The Field of Theosophy.' During this year, Rudolf Steiner also first meets Ita Wegman (1876–1943), who will become his close collaborator in his final years.

1903:   Rudolf Steiner holds about 300 lectures and seminars. In May, the first issue of the periodical *Luzifer* appears. In June, Rudolf Steiner visits London for the first meeting of the Federation of the European Sections of the Theosophical Society, where he meets Colonel Olcott. He begins to write *Theosophy* (CW 9).

1904:   Rudolf Steiner continues lecturing at the Workers' College and elsewhere (about 90 lectures), while lecturing intensively all over Germany among theosophists (about 140 lectures). In February, he meets Carl Unger (1878–1929), who will become a member of the board of the Anthroposophical Society (1913). In March, he meets Michael Bauer (1871–1929), a Christian mystic, who will also be on the board. In May, *Theosophy* appears, with the dedication: 'To the spirit of Giordano Bruno.' Rudolf Steiner and Marie von Sivers visit London for meetings with Annie Besant. June: Rudolf Steiner and Marie von Sivers attend the meeting of the Federation of European Sections of the Theosophical Society in Amsterdam. In July, Steiner begins the articles in *Luzifer-Gnosis* that will become *How to Know Higher Worlds* (CW 10) and *Cosmic Memory* (CW 11). In September, Annie Besant visits Germany. In December, Steiner lectures on Freemasonry. He mentions the High Grade Masonry derived from John Yarker and represented by Theodore Reuss and Karl Kellner as a blank slate 'into which a good image could be placed'.

1905:   This year, Steiner ends his non-theosophical lecturing activity. Supported by Marie von Sivers, his theosophical lecturing—both in public and in the Theosophical Society—increases significantly: 'The German Theosophical Movement is of exceptional importance.' Steiner recommends reading, among others, Fichte, Jacob Boehme, and Angelus Silesius. He begins to introduce Christian themes into Theosophy. He also begins to work with doctors (Felix Peipers and Ludwig Noll). In July, he is in London for the Federation of European Sections, where he attends a lecture by Annie Besant: 'I have seldom seen Mrs Besant speak in so inward and heartfelt a manner... Through Mrs Besant I have found the way to H.P. Blavatsky.' September to October, he gives a course of 31 lectures for a small group of esoteric students. In October, the annual meeting of the German Section of the Theosophical Society, which still remains very small, takes place. Rudolf Steiner reports membership has risen from 121 to 377 members. In November, seeking to establish esoteric 'continuity,' Rudolf Steiner and Marie von Sivers participate in a 'Memphis-Misraim' Masonic ceremony. They pay 45 marks for membership. 'Yesterday, you saw how little remains of former esoteric institutions.' 'We are dealing only with a "framework" . . for the present, nothing lies behind it. The occult powers have completely withdrawn.'

1906:   Expansion of theosophical work. Rudolf Steiner gives about 245 lectures, only 44 of which take place in Berlin. Cycles are given in Paris, Leipzig, Stuttgart, and Munich. Esoteric work also intensifies. Rudolf Steiner begins writing *An Outline of Esoteric Science* (CW 13). In January, Rudolf Steiner receives permission (a patent) from the Great Orient of the Scottish A & A Thirty-Three Degree Rite of the Order of the Ancient Freemasons of the Memphis-Misraim Rite to direct a chapter under the name 'Mystica Aeterna.' This will become the 'Cognitive-Ritual Section' (also called 'Misraim Service') of the Esoteric School. (See: *Freemasonry and Ritual Work: The Misraim Service,* CW 265.) During this time, Steiner also meets Albert Schweitzer. In May, he is in Paris, where he visits Édouard Schuré. Many Russians attend his lectures (including Konstantin Balmont, Dimitri Mereszkovski, Zinaida Hippius, and Maximilian Woloshin). He attends the General Meeting of the European Federation of the Theosophical Society, at which Col. Olcott is present for the last time. He spends the year's end in Venice and Rome, where he writes and works on his translation of H.P. Blavatsky's *Key to Theosophy.*

1907:   Further expansion of the German Theosophical Movement according to the Rosicrucian directive to 'introduce spirit into the world'—in education, in social questions, in art, and in science. In February, Col. Olcott dies in Adyar. Before he dies, Olcott indicates that 'the Masters' wish Annie Besant to succeed him: much politicking ensues. Rudolf Steiner supports Besant's candidacy. April–May: preparations for the Congress of the Federation of European Sections of the Theosophical Society—the great, watershed Whitsun 'Munich Congress,' attended by Annie Besant and others. Steiner decides to separate Eastern and Western (Christian–Rosicrucian) esoteric schools. He takes his esoteric school out of the Theosophical Society (Besant and Rudolf Steiner are 'in harmony' on this). Steiner makes his first lecture tours to Austria and Hungary. That summer, he is in Italy. In September, he visits Édouard Schuré, who will write the Introduction to the French edition of *Christianity as Mystical Fact* in Barr, Alsace. Rudolf Steiner writes the autobiographical statement known as the 'Barr Document.' In *Luzifer-Gnosis*, 'The Education of the Child' appears.

1908: The movement grows (membership: 1,150). Lecturing expands. Steiner makes his first extended lecture tour to Holland and Scandinavia, as well as visits to Naples and Sicily. Themes: St John's Gospel, the Apocalypse, Egypt, science, philosophy, and logic. *Luzifer-Gnosis* ceases publication. In Berlin, Marie von Sivers (with Johanna Mücke (1864–1949) forms the *Philosophisch-Theosophisch* (after 1915 *Philosophisch-Anthroposophisch) Verlag* to publish Steiner's work. Steiner gives lecture cycles titled *The Gospel of St. John* (CW 103) and *The Apocalypse* (104).

1909: *An Outline of Esoteric Science* appears. Lecturing and travel continues. Rudolf Steiner's spiritual research expands to include the polarity of Lucifer and Ahriman; the work of great individualities in history; the Maitreya Buddha and the Bodhisattvas; spiritual economy (CW 109); the work of the spiritual hierarchies in heaven and on earth (CW 110). He also deepens and intensifies his research into the Gospels, giving lectures on the Gospel of St Luke (CW 114) with the first mention of two Jesus children. Meets and becomes friends with Christian Morgenstern (1871–1914). In April, he lays the foundation stone for the Malsch model—the building that will lead to the first Goetheanum. In May, the International Congress of the Federation of European Sections of the Theosophical Society takes place in Budapest. Rudolf Steiner receives the Subba Row medal for *How to Know Higher Worlds*. During this time, Charles W. Leadbeater discovers Jiddu Krishnamurti (1895–1986) and proclaims him the future 'world teacher,' the bearer of the Maitreya Buddha and the 'reappearing Christ.' In October, Steiner delivers seminal lectures on 'anthroposophy,' which he will try, unsuccessfully, to rework over the next years into the unfinished work, *Anthroposophy (A Fragment)* (CW 45).

1910: New themes: *The Reappearance of Christ in the Etheric* (CW 118); *The Fifth Gospel; The Mission of Folk Souls* (CW 121); *Occult History* (CW 126); the evolving development of etheric cognitive capacities. Rudolf Steiner continues his Gospel research with *The Gospel of St. Matthew* (CW 123). In January, his father dies. In April, he takes a month-long trip to Italy, including Rome, Monte Cassino, and Sicily. He also visits Scandinavia again. July–August, he writes the first mystery drama, *The Portal of Initiation* (CW 14). In November, he gives 'psychosophy' lectures. In December, he submits 'On the

1911:

Psychological Foundations and Epistemological Framework of Theosophy' to the International Philosophical Congress in Bologna. The crisis in the Theosophical Society deepens. In January, 'The Order of the Rising Sun,' which will soon become 'The Order of the Star in the East,' is founded for the coming world teacher, Krishnamurti. At the same time, Marie von Sivers, Rudolf Steiner's co-worker, falls ill. Fewer lectures are given, but important new ground is broken. In Prague, in March, Steiner meets Franz Kafka (1883–1924) and Hugo Bergmann (1883–1975). In April, he delivers his paper to the Philosophical Congress. He writes the second mystery drama, *The Soul's Probation* (CW 14). Also, while Marie von Sivers is convalescing, Rudolf Steiner begins work on *Calendar 1912/1913*, which will contain the 'Calendar of the Soul' meditations. On March 19, Anna (Eunike) Steiner dies. In September, Rudolf Steiner visits Einsiedeln, birthplace of Paracelsus. In December, Friedrich Rittelmeyer, future founder of the Christian Community, meets Rudolf Steiner. The *Johannes-Bauverein,* the 'building committee,' which would lead to the first Goetheanum (first planned for Munich), is also founded, and a preliminary committee for the founding of an independent association is created that, in the following year, will become the Anthroposophical Society. Important lecture cycles include *Occult Physiology* (CW 128); *Wonders of the World* (CW 129); *From Jesus to Christ* (CW 131). Other themes: esoteric Christianity; Christian Rosenkreutz; the spiritual guidance of humanity; the sense world and the world of the spirit.

1912:

Despite the ongoing, now increasing crisis in the Theosophical Society, much is accomplished: *Calendar 1912/1913* is published; eurythmy is created; both the third mystery drama, *The Guardian of the Threshold* (CW 14) and *A Way of Self-Knowledge* (CW 16) are written. New (or renewed) themes included life between death and rebirth and karma and reincarnation. Other lecture cycles: *Spiritual Beings in the Heavenly Bodies and in the Kingdoms of Nature* (CW 136); *The Human Being in the Light of Occultism, Theosophy, and Philosophy* (CW 137); *The Gospel of St. Mark* (CW 139); and *The Bhagavad Gita and the Epistles of Paul* (CW 142). On May 8, Rudolf Steiner celebrates White Lotus Day, H.P. Blavatsky's death day, which he had faithfully observed for the past decade, for the last time. In August, Rudolf Steiner suggests the 'independent association' be called the 'Anthroposophical Society.' In September, the first eurythmy course takes place. In October, Rudolf Steiner declines recognition of a Theosophical Society lodge dedicated to the Star of the East and decides to expel all Theosophical Society members belonging to the order.

Also, with Marie von Sivers, he first visits Dornach, near Basel, Switzerland, and they stand on the hill where the Goetheanum will be built. In November, a Theosophical Society lodge is opened by direct mandate from Adyar (Annie Besant). In December, a meeting of the German section occurs at which it is decided that belonging to the Order of the Star of the East is incompatible with membership in the Theosophical Society. December 28: informal founding of the Anthroposophical Society in Berlin.

1913: Expulsion of the German section from the Theosophical Society. February 2–3: Foundation meeting of the Anthroposophical Society. Board members include: Marie von Sivers, Michael Bauer, and Carl Unger. September 20: Laying of the foundation stone for the *Johannes Bau* (Goetheanum) in Dornach. Building begins immediately. The third mystery drama, *The Soul's Awakening* (CW 14), is completed. Also: *The Threshold of the Spiritual World* (CW 147). Lecture cycles include: *The Bhagavad Gita and the Epistles of Paul* and *The Esoteric Meaning of the Bhagavad Gita* (CW 146), which the Russian philosopher Nikolai Berdyaev attends; *The Mysteries of the East and of Christianity* (CW 144); *The Effects of Esoteric Development* (CW 145); and *The Fifth Gospel* (CW 148). In May, Rudolf Steiner is in London and Paris, where anthroposophical work continues.

1914: Building continues on the *Johannes Bau* (Goetheanum) in Dornach, with artists and co-workers from seventeen nations. The general assembly of the Anthroposophical Society takes place. In May, Rudolf Steiner visits Paris, as well as Chartres Cathedral. June 28: assassination in Sarajevo ('Now the catastrophe has happened!'). August 1: War is declared. Rudolf Steiner returns to Germany from Dornach—he will travel back and forth. He writes the last chapter of *The Riddles of Philosophy*. Lecture cycles include: *Human and Cosmic Thought* (CW 151); *Inner Being of Humanity between Death and a New Birth* (CW 153); *Occult Reading and Occult Hearing* (CW 156). December 24: marriage of Rudolf Steiner and Marie von Sivers.

1915: Building continues. Life after death becomes a major theme, also art. Writes: *Thoughts during a Time of War* (CW 24). Lectures include: *The Secret of Death* (CW 159); *The Uniting of Humanity through the Christ Impulse* (CW 165).

1916: Rudolf Steiner begins work with Edith Maryon (1872–1924) on the sculpture 'The Representative of Humanity' ('The Group'— Christ, Lucifer, and Ahriman). He also works with the alchemist Alexander von Bernus on the quarterly *Das Reich*. He writes *The Riddle of Humanity* (CW 20). Lectures include: *Necessity and Freedom in World History and Human Action* (CW 166); *Past and Present in the*

Human Spirit (CW 167); *The Karma of Vocation* (CW 172); *The Karma of Untruthfulness* (CW 173).

1917:　Russian Revolution. The U.S. enters the war. Building continues. Rudolf Steiner delineates the idea of the 'threefold nature of the human being' (in a public lecture March 15) and the 'threefold nature of the social organism' (hammered out in May–June with the help of Otto von Lerchenfeld and Ludwig Polzer-Hoditz in the form of two documents titled *Memoranda,* which were distributed in high places). August–September: Rudolf Steiner writes *The Riddles of the Soul* (CW 20). Also: commentary on 'The Chymical Wedding of Christian Rosenkreutz' for Alexander Bernus (Das *Reich*). Lectures include: *The Karma of Materialism* (CW 176); *The Spiritual Background of the Outer World: The Fall of the Spirits of Darkness* (CW 177).

1918:　March 18: peace treaty of Brest-Litovsk—'Now everything will truly enter chaos! What is needed is cultural renewal.' June: Rudolf Steiner visits Karlstein (Grail) Castle outside Prague. Lecture cycle: *From Symptom to Reality in Modern History* (CW 185). In mid-November, Emil Molt, of the Waldorf-Astoria Cigarette Company, has the idea of founding a school for his workers' children.

1919:　Focus on the threefold social organism: tireless travel, countless lectures, meetings, and publications. At the same time, a new public stage of Anthroposophy emerges as cultural renewal begins. The coming years will see initiatives in pedagogy, medicine, pharmacology, and agriculture. January 27: threefold meeting: 'We must first of all, with the money we have, found free schools that can bring people what they need.' February: first public eurythmy performance in Zurich. Also: 'Appeal to the German People' (CW 24), circulated March 6 as a newspaper insert. In April, *Towards Social Renewal* (CW 23) appears—'perhaps the most widely read of all books on politics appearing since the war'. Rudolf Steiner is asked to undertake the 'direction and leadership' of the school founded by the Waldorf-Astoria Company. Rudolf Steiner begins to talk about the 'renewal' of education. May 30: a building is selected and purchased for the future Waldorf School. August–September, Rudolf Steiner gives a lecture course for Waldorf teachers, *The Foundations of Human Experience (Study of Man)* (CW 293). September 7: Opening of the first Waldorf School. December (into January): first science course, the *Light Course* (CW 320).

1920:　The Waldorf School flourishes. New threefold initiatives. Founding of limited companies *Der Kommende Tag* and *Futurum A.G.* to infuse spiritual values into the economic realm. Rudolf Steiner also focuses on the sciences. Lectures: *Introducing Anthroposophical*

Medicine (CW 312); *The Warmth Course* (CW 321); *The Boundaries of Natural Science* (CW 322); *The Redemption of Thinking* (CW 74). February: Johannes Werner Klein—later a co-founder of the Christian Community—asks Rudolf Steiner about the possibility of a 'religious renewal,' a 'Johannine church.' In March, Rudolf Steiner gives the first course for doctors and medical students. In April, a divinity student asks Rudolf Steiner a second time about the possibility of religious renewal. September 27–October 16: anthroposophical 'university course.' December: lectures titled *The Search for the New Isis* (CW 202).

1921:   Rudolf Steiner continues his intensive work on cultural renewal, including the uphill battle for the threefold social order. 'University' arts, scientific, theological, and medical courses include: *The Astronomy Course* (CW 323); *Observation, Mathematics, and Scientific Experiment* (CW 324); the *Second Medical Course* (CW 313); *Colour.* In June and September–October, Rudolf Steiner also gives the first two 'priests' courses' (CW 342 and 343). The 'youth movement' gains momentum. Magazines are founded: *Die Drei* (January), and—under the editorship of Albert Steffen (1884–1963)—the weekly, *Das Goetheanum* (August). In February–March, Rudolf Steiner takes his first trip outside Germany since the war (Holland). On April 7, Steiner receives a letter regarding 'religious renewal,' and May 22–23, he agrees to address the question in a practical way. In June, the Klinical-Therapeutic Institute opens in Arlesheim under the direction of Dr Ita Wegman. In August, the Chemical-Pharmaceutical Laboratory opens in Arlesheim (Oskar Schmiedel and Ita Wegman are directors). The Clinical Therapeutic Institute is inaugurated in Stuttgart (Dr Ludwig Noll is director); also the Research Laboratory in Dornach (Ehrenfried Pfeiffer and Gunther Wachsmuth are directors). In November–December, Rudolf Steiner visits Norway.

1922:   The first half of the year involves very active public lecturing (thousands attend); in the second half, Rudolf Steiner begins to withdraw and turn toward the Society—'The Society is asleep.' It is 'too weak' to do what is asked of it. The businesses—*Der Kommende Tag* and *Futurum A.G.*—fail. In January, with the help of an agent, Steiner undertakes a twelve-city German lecture tour, accompanied by eurythmy performances. In two weeks he speaks to more than 2,000 people. In April, he gives a 'university course' in The Hague. He also visits England. In June, he is in Vienna for the East–West Congress. In August–September, he is back in England for the Oxford Conference on Education. Returning to Dornach, he gives the lectures *Philosophy, Cosmology, and Religion*

(CW 215), and gives the third priests' course (CW 344). On September 16, The Christian Community is founded. In October–November, Steiner is in Holland and England. He also speaks to the youth: *The Youth Course* (CW 217). In December, Steiner gives lectures titled *The Origins of Natural Science* (CW 326), and *Humanity and the World of Stars: The Spiritual Communion of Humanity* (CW 219). December 31: Fire at the Goetheanum, which is destroyed.

1923: Despite the fire, Rudolf Steiner continues his work unabated. A very hard year. Internal dispersion, dissension, and apathy abound. There is conflict—between old and new visions—within the Society. A wake-up call is needed, and Rudolf Steiner responds with renewed lecturing vitality. His focus: the spiritual context of human life; initiation science; the course of the year; and community building. As a foundation for an artistic school, he creates a series of pastel sketches. Lecture cycles: *The Anthroposophical Movement; Initiation Science* (CW 227) (in Wales at the Penmaenmawr Summer School); *The Four Seasons and the Archangels* (CW 229); *Harmony of the Creative Word* (CW 230); *The Supersensible Human* (CW 231), given in Holland for the founding of the Dutch society. On November 10, in response to the failed Hitler-Ludendorff putsch in Munich, Steiner closes his Berlin residence and moves the *Philosophisch-Anthroposophisch Verlag* (Press) to Dornach. On December 9, Steiner begins the serialization of his *Autobiography: The Course of My Life* (CW 28) in *Das Goetheanum*. It will continue to appear weekly, without a break, until his death. Late December–early January: Rudolf Steiner re-founds the Anthroposophical Society (about 12,000 members internationally) and takes over its leadership. The new board members are: Marie Steiner, Ita Wegman, Albert Steffen, Elisabeth Vreede, and Gunther Wachsmuth. (See *The Christmas Meeting for the Founding of the General Anthroposophical Society,* CW 260.) Accompanying lectures: *Mystery Knowledge and Mystery Centres* (CW 232); *World History in the Light of Anthroposophy* (CW 233). December 25: the Foundation Stone is laid (in the hearts of members) in the form of the 'Foundation Stone Meditation.'

1924: January 1: having founded the Anthroposophical Society and taken over its leadership, Rudolf Steiner has the task of 'reforming' it. The process begins with a weekly newssheet ('What's Happening in the Anthroposophical Society') in which Rudolf Steiner's 'Letters to Members' and 'Anthroposophical Leading Thoughts' appear (CW 26). The next step is the creation of a new esoteric class, the 'first class' of the 'University of Spiritual Science' (which was to have been followed, had Rudolf Steiner lived longer, by two more advanced classes). Then comes a new language for

Anthroposophy—practical, phenomenological, and direct; and Rudolf Steiner creates the model for the second Goetheanum. He begins the series of extensive 'karma' lectures (CW 235–40); and finally, responding to needs, he creates two new initiatives: biodynamic agriculture and curative education. After the middle of the year, rumours begin to circulate regarding Steiner's health. Lectures: January–February, *Anthroposophy* (CW 234); February: *Tone Eurythmy* (CW 278); June: *The Agriculture Course* (CW 327); June–July: *Speech Eurythmy* (CW 279); *Curative Education* (CW 317); August: (England, 'Second International Summer School'), *Initiation Consciousness: True and False Paths in Spiritual Investigation* (CW 243); September: *Pastoral Medicine* (CW 318). On September 26, for the first time, Rudolf Steiner cancels a lecture. On September 28, he gives his last lecture. On September 29, he withdraws to his studio in the carpenter's shop; now he is definitively ill. Cared for by Ita Wegman, he continues working, however, and writing the weekly installments of his *Autobiography* and *Letters to the Members/ Leading Thoughts* (CW 26).

1925:   Rudolf Steiner, while continuing to work, continues to weaken. He finishes *Extending Practical Medicine* (CW 27) with Ita Wegman. On March 30, around ten in the morning, Rudolf Steiner dies.

Index